CONTENTS

ACTIVITIES

EXPRESSIVE USE OF THE BODY AND VOICE

BODY: This section develops body awareness and spatial perception.

Dramatizing Literary Selections

AESTHETIC GROWTH THROUGH APPRECIATION OF THEATRICAL EVENTS

Attending a play is the class activity in this instance. The recommended sequence of preparation and follow-up is as follows:

FOREWORD

I must confess to a facetious quality in me that at times is discomforting to my students. How often they defend a curricular practice with the observation, "Children love it." The devil's advocate in me rises to the surface as I respond, "Children love dessert. Does that justify a menu of cakes and puddings?"

Professor McCaslin carefully reminds us that dramatic activities in the classroom are not the frills added on to the diet but an essential and integral component of a curriculum that responds to children's healthy development. The wealth of recent research in language acquisition cannot be ignored. Programs that promote oral language development in young children are based on a quest for literacy; meaningful use of symbol systems in reading and writing are viewed as an extension of a rich environment in which a wide variety of oral communication opportunities exists for young children. Nellie McCaslin begins there and takes us into a world in which we can safely say, "Children love it but, even more importantly, they need it."

I cannot forget Eddie and Ezra, who were about 10 or 11 at the time. One day they appeared in my classroom, the excited authors of a pair of "operettas," complete with librettos and musical scores both sophisticated and childlike. There was no way in which these musical extravaganzas could be ignored. They had to be *performed* and so they were—a number of times—with the polish demanded by the composers. Professor McCaslin tells us that a carefully rehearsed finished product has its place but that day-to-day dramatic activities are the substance of a sound curriculum. To that end she suggests many possibilities, in rich illustrations aimed at realizing the important threads in education—to help children verbalize as well as recall, to encourage children to clarify *their* perceptions as well as those of others, and to promote children's working together to develop group living.

The ideas McCaslin presents help put to rest one of education's biggest myths—that the more valued the experience, the more money we must invest. A classroom can be turned into unending settings for a world of drama, she tells us; the investment must be one of commitment and creativity.

I remember, too, a group of 7- and 8-year-olds for whom "Rapunzel" was a cherished commodity. I never ceased to be amazed at how, at a moment's notice, a new interpretation of the story emerged, always with new dialogue, makeshift props, and new performers. What did not change was the children's joy and their ever-deepening feeling of belonging to a group. I treasure most a parent's saying, "The biggest thing I notice in Jimmy this year is that he doesn't say 'I' as much. When he talks about school, he always says 'we.'" McCaslin highlights this as an important goal for drama in the classroom.

Nellie McCaslin's book has both a timely and a timeless quality. As individual states mandate drama in the classroom, it serves as an immediate resource for teachers. But at the same time, it speaks to universals, reminding us of the need for the classroom to be a world of childhood.

The theme of my college yearbook returns to me—"Children's Faces Looking Up, Holding Wonder Like a Cup." Nellie McCaslin presents us with many ways in which we can fill the cup.

Robert Clausen
Professor of Education
New York University

PREFACE

Surely the arts need no justification for inclusion in the curriculum; they have been an important part of human life from prehistoric times. We first communicated through the arts: we embellished our tools with designs; we expressed our deepest emotions and worshiped our gods through the dance; we created and passed on our myths and legends before we had a written language with which to preserve them; we wore costumes, jewelry, and face paint for our celebrations. The young have learned, been entertained, and, in time, expressed themselves through the visual and performing arts.

During the greatest periods of history, the arts have flourished. It seems odd, therefore, that today, in an affluent, democratic society, we must find a rationale for including them in our educational system. In the 1977 Rockefeller Report, *Coming to Our Senses*, the majority of Americans expressed their belief in the arts as an important component of a liberal education. It is up to us to see that this professed belief is implemented, for to deny the arts is to rob our children of some of life's most enriching and humanizing experiences. It is heartening to know that despite budget cuts and a "back-to-basics" movement, the theatre arts, as well as music and the visual arts, are being mandated into the curricula of a number of states, not just as means to other more utilitarian goals but as ends in their own right.

Creative Drama in the Primary Grades and its companion, *Creative Drama in the Intermediate Grades*, are based on a philosophy of education that regards child drama as a subject in its own right and as an important component of the curriculum. While drama is unquestionably an effective tool for teaching, the thrust of these two books is the involvement in a process that enriches the participant on many levels, the primary one being the aesthetic experience. Unlike my other creative-drama texts, which were designed for use in the college classroom, these handbooks are written specifically for teachers of grades 1, 2, and 3 and of grades 4, 5, and 6.

Although there is no philosophic difference between *Creative Drama in the Classroom* and these two new books, the former is primarily theoretical, whereas the latter are, by intent, practical. Although some of the material in the first handbook can be used equally well with children in the upper grades, the reverse is not always true. Many of the stories, poems, and activities suggested for older children are too long or complex for boys and girls just starting school. The goals and procedures, however, are identical; it is only the materials and expectations that differ.

Through my own teaching, I long ago discovered that most classroom teachers, no matter how experienced, feel insecure when it comes to the theatre arts. They have had little, if any, drama in their own professional preparation. What experience they have had generally has been acting in high-school and college plays, where performance and production were paramount. Enjoyable and valuable as this activity undoubtedly was, participation in formal theatre for adults is in no way preparation for work in creative drama with children. The familiar practice of "putting on a play for assembly" conjures up visions of hours of rehearsal, wooden performances by bored or self-conscious actors, vast auditoriums that strain young voices, and valuable time lost from studies. The picture has changed, however, as a result of the pioneering efforts of Winifred Ward at Northwestern University and her successors, who not only first practiced a new approach to this art form with children, but also gave us our first books on the subject. They clarified the concepts of drama and theatre by defining *drama* as that which a child does or creates and *theatre* as that which a child views as a spectator. Both have value, but the goals and experiences differ. An ideal drama/theatre program provides a time and a place for each, but for the younger child, creative drama should take priority. Understanding the difference between drama and theatre and relieved of the necessity of putting on a play, teachers today can relax and enjoy the experience with their classes. For, indeed, children love to try on the roles of others, to enact favorite stories and create plays of their own, to move, and to mime. The teacher who is able to guide these activities and encourage the creative energy that children bring into the classroom will find not only that the classroom is a livelier place, but also that learning is enhanced and social relationships are strengthened.

Most teachers are aware of the interests, tastes, and backgrounds of their pupils. What they seek is guidance in the planning of lessons and the adaptation of material that is appropriate not only for creative drama and language arts classes, but also for all classes across the curriculum. With these needs in mind, these two handbooks were written. The contents include a rationale for the inclusion of drama in the curriculum, suggestions for pantomime and improvisation, a discussion of simple play structure, and a few basic steps to follow if or when a class shares its work with an audience. I recognize that a class occasionally wants to show its work or put on a play. When it does, new problems are posed. Suggestions for solving those problems are not intended to encourage the practice, but to help make the transition from process to presentation. I must add that very little creative drama ever reaches the performance level, especially in the first and second grades, frequently in the fourth to sixth. When it does, it should be recognized as growth and therefore supported, not with elaborate costumes and settings but with respect for the ideas and honest work of the group. The teacher provides the showmanship at this point in order that new goals may be realized and the young participants may find satisfaction in their efforts. Showmanship, incidentally, does not mean learning special techniques, but helping the group present itself as well as possible.

Because puppets provide an opportunity for an extension of creative drama, a chapter on puppet construction and handling is included. Very young children can make simple puppets, and they enjoy using them, especially under circumstances and in situations where large body movement is not possible. As for the shy youngster, hiding behind the puppet is an excellent first step toward communication with others. Mask making is also a popular activity, hence the inclusion of a section on the construction of masks. The combining of puppets, masks, and human actors, regarded as innovative in adult theatre, is a natural solution to staging problems for a child, whose approach to drama often includes incorporating all three without hesitation or apology.

Many teachers and principals have expressed a concern regarding audience behavior when a touring company performs for assembly or when a class goes on a field trip to a local community or college theatre. Therefore, a chapter on preparing children for the experience, the role of the audience, and suggestions for follow-up activities is included. Appreciation of any art is difficult to measure, if indeed it can be measured at all, but there are things the teacher can do to introduce children to a program or play so as to make it an enjoyable and meaningful experience. For some children, this may be the first live theatre they have ever seen, and we want it to be memorable—entertaining and worthy of their attention. Because most children enjoy live performance, the preparation, including observing a few ground rules, is relatively easy. Assuming that the children can see and hear well and are physically comfortable, discipline should not be a problem.

Activities are suggested throughout the text, not as ends in themselves but as springboards to later, more extensive projects. Stories, verse, and suggestions for dramatization are included as illustrations of what can be used and how; with a point of view and a creative approach, the leader will find other materials relevant to his or her own and the group's interests.

Finally, for teachers who are interested in further reading on the subject, I have included an annotated bibliography. Books on creative drama, children's theatre, choral speech, rhythms and movement, and literature for use in the elementary grades have been selected with the classroom teacher in mind. The growing number of states that are mandating drama in the curriculum to be taught along with music and art requires guidance based on a philosophy of aesthetic education with some practical suggestions and sample materials: ideas for pantomime and improvisations; appropriate stories, poetry, rhythms, and movement; and the steps to take in planning and conducting such activities. Once teachers have used creative drama with their classes, they will discover a wealth of ideas of their own.

The arrangement of chapters suggests a good way of using this book. Throughout, theory is demonstrated by activities. The chapters begin with simple basic exercises and move on to more complex ones. By following this outline, students build on a foundation of what they have done and learned. Chapter 12, "Putting It All Together," offers a few examples of ways that specific objectives can be reached through activities followed by class discussion.

For assistance in the preparation of this manuscript, I want to thank the teachers and principals who gave so generously of their time and thought and whose suggestions have guided me. I hope that my efforts on their behalf may prove as valuable to them as their help has been to me.

Nellie McCaslin

HOW TO USE THIS BOOK

This book is for teachers—for teachers who have some or no experience in creative drama, for teachers who plan to teach creative drama in the future, for teachers who want to or who are required to introduce and integrate creative drama into their elementary curricula.

Creative Drama in the Primary Grades really contains two courses of instruction—a methodology for teachers and curriculum material for students. Based on the theory that one learns best by doing, the book is designed so that the teacher with no experience can immediately begin teaching creative drama in the elementary grades. It is paced developmentally from simple to complex. As the teacher acquires skills for teaching creative drama, the students acquire creative drama skills. Thus, in the early lessons, a teacher needs only minimal information and skill in order to teach because these lessons comprise the least sophisticated components of creative drama. As the teacher practices and masters teaching skills, so the students learn increasingly sophisticated creative drama skills.

The book contains all the methodology, all the content, all the lesson components necessary to teaching several sequences of creative drama in the three primary grades. There are two basic components—text and activities. The text explains methods and theories of teaching creative drama. The numbered activities, which follow the text in each chapter and are printed in a different type style, comprise the practical core of the book. They detail the specifics of what goes on in the creative drama class. Each activity is a self-contained "recipe" for a creative drama event and includes:

1. The educational objective for the activity.
2. A step-by-step guide on how to conduct the activity.
3. Complete subject matter of the event—for example, if the activity is to be a game, full instructions for the game are provided. If the subject is a story, even a well-known story, the full story is provided. (A teacher does not have to rely on memory or refer to other sources to conduct any activity.)
4. Follow-up questions and discussion topics.

As the book progresses and teachers become more sophisticated, less detail is provided in the activities. At all stages, however, the teacher can enter the classroom with the confidence that unless special equipment such as costumes, music, or props is desired, the book contains all the components necessary to conduct the activity he or she has planned for the day's lesson.

So the ideal way to use the book is sequentially. As the teacher reads the book he or she selects the activities for presentation in the classroom.

However, not all teachers have the leisure for such careful reading and selection. For these teachers the following ways of using the book might be preferable.

ESSENTIAL ELEMENTS

The list of activities that follows the Contents is organized by essential elements and therefore can be used to develop a sequence of lessons containing all the elements. Within each category, the activities are listed in order of complexity—from simple to complex. Individual lesson plans can be based on the activities in a single category or activities selected from a number of different categories.

As states recommend or mandate the inclusion of creative drama in the curriculum, teachers are called on to demonstrate that a comprehensive sequence of creative drama is presented in class. The state of Texas has mandated the teaching of creative drama. In order to clarify the requirement, a taxonomy of essential elements was developed. The essential elements of the activities list in this book are derived from that taxonomy. In Table 1, the Texas classification system is correlated with the treatment of the elements in this book. For a teacher who wants to take the approach of teaching essential elements, it is recommended that he or she read the relevant chapters listed in Table 1 before presenting the activities in class.

TABLE 1. *Correlation of Essential Elements and Contents of the Text*

Essential Elements	*Creative Drama in the Primary Grades*
1. Expressive use of the body and voice	Chapters 2, 3, 4, 5, 6, 7
1.1 Develop body awareness and spatial perception using	Chapter 3
Rhythmic movement	Chapter 3: Activities 3.1, 3.2 Chapter 7: Activity 7.3 Chapter 10: Activity 10.2
Imitative movement	Chapter 3: Activities 3.1, 3.2, 3.3 Chapter 7: Activities 7.3, 7.10, 7.11
Sensory awareness	Chapter 2: Activities 2.5, 2.6 Chapter 4: Activity 4.6
Pantomime	Chapter 4: Activities 4.1, 4.2, 4.3, 4.4, 4.5, 4.8, 4.9 Chapter 7: Activities 7.4, 7.6, 7.7
1.2 Imitate sounds and dialogue	Chapters 5, 6, 7, 8
1.3 Recall sensory and emotional experiences	Chapters 2, 4, 5, and 8 Sensory Chapter 2: Activities 2.5, 2.6 Chapter 4: Activity 4.6 Emotional Chapter 4: Activity 4.5 Chapter 5: Activity 5.9 Chapter 8: Activity 8.3
2. Creative drama	Chapters 5, 6, 7, 8
2.1 Dramatize limited-action stories and poems using	Chapters 4, 5, 6, 7
Simple pantomime	Chapter 4: Activities 4.1, 4.2, 4.3, 4.4, 4.5, 4.9 Chapter 6: Activities 6.3, 6.4 Chapter 7: Activities 7.3, 7.4, 7.6
Puppetry	Chapter 8: Activities 8.1, 8.2, 8.4, 8.5, 8.6
2.2 Dramatize literary selections using	Chapters 4, 7, 8
Shadow play	Chapter 8: p. 124, and Activities 7.6, 7.10
Pantomime	Chapter 4: Activities 4.6, 4.7 Chapter 6: Activities 6.5, 6.8 Chapter 7: Activities 7.7, 7.8, 7.9, 7.11
Imitative dialogue	Chapter 6: Activities 6.2, 6.3, 6.4, 6.5, 6.6, 6.7, 6.8 Chapter 8: Activity 8.2
3. Aesthetic growth through appreciation of theatrical events	Chapter 11
3.1 View theatrical events emphasizing	
Player-audience relationship	Chapter 11: pp. 177–181
Audience etiquette	Chapter 11: p. 179

SCOPE AND SEQUENCE

With the exception of the few activities that are identified as more appropriate for one grade level, most activities can be used effectively with all three primary grades. If teachers wish to prepare sequences designed specifically for one grade or for all three grades, they can use the scope and sequence chart in Table 2 as a guide.

The following sample sequences for grades one, two, and three can be taught sequentially as a class progresses from one grade to the next. Likewise, a school that wants to adopt this program and to establish three different grade sequences could assign the sequences concurrently. All three sequences include all the essential elements.

Grade One

This section develops expressive use of the body and voice.

Rhythmic movement

Nonlocomotion (10 minutes) p. 37

Walking, skipping, hopping, galloping, slowing down, stopping (only large body movements are recommended for the first class session of about 15 minutes) p. 37

Animals (15 minutes) 3.2

Imitative movement

Animals (15 minutes; can be repeated in the next session if enjoyed) 3.2

Pantomime

Seeds (10 minutes) 2.3

Nursery Rhymes (20 minutes) 3.3

Imagination and Pantomime (15 to 20 minutes) 4.2

Imaginative movement

The Snowman (10 minutes) 2.2

Locomotion (15 to 20 minutes) 3.1

Sensory awareness

Using Our Five Senses (discussion; 2 or 3 of the exercises, 15 minutes) 2.5

Expressive use of the voice

Simple Improvisations Based on Situations (imitate sounds and dialogue in the toy shop, 15 or 20 minutes) 5.1

TABLE 2. *Scope and Sequence for Primary Grades*

	Theatre Arts Curriculum			
A theatre arts program in the elementary grades should include the following elements	*The student shall be provided opportunities to:*			
Theatre Arts	*K*	*Grade I*	*Grade II*	*Grade III*
Expressive use of the body and voice	Develop body awareness and spatial perception through Rhythmic movement Imitative movement Imitate sounds	Continue with body awareness and spatial perception through Rhythmic movement Imitative movement Sensory awareness Imitate sounds	Continue body work Begin pantomime Imitate dialogue	Continue body modes and dance using Rhythmic movement Imitative movement Expressive movement Pantomime Imitate dialogue and create dialogue Recall sensory and emotional experiences
Creative drama	Dramatize limited-action stories and poems through simple pantomime	Dramatize simple stories and poems in pantomime Begin puppetry	Dramatize literature through Pantomime Shadow play Imitative dialogue Puppetry	Dramatize literature through Pantomime Shadow play Improvisation Puppetry
Aesthetic growth through the appreciation of theatrical events	Listen to stories told by teacher, librarian, or good storyteller	Listen to stories told by teacher, librarian, or professional storyteller	Listen to stories, attend puppet plays appropriate for age level	Attend theatrical events emphasizing Content Player-audience relationship Audience behavior and conventions Difference between live theatre and TV

Recall sensory and emotional experience
- Our Five Senses (select exercises that you think children can do and will enjoy, 15 to 20 minutes) — 2.6

This section develops creative drama skills.

Limited action stories and poems
- The Three Billy Goats Gruff (15 to 20 minutes) — 3.4
- Hallowe'en (20 minutes; can be repeated on a day in October) — 7.6

*Puppetry**—puppets can be continued for several sessions, using all the time allotted to creative drama.
- Bandana puppets — p. 150
  - The Three Billy Goats Gruff — 3.4
  - Expressing Emotions through Puppets — 8.6
- Paper bag puppets — p. 151
  - Nursery Rhymes — 7.4
  - Expressing Emotions through Puppets — 8.6
- Flat puppets — p. 152
  - Nursery Rhymes — 7.4
  - Expressing Emotions through Puppets — 8.6

*Shadow play**—shadow play, either with puppets or with class members, will take more than one session and, if popular, may be repeated during the year.
- Nursery Rhymes — 3.3
- Creating Silhouettes in Pantomime — 4.9
- Nursery Rhymes — 7.4
- Shadow puppets — p. 152

Imitative Dialogue
- The Boy Who Cried Wolf (15 minutes) — 6.3
- The Tortoise and the Hare (15 minutes) — 6.4

This section promotes aesthetic growth through appreciation of theatrical events.

- Player-audience relationship — p. 217
- Audience etiquette — p. 220

Postperformance activities: First-grade children will probably not attend school assembly plays. However, there may be storytellers in the school and children should learn how to listen, behave, and respond. Postperformance activities may or may not be appropriate; this will be up to the teacher.

* Most of the stories in this book can be enacted in puppetry or in shadow play.

Grade Two

This section develops expressive use of the body and voice.

Rhythmic movement	
Locomotion (20 minutes or more)	3.1
Imitative movement	
Animals (20 minutes or more)	3.2
Imaginative movement	
The Legend of the Shooting Star (2 or 3 class sessions required)	3.5
Pantomime	
Performing an Action in Pantomime (use an entire period and continue either next time or from time to time)	4.3
Imitate sounds and dialogue	
The First Night of Sleep (a sound and motion story; 1 session). Other stories can be handled in this way if children enjoy them and space for movement is limited.	4.1
Recall of sensory and emotional experiences	
Expressing Feelings in Pantomine (more than 1 session)	4.5

This section develops creative drama skills.

Limited-action stories and poems	
Telling a Story in Pantomime	4.4
Being Inanimate Objects in Pantomime (Sounds may be added if or when children feel they are needed.)	4.8
Simple pantomime	
Creating Silhouettes in Pantomime	4.9
The Little Scarecrow Boy (2 or 3 class periods with teacher reading the story)	p. 56
The Fir Tree Who Wanted Leaves (2 sessions)	p. 227
*Puppetry**—more than 2 class sessions, depending on the children's interest. Children may become so interested that several sessions are given to puppetry.	
Sock puppets	p. 153
Little Indian Two Feet's Horse	8.1
A Mistake	8.3

* Most of the stories in this book can be enacted in puppetry or in shadow play.

Glove puppets	p. 153
Space Traveler	8.4
George, the Timid Ghost	8.5

DRAMATIZE LITERARY SELECTIONS

*Shadow play**	
Shadow puppets	p. 152
Creating Silhouettes in Pantomime	4.9
Jack and the Beanstalk	p. 79
The Two Foolish Cats	6.5
The Fisherman and His Wife	8.2
Pantomime	
The Shining Fish (2 or 3 Sessions)	6.6
Sing a Song of Seasons (1 or 2 sessions)	7.7
Imaginings (1 session)	7.8
Imitative Dialogue	
Caps for Sale (1 or 2 sessions)	6.1
The Two Foolish Cats (1 session)	6.5
A Legend of Spring (2 or 3 sessions, more if tied in with a social studies unit on the Native American)	6.8

This section promotes aesthetic growth through appreciation of theatrical events.

VIEW THEATRICAL EVENTS, EMPHASIZING

Player-audience relationship	p. 217
Audience etiquette	p. 220
Postperformance activities	pp. 222, 267–274

Grade Three

You will note that some of the following exercises are also suggested for the second and even first grades. This is because the exercises are valuable on any level and there is no reason why they should not be repeated. Some stories and activities will be more popular with some groups than with others; although we do not encourage dropping an activity before it has been fully developed, we should be sensitive to

* Most of the stories in this book can be enacted in puppetry or in shadow play.

children's interests and respond to them. Activities have been suggested in order of increasing difficulty; therefore, the best results will be achieved by proceeding in the order outlined here.

This section develops expressive use of the body and voice.

Rhythmic movement

- Locomotion and Nonlocomotion (5 or 10 minutes in first session) — p. 37
- Fruit Bowl (a good warm-up for a new class) — 2.4
- Adding to the Action (10 or 15 minutes) — 10.1
- Making a Machine (10 or 15 minutes) — 10.2

Imitative movement

- Mobile (20 minutes to ½ hour) — 7.11
- The Turnip (20 minutes or more) — p. 40

Sensory awareness

- Our Five Senses (This may be a repeat for children who did the exercise last year; however, it does no harm to repeat it because as children mature, they recognize more than they did earlier.) — 2.6
- Some one (15 minutes, possibly more) — 7.9

Imaginative movement

- La Mer (1 or 2 periods) — 4.6
- Being Inanimate Objects in Pantomime (1 period) — 4.8

Pantomime

- Performing an Action in Pantomime (1 or 2 sessions) — 4.3
- Expressing Feelings in Pantomime (1 or 2 sessions) — 4.5

Imitate sounds and dialogue

- Humane Education (1 or more periods) — 5.8
- The Carlanco and the Goats (2 or 3 sessions) — 6.7
- Tick-Tock (15 minutes) — 7.2

Sensory and emotional recall

- Expressing Feelings in Pantomime (2 or more sessions) — 4.5

* Most of the stories in this book can be enacted in puppetry or in shadow play.

Improvisations for Two Children (2 or more sessions)	5.4

This section develops creative drama skills.

DRAMATIZE LIMITED-ACTION STORIES AND POEMS

Simple pantomime

Improvisations Suggested by Objects (1 period; may be repeated 2 or 3 times)	5.2
Improvising from Costumes (1 period; may be repeated, if enjoyed, at a later date)	5.3
Improvisations for Three Children (1 period; may be continued if enjoyed)	5.5

*Puppetry**—count on several sessions to make and manipulate the puppets, having them enact stories.

Glove puppets	p. 153
The Shining Fish	6.6
Sock puppets	p. 153
The Two Foolish Cats	6.5
The Carlanco and the Goats	6.7

DRAMATIZE LITERARY SELECTIONS

*Shadow play**—allow several sessions for shadow plays, whether done by the children or the puppets.

Bread and Honey (Although for younger children, this works well in shadow and a first grade could be invited in to see it.)	6.2
Little Indian Two Feet's Horse	8.1
The Fisherman and His Wife	8.2

Pantomime—these take time to develop; therefore allow at least 2 periods, more if the children are interested and the work is going well.

The Legend of the Shooting Star	3.5
Mei Li's New Year's Day	3.6
Greensleeves	4.7

Imitative dialogue

How the Soldier Crab Got His Name (2 sessions unless story is tied into unit on the Caribbean islands. In that case, it will take longer but the experience will be richer.)	6.9

* Most of the stories in this book can be enacted in puppetry or in shadow play.

This section promotes aesthetic growth through appreciation of theatrical events.

VIEW EVENTS, EMPHASIZING

Player-audience relationship	p. 217
Audience etiquette	p. 220
Preparing for performance and postperformance activities	pp. 219, 222, 267–274

1

CREATIVE DRAMA AND ITS PLACE IN THE CLASSROOM

Drama is the first art form we experience. From earliest childhood, we imitate the sounds we hear and the activities we see around us. We respond to new situations with movement and sound, and we delight in make-believe. In short, we play; and this play, when encouraged, develops into drama—an art form, a socializing activity, and a way of learning.

PLAY

The phenomenon of the young child's play has fascinated philosophers, educators, psychologists, and anthropologists. They have searched for its meaning and its role in human life. Theories range from its being an expression of surplus energy, an escape from reality, or simply a means of relaxation to its being important as a way of learning. While joy and freedom are the hallmarks of play, the rules are clearly established and observed by the players. A young child may play alone, but one of the basic characteristics of play is the teamwork involved. Dressing up is often an element of play, although it is not always included and is not necessary. It is, however, a reason for having costumes in the classroom, not as preparation for a production, but as an enhancement of play, when desired, and later on, of creative drama.

One has only to watch a group of children playing in an empty lot or playground to accept the truth of these observations. Children play almost as soon as they move, and through their play, they learn. They enter the various worlds of their families and neighbors, interpreting and reenacting. First they observe; then they respond, repeating in play those actions and events that have made the strongest impressions. Not unlike primitive peoples, young children express their feelings first through movement and then in words, creating more complex situations as they grow older, with the boundaries stretched but the rules still clearly established. By the time they are ready for school, they have learned much about the world they live in, and a great part of this learning has come about through their play. As Winifred Ward, pioneer drama teacher, noted, "Drama comes in the door of every school with the child."[1]

Most teachers realize the potential of play and have made it an integral part of their programs. While some teachers are known to reject play on the grounds that it is frivolous and therefore unrelated to learning, children give it their most serious attention. They become involved voluntarily in games and projects that attract them—solving problems imaginatively, often seeking information, and initiating further action. The "why" of the young child, when answered, often leads to the "how," with the solution up to them. Teachers who recognize this creative spark want to keep it alive so that it may enhance learning and thus enrich the lives of their pupils.

Jon Godden and Rumer Godden, in their recollections of a childhood spent in India, speak with feeling of play, its magic and privacy. When asked, as they often were by their parents, what they were playing, the reply was generally, "Nothing."

> *Or, if that were too palpable a lie, we would give a camouflage answer like "Mothers and Fathers," which we never played, or, with us, another improbable play, "Shops." . . . Yet if we had told them what we were playing no one would have been much the wiser, because our plays were like icebergs, only three-tenths seen, the rest hidden, inside ourselves. It was what we thought into our play that made its spell.*[2]

Games, sports, ritual, and drama are closely related to play. Whereas sports, like theatre, are designed for an audience, games and drama exist for the participants. A sport is held in a particular place; a game,

[1] Winifred Ward, *Drama with and for Children*, U.S. Department of Health, Education, and Welfare, Bulletin no. 30 (Washington, D.C.: U.S. Government Printing Office, 1960), p. 1.

[2] Jon Godden and Rumer Godden, *Two under the Indian Sun* (New York: Knopf, 1966), p. 55.

wherever players may assemble. Ritual may be defined as the observance of a set form or series of rites. We think of the ritual as having religious significance, but it is more inclusive. The repetition of an act or a series of acts is also ritual. This is important to remember when working with children, for their games assume a ritualistic form. Movement and chants play an important part in them. By beginning a creative-drama class with the familiar—movement, rhythms, songs, or group games that all know—the leader is using ritual to draw the members together and make them comfortable.

EDUCATIONAL OBJECTIVES

One of the most frequently stated aims of education is the maximal growth of the child both as an individual and as a member of society. In order to achieve this aim, certain educational objectives have been set up. Although these objectives vary somewhat, there is general agreement that knowledge and appreciation of and skills in the arts are essential. The modern curriculum tries to ensure that each child will:

1. *Develop basic skills in which reading, writing, arithmetic, science, social studies, and the arts are stressed*
2. *Develop and maintain good physical and mental health*
3. *Grow in his ability to think*
4. *Clarify his values and verbalize his beliefs and hopes*
5. *Develop an understanding of beauty, using many media, including words, color, sound, and movement*
6. *Grow creatively and thus experience his own creative powers*[3]

Although other objectives are mentioned, these six are most frequently listed in the development of educational programs designed for today's world and the complex problems that life offers.

The most enthusiastic proponent of creative drama would not go so far as to claim that its inclusion in the curriculum will ensure the meeting of these objectives. But many objectives of modern education and creative drama are unquestionably shared. Among them are:

1. Creativity and aesthetic development
2. The ability to think critically
3. Social growth and the ability to work cooperatively with others
4. Improved communication skills

[3] Robert S. Fleming, *Curriculum for Today's Boys and Girls* (Columbus, Ohio: Merrill, 1963), p. 10.

5. The development of moral and spiritual values
6. Knowledge of self

Before creative drama can be discussed in greater detail, some definitions are in order. The terms *dramatic play, creative drama, playmaking, role playing, children's theatre,* and *participation theatre* are often used interchangeably, although they have quite different meanings. The following definitions will clarify the meanings as they are used in this text.

DEFINITIONS

Dramatic Play

Dramatic play is the free play of the very young child, in which she explores her universe, imitating the actions and character traits of those around her. It is her earliest expression in dramatic form, but must not be confused with drama or interpreted as performance. Dramatic play is fragmentary, existing only for the moment. It may last for a few minutes or go on for some time. It even may be played repeatedly, if the child's interest is sufficiently strong; but when this occurs, the repetition is in no sense a rehearsal. It is, rather, the repetition of a creative experience for the pure joy of doing it. It has no beginning and no end and no development in the dramatic sense.

Dramatic play may be as simple as Susan's passing of imaginary cookies to a guest when her mother has a friend for coffee. The two or three minutes of spontaneous pantomime are indeed dramatic play, since they involve stepping into the role of the mother and performing an observed activity. Susan has seen how a hostess behaves and is taking advantage of an opportunity to learn what it is like to be a hostess.

Dramatic play may, on the contrary, follow the pattern of 6-year-old Erma, who was the youngest child on the block and, therefore, the last to go to school. She had heard about teachers and lessons and had longed for the day when she, too, could pack up her books and lunch in a bag and trot off after breakfast with the other boys and girls to the elementary school. When the time came, her curiosity may have been satisfied, but her fascination became even more intense. According to her family, she returned home every afternoon and set up her own class in the dining room. Whether or not the other children joined her, she played for an hour or more with an improvised desk and a blackboard. She assumed, in turn, the various roles of principal, teacher, and pupils. Most often, however, she was the teacher, who called the roll, disciplined the children, and, to the great amusement of her mother and older sister, reenacted everything that had taken place during the day. This situation held her interest for three years, although the content varied according to her daily experiences. Other parents have described similar preoccupations, some lasting for an extraordinarily long time, until the interest waned and another preoccupation took its place.

In dramatic play, children create a world of their own in which to master reality. They try in this imaginative world to solve real-life problems that, until now, they have been unable to solve. They repeat, reenact, and relive these experiences. According to Richard Courtney, "Play is the principal instrument of growth. Without play there can be no normal adult cognitive life; without play, no healthful development of affective life; without play, no full development of the power of will."[4]

One of the most delightful and insightful treatments of the subject is to be found in Virginia Glasgow Koste's *Dramatic Play in Childhood: Rehearsal for Life*. Koste offers three main reasons for valuing dramatic play.

> *That is the time when most people are most expert and constant in playing; that is the time when they most freely externalize their playing so that it is possible to see and hear it; and that is the time when the power of play as a means of growth and accomplishment can most effectively be nurtured for a stronger rising generation of adults.*[5]

The text is rich in examples of children at play. Although she purposely eschews the scholarly approach, Koste presents effective evidence of learning, imagination, and social growth as a result of dramatic play. Valuable insights are to be found in this early stage of human development, which is preparation for the next—creative drama. That it is the root of drama and theatre is an obvious conclusion.

Creative Drama and Playmaking

The terms *creative drama* and *playmaking* may be used interchangeably, since they refer to informal drama that is created by the participants. As the word *playmaking* implies, this activity goes beyond dramatic play in scope and intent. It may make use of a story with a beginning, a middle, and an end. It may also explore, develop, and express ideas and feelings through dramatic enactment. It is, however,

[4] Richard Courtney, *Play Drama and Thought* (New York: Drama Book Specialists, 1974), p. 204.

[5] Virginia Glasgow Koste, *Dramatic Play in Childhood: Rehearsal for Life* (New Orleans: Anchorage Press, 1978), p. 6.

always improvised. Dialogue is created by the players, whether the content is taken from a well-known story or an original plot. Lines are not written down or memorized. With each playing, the story becomes more detailed and better organized, but it remains extemporaneous and is at no time designed for an audience. Participants are guided by a leader rather than a director, and the leader's goal is the optimal growth and development of the players.

The replaying of scenes is therefore different from the rehearsal of a formal play, in that each member of the group is given an opportunity to play various parts. No matter how many times a story is played, it is done for the purpose of deepening understanding and strengthening the performers, rather than for that of perfecting a product. Scenery and costumes have no place in creative drama, although an occasional property or article of clothing may be permitted to stimulate the imagination. When these are used, they should not be considered costuming. Most groups do not feel the need of properties of any kind and are generally freer without them.

The phrase *creative drama* describes the improvised drama of children from age 5 or 6 and older, but it is not limited to a particular age level and may be used just as appropriately to describe the improvisation of high-school students.

Role Playing

The term *role playing* is used most often in connection with therapy or edu-cation. It refers to the assuming of a role for the particular value it may have to the participant, rather than for the development of an art. Although all art may be considered to have certain curative powers, it is not the primary purpose of either creative drama or theatre to provide therapy or solve social and emotional problems. Role playing is what the young child does in dramatic play, it is true, but it is also a tool used by psychologists and play therapists.

Children's Theatre

The phrase *children's theatre* refers to formal productions for child audiences, whether acted by amateurs or professionals, children or adults, or a combination of both. It is directed rather than guided; dialogue is memorized; and scenery and costumes usually play an important part. Since it is audience centered, it is essentially different from creative drama. The child in the audience is the spectator, and the benefits derived are aesthetic.

What do children gain from attending good children's theatre? They gain much. First of all, there is the thrill of watching a well-loved story come alive on a stage. Then, there is the opportunity for a strong, vicarious experience as the children identify with characters who are brave, steadfast, noble, loyal, and beautiful. Emotions are released as the audience shares the adventures and excitement of the play. And, finally, the children learn to appreciate the art of the theatre if the production is tasteful and well executed.

I am speaking now of the child in the audience, not the child in the play. While there is much that is creative and of value for the performer, it is generally agreed that participation in creative drama is far more beneficial than is public performance for all children up to the age of 10 or 11. Occasionally, there is an expressed desire to "put on a play," and when this comes from the children themselves, it is probably wise to grant the request. There are times, to be sure, when sharing is a wonderful experience, but it is to be hoped that formal play production will be infrequent. If it is done, the production should be simple and all precautions taken to guard against the competition and tension that so often characterize the formal presentation of a play. For junior-high-school students, however, a play is often the desired culmination of a semester's work. To deprive students of the experience would be to withhold the ultimate satisfaction of communicating an art.

Some creative drama leaders believe that any performance in front of an audience is harmful to children. I agree up to a point. But the theatre is, after all, a performing art; when the audience is composed of understanding and sympathetic persons, such as parents or members of another class, performance may be the first step toward communicating a joyful experience. Without question, however, very young children should not perform publicly. Those in the middle and upper grades may not be harmed if their desire and the right occasion indicate that the advantages outweigh the disadvantages. A performance is a highly disciplined and carefully organized undertaking, involving a variety of skills that children in the first, second, and even third grades do not and should not be expected to possess. When children are trained rather than guided, praised extravagantly instead of encouraged, or featured as individuals rather than helped to work cooperatively, they risk losing all the positive aspects of the experience. Ironically, this leads to poor theatre as well, for ensemble, that most desirable quality of good theatre, is achieved by working together, not by featuring individual players.

Participation Theatre

Participation theatre is a new technique that permits the audience to become vocally, verbally, and physically involved in the production of a play given by adult actors. Children are invited to suggest ideas to the actors from time to time. The audience, if it is not too large, frequently is invited to come into the playing space to assist the cast in working out these ideas. Skillfully handled, this can be an exciting experience. The younger the audience, the more natural the involvement. When the formal is combined with the informal, and the actors with the audience, a closer relationship is established, and the spectator becomes a participant. The most successful participation plays are those given arena style in an all-purpose room rather than on a stage. Actors assume responsibility for the children's involvement in the action.

VALUES IN CREATIVE PLAYING

There is general agreement among teachers of creative drama that important values can be gained from creative playing. Depending on the age of the children, the situation, and the orientation of the leader, these values may be ranked in varying order. It is the contention of the author, however, that in spite of these differences, certain values exist in some measure for all, regardless of age, circumstances, or previous experience. To be sure, the activities must be planned with the group in mind, and the emphasis placed on the needs and interests of those involved. The 5- or 6-year-old needs and enjoys the freedom of large movement and much physical activity, but a similar opportunity should not be denied to older boys and girls. Adult students in early sessions also gain freedom and pleasure when given an opportunity to move freely in space.

Ten year olds enjoy the challenge of characterization and often create with remarkable insight and understanding. Young children, however, can also create on their level, although they cannot be expected to compete with older children. In other words, it is not a question of assigning different values to various age levels; it is a matter of accepting basic values that exist on all levels, varying more in degree than in kind. Specifically, these values may be listed as follows:

AN OPPORTUNITY TO DEVELOP THE IMAGINATION

Imagination is the beginning. In order to work creatively, it is necessary, first of all, to push beyond the boundaries of the here and now, to project oneself into another situation or into the life of another person. Few activities have greater potential for developing the imagination than playmaking. Little children move easily into a world of make-believe;

but as they grow older, this amazing human capacity often is ignored or even discouraged.

The sensitive teacher will not demand too much in the beginning but will accept with enthusiasm the first attempts of the beginner to use imagination to solve a problem. Once the players have had the fun of seeing, hearing, feeling, touching, tasting, or smelling something that is not there, they will find that their capacity to imagine grows quickly.

An Opportunity for Independent Thinking

A particular value of creative drama is the opportunity it offers for independent thinking. Although the drama, both informal and formal, is a group art, it is composed of the contributions of each participant, and every contribution is important. As the group plans together, each member is encouraged to express his or her own ideas and thereby contribute to the whole. If the group is not too large, there will be many opportunities for creative thinking before the activity is exhausted. Thinking is involved in such questions as: Who are the characters? What are they like? What parts do they play? What scenes are important? How can we suggest the action or the place?

The evaluation that follows an improvisation is as important as the planning; indeed, it is preparation for a second playing. Children of all ages are remarkably perceptive, and their critical comments show the extent of their involvement. A well-planned session in creative drama provides exercises in critical thinking as well as an opportunity for creativity.

Freedom for the Group to Develop Its Own Ideas

As the members of a group of any age work together under sensitive leadership, they learn to accept, appreciate, and stimulate one another. Every teacher has experienced a class in which the dynamics were such that all students seemed to produce more because of their association. This is not to say that creative drama is a magic formula for successful teamwork, but it does offer a rare opportunity for sharing ideas and solving problems together.

An Opportunity for Cooperation

When a group builds something together, its members are learning a valuable lesson in cooperation. Social differences may be forgotten in the business of planning and acting scenes. As an illustration, Jack entered a neighborhood class in drama that several of his third-grade schoolmates attended. It was a Saturday-morning activity, and it was obvious from the start that he was an "outsider." For the first three or four sessions, he contributed nothing and was chosen by no one to join in their scenes.

Then one day, the children were dramatizing the story "The Stone in the Road." They needed a farmer to drive along the road with a donkey cart. Several children attempted to pantomime the action, but each time, the others insisted that "he didn't look like he was really driving." Suddenly Jack, who had been sitting on the sidelines, stood up and volunteered to try it. The vigorous and convincing pantomime he created as he guided his cart around the upturned chair that was the "stone" astonished the class. His position in the group changed at that moment. While he never became a leader, he was accepted and often sought out. Working together cooperatively is an experience in democratic partnership. It provides an opportunity for the Jacks in a group to offer their skills and have them accepted.

An Opportunity to Build Social Awareness

Putting oneself in the shoes of another is a way of developing awareness and human understanding. Even very young players may glimpse insights that help them in their future understanding of people. Both literature and original stories provide the players with this opportunity to study human nature.

A Healthy Release of Emotion

Much has been said and written about the thinking, both creative and critical, that characterizes creative drama. Another value is of equal importance: the opportunity to feel and release emotion. As children grow up, the chance for emotional release is too often restricted to responding to television shows and movies. While there is value in being a spectator, the deeper involvement of active participation is lacking.

Control of emotion does not mean suppression of emotion. It means the healthy release of strong feelings through appropriate and acceptable channels. At some time or another, all persons feel anger, fear, anxiety, jealousy, resentment, and negativism. Through the playing of a part in which these emotions are expressed, the player may release them and so relieve tension: "By permitting the child to play freely in a setting of security and acceptance, we enable him to deal satisfactorily and healthfully with his most urgent problems."[6]

[6] Ruth Hartley, Lawrence Frank, and Robert Goldenson, *Understanding Children's Play* (New York: Columbia University Press, 1964), p. 16.

Better Habits of Speech

To many teachers, a primary value of creative drama is the opportunity it affords for oral communication. There is a built-in motivation for the player who wishes to be heard and understood. Volume, tempo, pitch, and diction are involved in a natural way; no other form of speech exercise captures the child to the same degree or offers so good a reason for working on speech as does creative drama. The little girl who can barely be heard in a classroom recitation will be reminded by her fellow players to speak up so the lines will not be lost. And the boy with the strident tone will also be told when his voice is too loud for the character he is playing. Being, in turn, a giant, a prince, an old man, an animal, or a comic character in a modern story offers further opportunities for developing variation of tone and expression.

Vocabulary is also served through this form of oral expression. Conceptual thinking and the cognitive aspect of language are encouraged when words are put to practical use. For the young child, the culturally disadvantaged child, or the child whose native language is not English, vocabulary can be built and distinctions in the meanings of words made clear through taking part in creative drama.

An Experience with Good Literature

The story that is played makes a lasting impression. Therefore, the opportunity to become well acquainted with good literature, through dramatizing it, is a major value of creative drama. The teacher soon discovers that the stories that hold interest longest are those of the best literary quality. Both folk tales and modern tales provide fine opportunities for acting. Bruno Bettelheim has given powerful arguments for the folk and fairy tale, a genre that in recent years has been questioned as to its relevance for the modern child.[7] In addition to the narrative interest of these tales, there are important psychological reasons why they continue to have value and why they should be used—although, of course, not to the exclusion of contemporary literature. A program that includes a variety of material helps to build appreciation and set a standard for original writing. Television shows and comic books attract temporary interest, but compared with a story that has stood the test of time, these rarely sustain attention. Believable characters, a well-constructed plot, and a worthwhile theme make for good drama. What better way of discovering and learning to appreciate literature?

Poetry may also be played creatively. Both narrative and lyric verse stimulate the imagination, suggesting mood and feeling. Sometimes the

[7] Bruno Bettelheim, *The Uses of Enchantment* (New York: Knopf, 1976).

response is an original story; sometimes, an emotional reaction expressed in movement or dance. Most children enjoy poetry, particularly when they are encouraged to do something of their own with it.

An Introduction to the Theatre Arts

Art is said to represent the human being's interpretation of life, expressed in a way that can be universally recognized and understood. Creative drama is primarily participant centered and offers the young player his or her first taste of the magic and make-believe of the theatre. In her imagination, a chair becomes a throne or a rock; a stick, a wand or a cane; a change in lighting, a difference in time; and an actor, a character in whom she believes and with whom she can identify. Listening, watching, and becoming involved are required of the theatre audience. This is easy for the first and second grader. The child who is introduced to the theatre through creative drama is going to look for more than superficial entertainment when she attends a performance by live actors.

Recreation

Implicit in everything that has been said so far, yet different and of value in itself, is the opportunity for recreation, or "re-creation," that drama affords. In certain settings—such as camps, community centers, after-school-activity programs, and neighborhood clubs—the highest priority of drama may be recreation. Drama is fun. It exists for the pleasure of the players, and it expresses free choice. It may also, in time, lead to serious work or a lifelong avocation.

Values for the Special Child

Creative drama offers an opportunity for children with learning or physical disabilities to participate in the performing arts. Because of its flexibility, drama can be a freeing adventure for groups of all ages. Special needs can be served by adjusting the emphases and activities. The expectations of the teacher will be different from those held for the average group. Often, for special children the experience of participation in drama stimulates interest in other subjects and, in so doing, strengthens skills and awakens latent abilities.

Creative-drama class in Kendall Demonstration Elementary School for the Deaf at Gallaudet College, Washington, D.C. (Courtesy of Victoria Brown)

Values for the Teacher

What do teachers get from creative drama? Probably the most important thing is the perspective it gives on every child in the class. It reveals imagination in the least likely children, skill in problem solving, or the ability to work with others.

What if an exercise fails? Do not be discouraged. No activity is foolproof, and no idea stimulates every class equally well. But teachers learn as the children do, by doing. Be prepared; then take the risk. The worst thing that can happen is that that *one* lesson does not go as hoped. Teachers will discover more from the "flops" than from the successes.

While I do not suggest that special study of creative drama is unnecessary to its practice, I believe that the average classroom teacher, because of preparation and experience, is better equipped to teach it than he or she may realize. The reason? Because drama does not require mastery of the kinds of technical skills that are required for the teaching of music, dance, or the visual arts. Drama does, however, demand sensitivity to and a knowledge of children; the goals and principles of education and a knowledge of child psychology—these the classroom teacher already possesses. If he or she enjoys the theatre, and most of us do, then sharing this interest with children should be a pleasure.

Skill comes with experience. Experience, combined with study under well-prepared leaders, leads to an ease and ability that marks the professional.

PROBLEMS IN CREATIVE PLAYING

Sooner or later, the teacher of creative drama is bound to encounter problems of one sort or another. They may be the simple ones of time and space: periods that are too short to accomplish curriculum goals; space that is inadequate for movement; classes that are too large. These problems usually can be solved, although the solutions are not always easy. Other problems confronting the teacher, even under ideal conditions, are the individual behavioral problems that he or she finds in the group.

Self-Consciousness

Self-consciousness is the greatest obstacle to creativity. Self-consciousness or fear takes many forms. The shy child and the show-off are examples of the two forms in which self-consciousness is most often encountered. The insensitive child is also a problem, for he or she usually lacks friends and so finds it difficult to work cooperatively in a group. And, finally, there is the disabled child, whose physical, mental, or emotional needs pose special problems for the leader.

Teachers must keep in mind that in drama, players are exposing themselves more than in any other art or activity. Therefore, the handling of behavior problems implies awareness of their causes. If the problem is severe, it should be handled by a therapist and not by the classroom teacher; in many cases, an intelligent, sympathetic effort to build self-respect and bring fun into the lives of the players can go a long way toward solving problems.

Timidity

The timid child is the most common problem of all, but one that creative drama can help. Such children are usually quiet in class, preferring to sit in the back of the room and let others do the talking. Their fear of making a mistake, or even of being noticed, causes them to withdraw, even though they may want to participate. Children who never volunteer need special encouragement. The teacher who gives them an opportunity to show what they can do may be taking the first step in helping them build a better self-image. Warm praise for whatever contribution they make invariably leads to a second effort.

As an example, there was 8-year-old Patty, who was referred to a Saturday-morning play group because of her extreme shyness. At first, she took part only when the whole group was moving, and then, I suspected, because it would have been more conspicuous to remain seated than to get up with the others. After several weeks, she did a pantomime of a child finding a kitten. Her pleasure and tenderness as she fondled its soft body drew spontaneous admiration from the other children in the class. This was the breakthrough. From that day, Patty's eagerness to enter into the activities was apparent. Her voice was almost inaudible at first, but it grew stronger in proportion to her growing self-confidence. This was no sudden miracle; indeed, it took three years for a transformation to take place. Patty's feelings of inadequacy had been so deep-seated that many successes were necessary to convince her that she had something to offer that her peers would accept. Whether or when she would have found her way anyhow, no one can say. Creative drama as a technique was deliberately used, and the change during the three years she attended the class was striking.

Exhibitionism

The show-offs are just as much in need of help as the shy children, but rarely elicit sympathetic attention. Their problem is also one of uneasiness, and in trying to prove their importance, they do all the wrong things. Their behavior ranges from monopolizing class discussion to interfering with the work of others. They may deliberately use a wrong word for the sake of a laugh or play the clown so as to give their peers something to laugh at. Because they are so focused on the effect they are having, they have difficulty concentrating on what they are supposed to be doing.

I remember John, a nervous little fellow of 7, with facial mannerisms and a habit of interrupting. John was accepted by the others for a while because he amused them. Nevertheless, he was unable to remain involved in a role for more than a few minutes. Then he would look around the room to see how he was affecting the other children. In John's case, there was no sudden incident that accounted for the change that took place. Rather, it was a matter of working patiently, taking every opportunity to praise his honest expression and helping him find satisfaction in getting attention legitimately. By the end of the year, John was able to work cooperatively with the group much of the time and to forgo the need to show off. His problem was still not entirely solved, but he had learned something of the give-and-take of working with others and the pleasure that comes from honest work.

Sometimes the teacher may be forced to ask a disruptive child to return to his or her seat—not as punishment, but as the consequence of unacceptable behavior. Creative drama demands, above all, teamwork and respect for others. The player who cannot work with the team must withdraw until he or she is willing and able to accept the ground rules.

Isolation

The isolate, or loner, is often a child who cannot relate to the group. Loners may work hard and have good ideas and the ability to present them, but always in isolation. This may, of course, be an indication of superior talent and high motivation. Independence is a desired goal, but when withdrawal is the result of an inability to relate to others, it is a serious problem. Through movement and group activities, the isolate may be drawn into the group naturally. The isolate who has good ideas should be urged to share them; this expressed desire to use the ideas may bring about the desired result. If not successful at once, the teacher should persist, explaining that drama is a *group* art and needs the contributions of every participant. If nothing works, the school psychologist should be consulted; the problem would appear to be deep-seated and, therefore, serious.

Insensitivity

The insensitive child is similar to, but different from, the show-off because he or she usually is rejected by the others and does not understand why. Insensitive children tend to ridicule the ideas of others and criticize their efforts, often harshly. Playing a variety of roles may help them gain insights into and develop an awareness of the feelings of others. This takes time, but patient attention to the problem in human relations may eventually help insensitive children to listen and accept suggestions from their peers.

Because of their insensitivity, such children can be dealt with quite directly by calling attention to the fact that they are harsh and that others are hurt or angered by their criticism. Insensitive persons do not realize this and have to have it pointed out to them. They may be very intelligent children, but they have a blind spot in dealing with others; teachers do not do them a service by ignoring it.

Distraction

Every teacher has known the easily distracted child—the one whose concentration is broken at any unexpected sight or sound. Work to strengthen concentration is the best approach to the problem. But success may take a long time, and the teacher may have to find satisfaction in the slightest improvement—a longer attention span and the child's ability to remain focused beyond the point where he or she used to be thrown off. Again, if the problem persists, professional help for the child should be sought, for it may be a symptom of something serious.

Physical Disabilities

Children with special handicaps need special attention. They need sympathy, understanding, and encouragement. The teacher is not equipped to practice therapy, but he or she must know what to expect of disabled children and try to adapt the activities to their capabilities. Such children often are in therapy, and if the teacher can work with the therapist, she or he will be able to receive helpful suggestions about the proper approach.

Stuttering, a harelip, any condition that interferes with locomotion, or a hearing loss presents problems that must be faced within the context of a class; most classroom teachers have had little or no experience with them.

The first thing to remember is that all persons gain in self-respect when their ideas are accepted. The child with a problem has a special need for acceptance, and the teacher must try to find the best way in which to meet it. Creative drama provides an ideal opportunity to help the timid child overcome inhibitions; to provide the show-off with a better way of getting attention; to guide the insensitive child to some awareness of the feelings of others; to help the disabled child find an avenue of expression. In each case, imagination is the first step in discovering ways to see beyond the problem and create a solution. It takes imagination both on the child's part and on the teacher's, and the task is not easy.

Today's children are subjected to pressures and demands that, if not greater than in the past, are certainly new and different. Not only inner-city children but also affluent, suburban children reflect these changes in values and mores. The pressures and demands often result in unpredictable behavior, causing problems for teachers and creating difficulties when freedom is encouraged. Creative-drama teachers are particularly vulnerable to these problems, for they deal with the emotional and social, as well as the intellectual, aspects of child development.

Although freedom is essential to creativity, it often is necessary to impose restraints in the beginning, or at least until the children become comfortable with the group, the leader, and the activity. It is important that teachers be sensitive to unusual behavior and try to handle it with understanding and firmness. While they cannot accept certain antisocial behavior in a child, it is important for the child to know what is being rejected. In other words, teachers do not reject the child but do reject behavior that interferes with the freedom of others to express their ideas and feelings.

EVALUATING CHILDREN'S RESPONSES

A question that always comes up is how to evaluate children's responses. This is difficult to answer, for progress varies from one child to the next. The teacher has different expectations for each child, and what may be extraordinary growth for one is scarcely an adequate performance for another. With that in mind, the teacher should ask:

1. Have the individuals in the class become a group, willing and able to work together? Is there easy give-and-take?
2. Is each child an integral part of the group, sharing ideas without fear of failure or need to impress?
3. Is the work sincere?
4. Has physical movement become more free and more expressive?
5. Have verbal skills—speech, voice and diction, vocabulary, and oral expression—improved?
6. Depending on the focus, have other goals—use of resource materials, integration of learning, and involvement in subject—been met?
7. Does the group exhibit vitality—eagerness to begin and reluctance to stop at the end of the period?
8. Does the noise level reflect industry and enthusiasm?

It is easier in many ways to evaluate the work of the older child than that of the younger because of the older child's better handling of materials. The younger child lacks the experience, vocabulary, and background that can be assumed in the middle and upper grades. Evaluation of the younger child must focus, therefore, on attitude, freedom of movement, and imagination, rather than on the more objective aspects of a performance, which are developed later. The assessment of students of any age is difficult at best, particularly for the teacher who is deeply involved in the work of the group.

SUMMARY

Creative drama may be regarded as a way of learning, a means of self-expression, a therapeutic technique, a social activity, or an art form. Children are helped to assume responsibility, accept group decisions, work cooperatively, develop new interests, and seek new information.

It is often observed that few persons perform on their highest level. This is true of the beginner, child or adult, who, through shyness or fear, needs encouragement and acceptance. The sensitive teacher recognizes this and tries to create an atmosphere of mutual trust in the classroom. In the acceptance of every child and what he or she has to offer, the leader has taken the first big step toward building the child's self-confidence. Freedom will follow; learning will occur; and an ordinary schoolroom will become a place in which wonderful things can happen.

2

IMAGINATION: THE STARTING POINT

The *fact* of imagination has long been known, but it is only recently that the *value* of imagination has been recognized. Today, not only artists but also businesspeople, scientists, military leaders, and educators describe imagination as the magic force that goes beyond the mastery of facts and techniques in the search for new ideas. The child brings this magic force into the classroom, but it is up to the teacher to encourage its use. For imagination leads to creation, and the creative child is the one who can transform the *ordinary* into the *extraordinary* and unique.

CREATIVITY

Creativity may be defined in a number of ways. It may be thought of in terms of process or product, depending on whether we are concerned with the way in which a problem is solved or with the solution itself. If creativity is interpreted as process, it is considered as a new way of seeing, a different point of view, an original idea, or a new relationship between ideas. Inventiveness and adaptation are often included in the thinking of those who believe creativity to be a way of working.

If, however, creativity is defined in terms of product, it is best illustrated by works of art (poems, stories, paintings, music, dance), scientific inventions, and new arrangements or designs. There has been great interest in the study and measurement of creativity in recent years,

Encouraging imagination through a puppet. (Courtesy of Tamara Hunt, University of Hawaii at Manoa)

and a considerable body of data has appeared. One assumption accepted by psychologists is that creativity is not a special gift possessed by a fortunate few, but a human capacity possessed to some degree by everyone.

According to some authorities, the beginning of creative thinking may be found early in the life of the infant, in its manipulative and exploratory activities. In its awareness of human facial expressions, gestures, and sounds, the baby is first observer and then investigator. It is but a short step from here to experimentation, at which point the child becomes creator. The words *observer, investigator, creator* are of particular interest to the teacher.

One of the most delightful views about creativity was expressed by Professor Franz Čižek of the Vienna School of Arts and Crafts in 1921. Although he was not referring to drama, his attitude is that of many successful teachers in any of the arts. The following conversation with Čižek is included verbatim for its insight and its relevance to this chapter.

> *"How do you do it?" we asked at last, when we had looked at some hundreds of the productions of Professor Čižek's pupils, each more delightful and original than the last.*

"But I don't do," he protested with a kind of weary pity for our lack of understanding. "I take off the lid, and other masters clap the lid on—that is the only difference.

"Children have their own laws which they must needs obey. What right have grown-ups to interfere?"

"And do many of your children go in for art afterward?" we queried.

"Not as a rule. They go into all sorts of professions and trades. That's quite right. That's what I like. I like to think of art coloring all departments of life rather than being a separate profession."

". . .What a pity all children don't come to you."

"Yes, it is a pity," he assented, shaking his head rather mournfully. "There is so much of the summer and the autumn but the spring never comes again."[1]

BEGINNING EXERCISES FOR IMAGINATION

The first day the class meets, the teacher will do well to begin with the simplest exercises in which imagination is involved. Regardless of age level, the participants must be given an opportunity to go beyond the here and now, but they cannot and should not be expected to handle an entire story or create an improvisation. It is wise to start work with the whole group, if space permits. This removes all thoughts of actors and audience, thereby diminishing fear and self-consciousness.

How the teacher begins will be determined by the age, experience, and number of children in the group, as well as by the size of the playing space. With young children, large physical movement is the best opening exercise. Music or a drumbeat will help to focus the attention. One simple and very effective way of beginning is to have the group walk to the beat of the drum. As the group becomes more comfortable and relaxed, the beat can be changed: rapid, double time, slow, and so on. The children, in listening for the change in beat, forget themselves and are able to use their entire bodies more freely. Galloping, skipping, and hopping are good exercise and fun for younger children.

From the purely physical body movement, the teacher may move on to feelings. For example, if the group has been walking to a slow beat, she may suggest that there is green grass underfoot: "How does it feel to you? Your feet are tired. Imagine what it is like to put them down on soft, cool grass. Take off your shoes. [Some children will do so at this suggestion.] Walk on it. Feel it." Activities 2.1 to 2.3 carry the idea further into a simple narrative.

[1] Franz Čižek, "Some Conversations with Čižek," in *The Child as Artist* (Children's Art Exhibition Fund, 1921).

Concentration

If imagination is the beginning, concentration—the capacity to hold an idea long enough to do something about it—must come next. It is not enough to glimpse an idea; action must follow. Inexperienced players of any age may have difficulty concentrating, for self-consciousness and fear of failure are distracting agents. It is now that the teacher has to encourage every effort, however small, in order to free the child of self-doubt. A game often is helpful, for it provides structure and discipline. Because of the social nature of the game, the interpersonal relationships involved are of primary value. One that most children love is "Fruit Bowl" (Activity 2.4).

Organization

Once concentration has been established, the next step is the organization of ideas. No matter how simple the problem, some arrangement of the parts is necessary in order to give meaning to the ideas and to convey that meaning to spectators. This consists of a beginning or introduction, a logical succession of parts, and an ending. There may be only two or three parts or there may be several, but as children gain experience, they will find ways to organize their ideas into a cohesive structure that adds clarity and interest.

SENSORY AWARENESS

This may be the time to introduce sensory awareness. While little children cannot and should not be burdened with long discussions, they are well aware of the ways in which they find out what is going on around them, and they usually are eager to talk about the five senses: sight, hearing, touch, smell, and taste. Activities 2.5 and 2.6 help to enliven the discussion.

SUMMARY

Imagination is the spark that sets off the creative impulse. Concentration (the capacity to hold an idea long enough to do something about it) and organization (the arrangement of the parts) are necessary to satisfying self-expression. Communication (the bridge to others) comes last and is less the concern of creative drama than of the formal play.

In all creative work, there are obstacles that must be recognized and, as much as possible, overcome. Wise leaders learn first to identify the problems and then to look for solutions. They will remember that they are neither therapists nor theatre directors but teachers, guiding players through the medium of informal drama. Brian Way has defined their role: "Schools do not exist to develop actors but to develop people, and one of the major factors in developing people is that of preserving and enriching to its fullest the human capacity to give full and undivided attention to any matter in hand at any given moment."[2]

[2] Brian Way, *Development through Drama* (New York: Humanities Press, 1967), p. 15.

ACTIVITY 2.1

GOING ON A JOURNEY

"Going on a Journey" is an exercise that children of all ages enjoy, but it is particularly popular with younger boys and girls. Besides stimulating the imagination, it develops concentration and organizes ideas.

Objective: To stimulate the imagination

Suggestions for the Teacher

Clear the room in order to allow for as much space as possible. Then divide the class into several groups of seven or eight children. Each group will have a turn to play while the others watch. Explain to them that they are going on a long journey. Allow time for them to follow each direction:

1. Walking down a country road
2. Running across hot sand in a desert
3. Stepping over puddles
4. Going through tall grass
5. Climbing a hill
6. Wading through snow
7. Reaching the top of a mountain
8. Finding a cottage

In this exercise, the point is to help the players see the different terrains they must cover. After they have found the cottage, some groups like to return home, making the trip in reverse. If the children enjoy this exercise, more areas can be added, lengthening the journey.

Questions for the Observers

1. Could you see the travelers crossing the sand? the puddles? the tall grass?
2. How would you have known when they reached the end of the journey if I had not told you?
3. Were there other things the travelers might have done?

Questions for the Players

1. How did the sand feel under your feet?
2. Could you see the puddles you crossed?
3. What does tall grass feel like when you try to walk through it?
4. How were the snow drifts different from the grass?
5. What did you see at the top of the mountain?
6. Describe the cottage.

ACTIVITY 2.2

THE SNOWMAN

Objective: To stimulate the imagination and relax the entire body

Suggestions for the Teacher

The entire class can take part if there is enough space. Otherwise, divide the class into two groups; each group will be snowmen while the other watches. Those who are snowmen should stand far enough apart that they do not touch.

Ask how many children have ever seen a snowman melt when the weather suddenly grows warmer: What happens to the snowman? Does it change its shape? How?

Ask the children to imagine themselves as large, white snowmen with hats and canes and then to listen carefully as you give them the following directions.

1. The sun begins to shine, and for the first time, your body feels warm.
2. You grow warmer and warmer. Your hat slips—and slides—and falls off.
3. Now you feel the sun shining on your shoulders. Your arms and legs are melting. Your cane slips from your hand and falls to the ground.
4. Your legs no longer hold you up, and you, too, slide down. Finally, you are completely melted and become a puddle.

Questions for the Players

1. What did it feel like when the sun began to shine on your head? your shoulders? your legs and body?
2. How did your body feel when you became a puddle?
3. What happens to the water after a snowstorm, when all the snow melts?

2.3

"Seeds" is a good exercise after a discussion of growth and growing. Most children enjoy it and the vivid imagery it stimulates.

Objective: To contract and stretch the entire body

Suggestions for the Teacher

Like "The Snowman," "Seeds" can be done by the entire group if the space is large enough. If not, divide the class into two groups; each group will be seeds while the other watches. Suggest that the seeds imagine themselves either planted in rows or growing wild.

Ask the children to think of themselves as buried deep in the earth. It is winter. The hard earth is cold and quiet. Then ask them to listen as you describe what happens when the seasons change.

1. Spring comes—first with rain, and then with sun and wind. What happens to the little seeds? Do you try to break through the hard earth? Can you push and push and *push*—and grow?
2. Summer comes. The little plants are growing taller and stronger. What do they become—flowers or bushes or trees? Are you tall, weak, or strong?
3. Now feel the warm rain, the hot sun, and the breeze blowing.
4. It is fall, and you have reached your full growth.

This exercise can be extended and lead into further discussion, depending on when and how it is introduced.

Questions for the Players

1. Describe your feelings as you began to grow.
2. What were you—a flower? a weed? a young tree?
3. What will happen to you in the fall, when the weather becomes colder again?

ACTIVITY 2.4

FRUIT BOWL

"Fruit Bowl" is adaptable to groups of all ages and abilities. The game may be used as a warm-up while waiting for everyone to assemble or as an activity to help shy players focus attention.

Objective: To create relaxation

Suggestions for the Teacher

As the children enter the room, give them names of a fruit to remember—say, apple, banana, and peach. Players sit in a circle, and you stand in the center. When you call out "apple," all the apples change places; when you call out "banana," those players who are bananas change places. When you call out "fruit bowl," each child in the circle gets up and changes places with someone else.

Variations on the game can be made, but however it is played, turn to another activity or begin the lesson before the players become bored.

ACTIVITY 2.5

USING OUR FIVE SENSES

Objective: To discover how many things there are right around us when we use our senses.

Suggestions for the Teacher

Ask the players to do the following for a minute or two.

1. Close your eyes for a minute and listen to all the sounds you can hear from where you sit. Then tell the class what you heard.
2. Look down at the floor and, when a minute is up, tell what things you saw. You will be surprised at all you see when you really look.
3. Close your eyes and feel an object. After a minute, describe it as completely as you can.
4. Look at a picture and tell us everything you saw in it. [The teacher shows it, and then takes it away so that the class has to remember the objects in and arrangement of the picture.]
5. Try to discover any odors in the room. They may be pleasant or unpleasant, familiar or strange. What are they?
6. Go into a corner or another area of the room and touch and examine three objects or surfaces. Then come back and tell what you have seen in as much detail as possible.

What we are trying to do is

lead children into experiences that will involve them in touching, seeing, tasting, hearing, and smelling the things in their world. We also want them to become involved in experiences that will lead to imagining, exploring, reasoning, inventing, experimenting, investigating, and selecting, so that these experiences will not only be rich in themselves but lead to personal creative growth. *

* Earl Linderman and Donald W. Herberholz, *Developing Artistic and Perceptual Awareness* (Dubuque, Ia.: Brown, 1964), p. x.

ACTIVITY 2.6

OUR FIVE SENSES

Objective:* *To imagine situations in which we use our five senses

Suggestions for the Teacher

Have the children try the following exercises—first in groups, and then individually, if they are ready for individual work. With a very large class, you may want to do only one or two of the exercises at a time in order to avoid having the children become bored.

Exercises for the sense of *sight*

1. Looking for a missing piece of a puzzle that you have just dropped
2. Watching your favorite program on television
3. Waiting at the airport for a plane that is bringing your grandmother and grandfather to visit you; it is taking the plane a long time to land
4. Looking at a big tray of cookies and trying to decide which ones to buy
5. Looking in your sweater drawer for your favorite sweater

Exercises for the sense of *hearing*

1. Listening to a marching band, far in the distance, as it comes closer and closer to your home
2. Trying to hear what your friend is calling to you from across the playground
3. Trying to discover where a small noise is coming from and what it is (Is it in your house or next door? Is it a small animal or an insect? a dripping pipe?)
4. Listening to a familiar voice on the telephone; you have a poor connection, but you can hear words now and then
5. Listening to the radio as it plays a piece of music that you like

Exercises for the sense of *smell*

1. Coming home from school and smelling cookies baking in the kitchen
2. Walking in the woods and smelling a campfire
3. Smelling different flowers in a vase
4. Smelling something very unpleasant and trying to decide what it is

Exercises for the sense of *taste*

1. Eating a piece of delicious chocolate candy

2. Trying a foreign food that you never have tasted and deciding that you like it
3. Biting into a sour apple
4. Eating a sandwich and trying to decide what is in it

Exercises for the sense of *touch*

1. Touching a piece of velvet
2. Touching a hot stove
3. Touching or holding an ice cube
4. Stroking the soft fur of a rabbit

These are only a few suggestions, and you will think of many more. Whatever is suggested, however, should always be within the experience of the players.

3

DEVELOPING BODY AWARENESS AND SPATIAL PERCEPTION

Movement is a natural response to a stimulus and an important element of drama. Theatre began with movement; its origins were closely linked with religious and magical rites. The elements of conflict, character, plot, and dialogue gradually were added. With these additions, theatre as an art form was born.

Primitive peoples—in attempting to order their universe, explain natural phenomena, and pray to their gods—used rhythmic movement to express themselves. In time, this movement evolved into dance. An entire tribe might take part, or perhaps only the most skilled dancers. As the movements were repeated, they took on special meanings. These meanings were understood by both performers and spectators and were taught to the young, thus serving an educational as well as a religious purpose.

CHILDREN AND MOVEMENT

Creative movement deals with the elements of dance but is more spontaneous. Children move naturally; by encouraging such movement, the teacher can help children to express themselves through physical activity, thereby creating their own styles of movement, gaining confidence in their bodies, and developing spatial awareness. It is easy to move from creative movement to either dance or drama.

Drama differs from dance because it involves a linguistic element; the older the players, the greater the dependence on words to communicate meaning. The teacher of creative drama hopes to develop children's ability and ease in the use of both verbal and nonverbal expression; starting early is an important factor in achieving these goals.

Like primitive peoples, preschool children use their bodies to express their strongest emotions and communicate their needs and desires. Children's posture, for instance, reflects how they feel, regardless of what they may say. We read much about body language these days. This form of nonverbal communication includes any posture as well as reflexive or nonreflexive movement of the body that conveys emotion to the observer. Although most of this popular writing concerns adults, the attitudes and feelings of children are just as clearly revealed by their movements and facial expressions. A teacher can learn much about the members of a class of any age from the postures they assume and the use they make of the various parts of their bodies.

A young child tends to express physically what an adult states in words. For example, when asked how a horse moves, a small child is more apt to gallop than to describe the gait. Asked the height of a very tall person, the preschool child stands on tiptoe to reach as high as possible.

Rhythm classes for young children build on this natural impulse. What happens in the class was well described by an experienced teacher of rhythms and dramatic play.[1] The children remove their shoes and stockings as they enter a gym or a large, free, unencumbered space. Music is provided by a pianist or a recording, or "if we are lucky, it is music created by the children themselves." Then, as if by signal, the children respond to changing rhythms. If the music is fast, wild, and free, so are their movements. If it becomes slower, quieter, and softer, so will their movements. The idea is for the children to listen to what the music says and then to transfer its meaning into bodily activity. "To one child the rhythm may suggest the rhythm of a galloping pony; to another it may mean the branches of a tree buffeted in a wind storm; a third may think of the whirling arms of a threshing machine." The teacher neither suggests what the children should do nor asks them questions; but by watching, she usually is able to tell what is in the mind of each. In the middle grades, rhythms may be based on units of study: Indians, Greek mythology, the Old West, the jungle. "These are samples of the big

[1] All the quotations in this paragraph are from *Rhythms by Mary Perrine*, as told to Henrietta O. Rogers (New Canaan, Conn.: The New Canaan Country School Monograph, 1951).

rhythmic activities that appeal so strongly to growing, energetic youngsters."

In addition, there is the physical pleasure a child derives from moving, a pleasure that leads into play, dance, sports, and exercise for its own sake. Today, unfortunately, television constantly bombards the eyes and ears of children, giving information of all kinds, it is true, but at the expense of movement and natural creative response. In bringing children indoors, television helps to make them passive spectators rather than active participants in games and sports in open areas. Most children enjoy moving their bodies and discovering different ways of exploring a space. As they gain physical control, they prefer running to walking and enjoy finding new methods of locomotion that are energetic and fast. Running, skipping, galloping, hopping, jumping, leaping, and rolling stretch the muscles and help children gain a mastery of their bodies as they try out all the different things they can do with them. Because movement is so natural an expression, it is the ideal way of beginnning work in creative drama. Experienced teachers of young children know this and progress from rhythmic movement to dramatic play.

Children with language problems also tend to find great satisfaction in movement. The physicality of dance and movement circumvents their disadvantages in verbal skills, thus providing another reason for its inclusion, particularly in the beginning.

BEGINNING CLASSES IN MOVEMENT

Classes in movement are most successful when taught in a large room, where children have plenty of space in which to move freely. Too large an area, such as a gymnasium or a playground, presents problems, however, as large, unconfined space often leads to chaos, dispersing the group rather than bringing it together. Therefore, boundaries should be established and maintained.

Piano accompaniment is an asset, if the teacher can play or has an accompanist; if not, a drum is perfectly satisfactory. Later on, recorded music will help suggest mood and characterization. In the beginning and for most purposes, percussion instruments are all the leader needs to give the beat and suggest or change rhythms. One advantage of the drum is that it permits the leader to move freely and watch the group.

In a movement class, it is usually a good idea to begin work with the entire group, unless it is so large or the room is so small that the participants will bump into one another. In that case, the leader should divide the class into two groups, working first with one and then with the other, and alternating every few minutes in order to hold the chil-

The Frog

dren's interest. After gathering the children into a large circle, the leader should beat on a drum a good rhythm for walking. When everyone is moving easily and without self-consciousness, the beat can be changed to something faster, such as a trot or a run. Shifting the rhythm to a gallop, a skip, a hop, a jump, and then back to a slow walk not only stimulates good exercise, but also holds the attention as the children listen for the changes. Why rhythmic movement first? Because it encourages spontaneity within a disciplined framework. This is the goal of the teacher of creative drama as well as the teacher of dance.

As teachers, we have tended to think of creative drama as being concerned primarily with the development of intellectual and linguistic abilities, whereas we have thought of movement as being concerned with the control and use of the body. Actually, movement and body language are a part of drama. It is the combined mental, physical, vocal, and emotional involvement that distinguishes drama from all other art forms and gives it its special value.

Movement Vocabulary

Utilizing movements that young children have tried and probably mastered makes it easier to attempt explorations in space. Possibilities go far beyond this list, but the following are known by most children by the time they are in the first grade. They can be enjoyed at any time and later combined to make patterns.

Locomotion	*Nonlocomotion*
Walking	Bending
Running	Stretching
Jumping	Swinging
Hopping	Pulling
Galloping	Bouncing
Skipping	Shaking
Lunging	Pushing
Trotting	Twisting

The following is a quieting exercise to be used after vigorous movement. Sitting in a circle on the floor, the group creates different rhythms and sounds. Clapping hands, snapping fingers, tapping knees, and brushing the floor softly with the hands are among the sound-producing movements that can be made in this position. Have each child put two, then three, of these sounds together in a rhythmic sequence. The group listens carefully and tries to repeat the sequence.

Observation and Imitation

An exercise for observation and imitation that younger children enjoy suggests movement through the *ly* game. The entire class can play it together, or one person can begin and the others follow his or her interpretation. In this way, every child is ensured the opportunity to create a movement suggested by the word. Words used might be *lazily, quickly, slowly, curiously, wearily, sleepily, noiselessly, loudly, angrily, happily, joyfully, thankfully,* and *fearfully.* For example, if the first child says "lazily," he walks across the room in a *lazy* manner. The group follows, imitating the movements. The next child might say "happily" and interpret it as she feels it. Again, all follow her lead. This can continue as long as the interest holds. Incidentally, playing the *ly* game is also a way of learning new words.

The Wheel and the Cobra(Courtesy of Rachel Carr; photographs by Edward Kimball)

Similar to this game is the beating out of rhythms. Each child has a turn clapping a rhythm for the others to follow. After each has had a turn, variations of the game may be played. One child goes into the center of a circle and begins to clap a rhythm; after changing it suddenly, the child taps another child, who will begin the next rhythm. This has endless possibilities and is an excellent exercise for encouraging close observation and imitation.

Rhythm

Activities 3.1 and 3.2 are designed to help the child discover the drama in movement.

A variation on "Building a Zoo" is "Making a Train." It is a problem of precision for very young players. Each child follows another in a line, with all the children maintaining an equal distance between themselves and the children ahead of them. The teacher determines the speed, direction, and rhythm of the cars. Variations on this activity might involve being derailed, stopping suddenly, running out of fuel, or being wrecked.

TELLING STORIES THROUGH MOVEMENT

Storytelling through movement offers children an opportunity to express themselves in a way that is natural yet different from verbal exposition. For younger children, particularly those for whom English is a second language, this mode of communication has special significance. It gives them a chance to live the story, as they portray characters in action without struggling for words.

It is a good idea to begin with a simple story line and, as with a story to be told in dialogue, move on to more complex material. Nursery rhymes are good for "starters." They are familiar, provide dramatic action, and have different moods and tempos (Activity 3.3).

Once children have had some experience in performing a simple story in movement, rather than telling it through spoken lines, they are ready for a longer narrative. Portions of "The Elves and the Shoemaker" are good because there are parts for everyone: the shoemaker and any number of elves.

Dancing with a body puppet in creative movement. (Courtesy of Tamara Hunt, Hokulani School, Honolulu)

Now the class is ready for longer tales. The traditional folk tale of pulling up the turnip can be told completely in movement. Although it is about individuals rather than groups, there are so many characters and the tale is so short that everyone in the class can have a turn. It is a very amusing situation, but also one that requires skill and control to prevent its becoming a series of pratfalls. The teacher reads it slowly as the children move. Activities 3.4 to 3.6 involve longer and more complicated stories.

THE TURNIP

It was autumn and time for the turnips to be harvested. Grandfather went out to the garden and bent down to pull the first one. But this turnip was different from any turnips he had ever planted. It refused to come up! So, after trying unsuccessfully with all his might, he called his wife to help him.

When grandmother came out and saw what he wanted, she put her arms around his waist, and together they pulled and pulled. Still the turnip would not budge. Then granddaughter came out to the garden to see what was happening. Putting her arms around grandmother's waist, she pulled grandmother, who pulled grandfather, who pulled the turnip. But the turnip refused to come up.

[The story continues in this way with any number of characters included, each one pulling the one before him or her. Sometimes it is told with the granddaughter's dog pulling her and a beetle pulling the dog, followed by a second, third, and fourth beetle all pulling at the end of the line.]

Finally, when all pull together, the turnip comes up!

SUMMARY

Movement—the basis of play, ritual, games, dance, and theatre—is a natural beginning for work in creative drama. Physically, the whole body is involved: torso, arms, legs, head, and neck. Through the use of the body, muscles are stretched and relaxed. Posture and coordination improve with regular exercise. Because the entire group can take part at one time, the possibility of self-consciousness is lessened. Persons of all ages and backgrounds usually find it easier at first to become involved in drama through movement rather than through verbalization. This is particularly true of young children, children for whom English is a second language, and persons with special problems and needs. In the rhythms and patterns of a child's movement, the problems in his or her inner life often are revealed. This is why movement and dance are recommended as treatment, serving both diagnostic and therapeutic purposes.

Imitation and observation are as much a part of movement as is creativity. The leader encourages imagination but discourages cliché. Through movement, therefore, children experience both discipline and freedom. Moving into the rituals of the group (and here the word *rituals* is used in its broadest sense) engenders a feeling of belonging. Rhythm, that underlying flow and beat, captures the mover in an experience both objective and pleasurable. Taught together, rhythms and dramatic play provide a sound foundation for acting. "Dance-drama" encompasses the disciplines of both arts and thus is a powerful tool for creative expression.

ACTIVITY 3.1

LOCOMOTION

Objective: To create movement suggested by rhythms

Suggestions for the Teacher

Have the children listen as you beat a rhythm on a drum. Then ask them to imagine what kinds of people the following beats suggest.

1. ♩♩♩♩ ♩♩♩♩ ♩♩♩♩

   [This beat may suggest a soldier, a police officer, someone walking to a bus, an Indian chief.]

2. ♩♩ ♩♩ ♩♩ ♩♩

   [This may suggest a tired old person, a delivery boy with a heavy load, someone trudging up a hill.]

3. ♫♫♫♫

   [This may suggest a person hurrying home.]

4. ♬♬♬♬

   [This very rapid beat may suggest someone running for a train that is just pulling out of the station, a child late for school, a best friend knocking at the door.]

Now describe a character and make up a rhythm to guide the children in creating it.

1. A child jumping rope
2. A toddler walking, stumbling, walking again, falling down, then walking yet again
3. A thief escaping after robbing a house
4. A watchman on his rounds
5. A child skipping

ACTIVITY 3.2

ANIMALS

Objective: To find rhythms that suggest different animals

Suggestions for the Teacher

Call out the name of an animal. Ask one child to move as that animal does, either actively around the room or in place. Pick up the rhythm of the movement with a drum and ask the other children to follow.

1. A horse
2. A cat
3. A rabbit
4. A chicken
5. A kangaroo
6. A mouse
7. A toad
8. A bird
9. A caterpillar
10. An elephant

If the children enjoy being animals, here are two extensions of the animal-movement exercise. First, using this simple verse, have a few children take each line and cross the room in the manner of the animal named.

*JUMP AND JIGGLE**

EVELYN BEYER

Worms wiggle.
Bugs jiggle.
Rabbits hop.
Horses clop.
Snakes slide.
Sea gulls glide.
Mice creep.
Deer leap.
Puppies bounce.
Lions stalk—
But—
I walk.

Second, in "Building a Zoo," each child imitates a different animal in movement, eventually having the animals move into imagined zoo cages or natural habitats around the room. The teacher can be the zoo keeper, working "in role" with the class.

* Lucy Sprague Mitchell, ed., *Another Here and Now Storybook* (New York: Dutton, 1965).

ACTIVITY 3.3

NURSERY RHYMES

Objective: To suggest character through posture and body movement, and story through dance and movement

Suggestions for the Teacher

Familiarize the class with the verses they will interpret. Focus on the essential action; emphasize the structure—beginning, middle, and end. It is a good idea to have younger children try it in unison.

Music or percussion instruments will enhance the story and help the children to find the mood and tempo.

TO MARKET, TO MARKET

To market, to market To buy a fat pig.	*Gallop in one direction*
Home again, home again Jiggidy, jig.	*Gallop in the other direction*

JACK AND JILL

Jack and Jill went up the hill To fetch a pail of water.	*March, lifting knees high*
Jack fell down	*Bend over, resting the top of the head on the floor*
And broke his crown	*Somersault*
And Jill came tumbling after.	*Continue turning somersaults*

OLD KING COLE

Old King Cole was a merry old soul A merry old soul was he.	*Lift elbows up and down*
He called for his pipe [clap, clap]	*March 12 counts (light load)*
He called for his bowl [clap, clap]	*March 12 counts (heavy load)*
He called for his fiddlers three. [clap, clap]	*Bow one arm like a violin, play it with the other one*

ACTIVITY 3.4

THE THREE BILLY GOATS GRUFF

"The Three Billy Goats Gruff," a Scandinavian folk tale, is a great favorite of little children and lends itself to mime, improvisation, and puppetry. Because it is so familiar, it requires little preparation time; and because it is so short, it can be played again and again until every child in the class has had a turn.

Objective: To enact a simple story in movement

Suggestions for the Teacher

Read the story aloud slowly as the children act it. The rhythm of the goats' crossing the bridge is a good beginning and can be established by a simple drumbeat.

THE THREE BILLY GOATS GRUFF

Once upon a time, there were three billy goats. They were known as the Billy Goats Gruff. One day, they wanted to get some fresh green grass to eat. Now the green grass grew on the far side of a bridge, and under the bridge lived a Troll. After thinking it over, the Billy Goats decided to cross the bridge anyhow, for they were hungry.

They sent the smallest goat over first. He walked across the bridge, "trip-trap, trip-trap, trip-trap."

The Troll heard him and roared, "Who's that tripping over my bridge? I'm going to gobble you up."

"Oh, no, don't do that," cried the little Billy Goat. "Wait for the second Billy Goat Gruff. He's bigger than I am."

So the Troll let him cross. Soon there was another "trip-trap, trip-trap, TRIP-TRAP" on the bridge. It was the second Billy Goat Gruff. "Who's that tripping over my bridge?" roared the Troll. "I'm going to gobble you up."

"Oh, no," said the middle-size Billy Goat. "Wait for the big Billy Goat Gruff. He will be along soon." And the Troll let him cross.

And, sure enough, soon there was a "TRIP-TRAP, TRIP-TRAP, TRIP-TRAP." "Who's that?" roared the Troll. "It must be the big Billy Goat Gruff, and I'm coming to gobble you up."

This time, the Troll ran toward the big Billy Goat, but the goat was so big that he ate up the Troll instead. Then all the Billy Goats crossed the bridge and danced on the fresh green grass on the other side.

ACTIVITY 3.5

THE LEGEND OF THE SHOOTING STAR

"The Legend of the Shooting Star" can be done with children of all ages and even choreographed by adult dancers for audiences of children. The story is so simple that second and third graders can follow it easily. Children of this age like animal stories and enjoy the action that this one involves.

This legend offers an opportunity to learn about the Indians of the Southwest. It can also be part of a social-studies unit, in which the legends as well as the habits, clothing, homes, and land in which the people lived are discussed.

Objective: To encourage creative movement through acting a story

Suggestions for the Teacher

It is a good idea to experiment with different rhythms, letting the group suggest movements for Coyote and the stars. When the class is ready, read the story aloud very slowly, and the legend can be danced or played in its entirety.

Even though the story of Coyote can be danced by any number of children, it is a good idea to use no more than 12 or 14 and repeat it several times with different children being Coyote. There is no right or wrong way to do it, for it is the story that is important. It can be told in many different ways, but dancing it is one of the most effective.

THE LEGEND OF THE SHOOTING STAR

Many moons ago, Coyote was a great dancer.

More than anything else, Coyote loved to dance.

More than fishing, more than hunting, more than running through the hills, Coyote loved to dance.

Coyote was a dancer.

At night, Coyote looked up into the sky and watched the stars dancing.

I should like to dance with the stars, thought Coyote.

One night, Coyote climbed to the top of the highest hill.

"I want to dance with you," Coyote called to the stars, but the stars only laughed.

"But I am a great dancer," called Coyote. The stars laughed again.

"How can we dance with you if we're up in the sky and you are down on earth?"

"Let me dance with you," Coyote cried.

Suddenly, the North Star had an idea. "I will throw this rope down to earth and pull Coyote up into the sky."

Coyote caught the rope, and the stars pulled Coyote into the sky. They began dancing together.

The stars danced very quickly. Soon Coyote grew tired. "I want to stop!" cried Coyote, but the stars danced faster and faster.

Coyote tried to climb onto the back of one of the stars, but his paw slipped and he fell to earth instead . . . and made a great hole in the ground.

To this day, whenever you see a shooting star, it is really Coyote falling to earth.

ACTIVITY 3.6

MEI LI'S NEW YEAR'S DAY

Every country in the world has its myths, legends, and folk tales. "Mei Li's New Year's Day," a story from China, is particularly suitable for telling in movement.

Objective: To enact a story with a variety of movements

Suggestions for the Teacher

Probably the best approach is a combination of storytelling and rhythms. If a gong or other percussion instruments are available, they may be used to add variety. If not, a simple drum is adequate. Working with the music or dance teacher is helpful, although the story is so simple that it does not require a specialist.

MEI LI'S NEW YEAR'S DAY

Mei Li was a little girl who lived in North China many years ago. This story takes place one New Year's Day—a very important day in the lives of the Chinese people. Mei Li was busy that morning, helping her mother clean the house and prepare for the coming of the Kitchen God in the evening. Just as they were finishing, Mei Li's older brother came in and said he was going to the New Year's Fair inside the Great Wall. Mei Li begged her mother to let her go with him, for she had never been to the fair. Her mother gave her permission but warned the children to be home before dark.

The two started out. On the way, they met some friends, who joined them. When they reached the Great Wall, they saw performers on stilts, clowns, prancing ponies, acrobats, and even a dancing bear. They watched all day. Suddenly, Mei Li realized that the gates would be closing at dusk, and they must leave at once so as to get home in time for the arrival of the Kitchen God. The children rushed through the gate and ran all the way home. They came in the door just in time to see him appear in the incense their mother was burning. As was the custom, the children did a dance in his honor.

The story can be developed much further, or it can be done only once or twice; either way, it offers excellent opportunities for trying different rhythms, movement, and dance. The children's dance at the end of the story may be simple or more elaborate, depending on the experience of the teacher, the size of the room, and the time allowed for a class in movement.

Rhythm Patterns

1. A quick beat on the drum as the children walk down the road to the fair
2. A slow staccato rhythm for the performers on stilts
3. A fast staccato rhythm for the prancing ponies
4. A crescendo to suggest excitement when the acrobats perform
5. A slow rhythm to suggest the clumsiness of the dancing bear
6. A very rapid beat as the children run home
7. The gong may be struck when the gates of the city open and close

4 FROM MOVEMENT TO MIME

Pantomime is the art of conveying ideas without words. Children enjoy pantomime, which is an excellent way to introduce creative drama to young children. Since many of their thoughts are spoken entirely through the body, 6- and 7-year-olds find pantomime a natural means of expression. Group pan-tomimes of the simplest sort challenge the imagination and sharpen awareness. In kindergarten, such basic movements as walking, running, skipping, and galloping prepare children for the creative use of rhythms. Music can set the mood for people marching in a parade, horses galloping on the plains, toads hopping in a field, cars racing on a track, or children skipping on a fine autumn day. In other words, rhythmic movement becomes dramatic when participants make use of it to become someone or something other than themselves.

Pantomime is especially satisfying to children who do not speak English and those with hearing and speech problems. The child who has an idea but not the words to express it can convey meaning, often very successfully, through body language. I have had speech-handicapped students of all ages present characters, stories, and ideas in pantomime with clarity and artistry. Another benefit, in addition to the obvious one of building self-confidence, is motivation for skill in the language arts. Having succeeded in sign language, children are encouraged to express themselves in words and writing as well.

Pantomime, incidentally, has become a familiar art form in the past 10 or 15 years. One of the benefits of television is the opportunity it affords all persons to enjoy the performing arts, including skilled professional mime.

PRACTICAL CONSIDERATIONS

CLASS SIZE

While movement classes can be carried on successfully with almost any number, pantomime requires a group of no more than 15 to 20 participants. If a class is very large, the teacher should make every effort to divide it, so that half the group is involved in another activity at that hour. Pantomime demands individual attention, and every child should be ensured the opportunity of participation each time the class meets. This is true whatever the age level, for growth results from repeated experiences that increase in difficulty.

LENGTH OF CLASS PERIOD

The length and frequency of class meetings depend on the situation and the age of the players. With very young children, daily classes for 10 to 15 minutes are ideal, whereas with older children, 2 or 3 meetings a week for 45 to 60 minutes work well.

In schools in which creative drama is a definite part of the curriculum, the teacher can look forward to regular meetings throughout the year. Where it is not, it is up to the classroom teacher to introduce it whenever and however possible. Pantomime can be handled in connection with other subjects, which, if imaginatively done, can be of value as a tool for teaching as well as an experience with an art form.

PLAYING SPACE

A stage is generally used for formal rehearsals, whereas a large room is more desirable for creative drama. Little children enjoy moving all over a room and should be encouraged to do so. The younger the group, therefore, the larger the space required. If a large room is not available, a classroom in which all the chairs have been pushed aside will do. Space makes for freedom; a small or cramped area inhibits it. As was noted in Chapter 3, however, too large an area can present other problems, particularly for a beginning or an uncontrolled group. Boundaries are needed, as the leader soon discovers; there is greater freedom where there are clear boundaries of both time and space than where there are neither. An auditorium with a stage and chairs is least desirable as a playing space for a beginning group of any age, since it inevitably leads to a concept of performance before the players are ready for it. Under any circumstances, seating children on the floor in a semicircle so that all can see, hear, and be heard is the most satisfactory arrangement.

Time of Class

When should the class meet? Not the last hour on Friday, if it can be avoided. Whereas movement classes are welcomed at that time, serious work in creative drama may suffer if children are restless and eager to be out of doors. Otherwise, pantomime can take place any time, as a class in its own right or in conjunction with other classes: language arts, social studies, math, science, or health. Drama belongs everywhere, as long as it is used legitimately.

SOUND AND MOTION STORIES

A good introduction to pantomime is a sound and motion story, which is a simple form of drama that requires limited participation. Players describe action through the use of the body while seated, with all vocal parts spoken in unison. It is a technique that can be used in a room where the desks are fastened to the floor. The imagination is stimulated, creating freedom within the boundaries of space, time, or the ability of the children to handle more demanding material. Sound and motion stories are especially popular with children in the lower grades. If a class enjoys the participation, the teacher can find stories that lend themselves to this technique and mark suitable participation points accordingly.

Activity 4.1 presents a delightful story that children with whom I have worked love.

IMAGINATION AND PANTOMIME

Activity 4.2, a favorite among children, may be used now or much earlier, as it combines imagination and pantomime. It is better for third graders than for first or second graders, and should not be used in a very large class or with immature children. Although small groups are involved, the actions are done by individuals; this can lead to self-consciousness, which must be avoided at all times.

ACTIONS IN PANTOMIME

There is no right or wrong order and no prescribed length of time to spend on one activity. Generally speaking, the older the players, the longer their attention can be sustained, although this does not always hold true. A pantomime that is guaranteed to capture and hold the interest of every player, regardless of age, is that of making or doing something (Activity 4.3). In the beginning, the teacher will have to offer suggestions, but most second- or third-grade players will have ideas of their own.

Pantomimes of actions will grow more complicated as the players put them into new situations. They are often the first step in enacting such situations as those in Activity 4.4.

EMOTIONS IN PANTOMIME

Feelings eventually creep into pantomime. The teacher may want to talk about feelings or even ask the children what kinds of feelings they have experienced. Their responses often include many more than the teacher has anticipated. Anger, fear, happiness, excitement, pride, curiosity, vanity, anticipation, sorrow, and hatred are some of the emotions that I have heard 7- and 8-year-olds list.

This may be a time to break the class into groups of four or five, with each group choosing one emotion to pantomime. Delightful results are always forthcoming when working on mood. One group showed excitement through a scene on Christmas Eve, when they crept downstairs to look at the tree and presents. Another group chose fear and set their scene in a tent at a summer camp. They were campers who heard a strange noise at night and imagined it to be a bear, but it was only their counselor coming back.

It soon becomes obvious that more than one emotion is usually involved in a situation of any length. Therefore, the next step will be to show change of mood. Situations like those in Activity 4.5 help the players move from one mood to another.

MUSIC AND PANTOMIME

Music can be a great asset in stimulating creative response. It is also an excellent way of drawing a group together at the beginning of a session. Leaders of after-school-activity groups have long recognized this and often use music to hold the attention as children are assembling. I have seen boys and girls absorbed for 10 to 15 minutes, singing folk songs or other familiar songs to simple guitar accompaniment. Leaders who can play an instrument have a decided advantage, for they not only hold the children's interest, but also build group spirit and make the sometimes difficult transition from school to an after-school activity.

When creative drama is a part of the curriculum, the class is already assembled, and music serves another purpose—to establish mood and stimulate the imagination. We have already used rhythms to suggest different kinds of movement, characters, or animals. From that to the heightening of characterization is a natural step. Actually, only the beat of a drum is necessary, although music can enrich the activity enormously. Playing records of orchestral music is an effective way of establishing mood and creating a pattern of listening, reacting, and responding. A leader with no formal background in music can guide the group, not in the sense of a lesson in music appreciation, of course, but in the sense of encouraging listening and imaginative response. Young children seem to respond more spontaneously to music than do older children, who have learned to be concerned with structure, theme, and melody. Careful selection of the music to be used is necessary for good results.

After playing a piece of recorded music or music on the piano, the teacher might follow the procedure in Activity 4.6.

There is a wealth of music that will stimulate a creative response. Both classical music and folk songs can be used. A leader who plays the guitar will find folk songs to be very appealing to children of all ages (Activity 4.7).

To create even a simple story from music takes time, but after several experiences in listening and responding, the group may be ready to proceed with the creation of characters, an original plot suggested by the music, and, much later, perhaps some dialogue. Again, music is a way of inducing the flow of creative energy and, because of its abstract quality, produces a mood more readily than do other stimuli.

CHARACTERIZATION

Until now, we have been pantomiming activities and working to induce mood or feeling. The next step is characterization. Some children already will have suggested characters different from themselves, and the teacher can either use their suggestions or introduce new ones to start the group thinking in terms of characterization.

Again, situations involving groups are a good way to begin.

1. Suggest that the children are a group of people waiting for a bus on a city street. Each child should think of someone special to be—for example, an elderly woman going to see her grandchildren, a businessman late for work, a girl on her way to high school, a blind man who needs help getting on the right bus, or a young man beginning a new job.

2. The children are people in a bus terminal. Discuss who they might be and why they are there. Some are going on trips; others are returning; still others are meeting friends or relatives. There may be a porter, a woman selling tickets, and a man selling newspapers and magazines. By the way they act, the children should suggest who they are and how they feel as they wait for the buses to arrive and depart.

3. The supermarket is a familiar scene to every child, urban and rural, these days. Therefore, the supermarket provides an excellent place for a variety of characters to be observed, recollected, and enacted. Customers, clerks, delivery boys, the manager—all are a part of daily life in a supermarket, and even the youngest children enjoy entering into it. Because there is so little interaction, except for clerks and customers, it is easy for a large group of children to participate at one time.

PANTOMIME SUGGESTED BY OTHER MEANS

Some exercises are fun to do and stimulate inventiveness, but they have nothing to do with familiar actions, mood, or characters. These are good as a change and may be introduced any time the leader feels that the group needs a new type of stimulation. Activities 4.8 and 4.9 present some ideas.

Some teachers find that acting a story while it is read aloud is a good transition from pantomime to dramatization. Many stories can be acted in this way, although some lend themselves to it better than others. One story, which has met with success with more than one group, is "The Little Scarecrow Boy."

THE LITTLE SCARECROW BOY[1]

(Arranged for Creative Playing by Aurand Harris)

Once upon a time, in a cornfield, there lived a scarecrow [*he enters and takes his place*], and his scarecrow wife [*she enters and takes her place beside him*], and their little scarecrow boy [*he enters and joins his mother and father*].

Every day of the world old man scarecrow would go out into the cornfield to make faces at the crows. [*He crosses the room and takes up his position in the cornfield.*] And every day of the world little scarecrow boy would want to come, too. [*He goes to his father and*

[1] Margaret Wise Brown, *Fun and Frolic* (Lexington, Mass.: Heath, 1955).

pulls at his coat.] And every day of the world, old man scarecrow would say:

> No!
> No, little boy,
> You can't go.
> You're not fierce enough to scare a crow.
> Wait until you grow.

[*He shows how high little scarecrow boy will have to grow. The little boy is discouraged and returns to his mother.*]

So, little scarecrow boy would have to stay home all day and just grow. [*His mother holds up her hand to the height he will have to grow. First he stretches his neck, then he stands on his toes, and finally he jumps but does not reach her hand.*] Every morning when the sun came up [*the sun crosses the room, smiling happily*], old man scarecrow went out to the cornfield. He waved his arms and made terrible faces. Every day the crows cried, "Caw! Caw! Caw!" [*The crows fly in and circle around the corn; then one by one, each crow sees old man scarecrow, screams, and flies away.*] He made such terrible faces that the crows would fly far, far away.

Every night, when the sun went down [*the sun walks back across the playing space, smiling happily*], old man scarecrow would go home [*he goes to the mother and the little boy*], and there he would teach little scarecrow boy how to make fierce faces. [*He makes a face, and the little boy imitates it.*] One—two—three—four—five—six. Old lady scarecrow would clap her hands and whistle through her teeth at the looks of them.

One day after the little boy knew all six of his father's terrible faces so that he could make them one after the other, he decided to go out into the cornfield by himself and frighten a crow. [*The scarecrows have closed their eyes in sleep.*] So, the next morning, before the sun was up, or old man scarecrow was up, or old lady scarecrow was up, little scarecrow boy got out of bed. [*He steps forward cautiously.*] He dressed and went quietly . . . [*he takes one step*] . . . quietly . . . quietly . . . quietly out of the house and over to the cornfield. He stood in his father's place. [*He takes his father's position in the cornfield.*]

It was a fine morning and the sun came up. [*The sun crosses the stage, smiling.*] Far away over the trees, crows flew around and around. Little scarecrow boy waved his arms through the air. He had never felt fiercer in all his life. [*The little boy waves his arms and makes faces.*] In the distance the "caws" of the crows were heard. [*The leader enters, and all of the crows fly in, circling the corn. One crow at a time sees the little boy, screams, and flies off. Only the leader is left, and he is not afraid. He starts toward the little scarecrow boy.*]

"Oh!" said little scarecrow boy, and he made his first fierce face. Still came flying the big crow.

"Oh, oh!" said little scarecrow boy, and he made his second fierce face. Still came flying the big crow. He made his third fierce face. "Oh, oh, oh!" It was time to go. [*He jumps down and runs in a circle, covering very little ground but running hard. The crow flies after him.*]

So, little scarecrow boy ran and ran. Then he stopped. He made his fourth fierce face. Still came flying the big old crow. He ran and he ran and he made his fifth fierce face. Still came flying the big old crow. Little scarecrow boy had only one face left now. So he stopped. He held his arms wide above his head and he made his sixth fierce face. [*As he makes his sixth face, the old crow stops, backs up, turns, and flies off.*]

Whoa! The old crow stopped and then flew backward through the air, feathers flying everywhere, until there wasn't even the shadow of a crow in the cornfield. A scarecrow at last!

[*Meanwhile, old man scarecrow walks to his side.*] Then little scarecrow boy saw a shadow in front of him and he looked around. There beside him stood his father. Old man scarecrow was proud of his little boy and shook his scarecrow hand. [*They shake hands.*] Old lady scarecrow was proud of her little boy, who could make all six fierce faces. [*She pats him fondly.*] And when little scarecrow boy grew up, he was the fiercest scarecrow in all the cornfields in all the world.

This is a somewhat shortened version of the story, with action suggested by one group of children. All took turns playing the different parts and had a grand time creating fierce faces. One child read the story while the others acted in pantomime. The scarecrow story offers an opportunity to experiment with physical movement in addition to simple characterizations. Stories read while acted help the more timid or inexperienced children to follow the plot and feel the sense of accomplishment that comes from successful dramatization.

Performing a story in mime as it is read by the teacher or a student is, however, not restricted to younger children; it can be a challenging assignment for the older ones, whose skills are more developed.

SUMMARY

Pantomime, while good practice at any time, is usually the most satisfactory way of beginning work in creative drama. Although it is not necessary to follow a prescribed program of exercises, it is easier for many groups to begin with familiar activities and then move on to mood or feeling and, finally, characterization. By starting with movement and then advancing to pantomime, the players learn to express themselves through bodily action, without the additional problem of dialogue. Younger children accept this as a natural means of expression, and older children and adults find it easier to begin with pantomime than with improvisation or formal acting. Pantomime sharpens perception and stimulates the imagination as the players try to remember how actions are done and what objects are like, in terms of size, weight, and shape. Recalling emotion demands concentration and involvement: How do you feel when you are happy, tired, angry, excited, or anxious? Close observation of people is a means of developing believable characters whose bearing, movement, and gestures belong to them and whose behavior seems appropriate. Although pantomime is considered here as a medium of expression, it may become an art form in itself.

ACTIVITY 4.1

THE FIRST NIGHT OF SLEEP

In African mythology, Ananse the Spider is often depicted as a clever god who enjoys practical jokes. The Abure tribes of West Africa also think of him as the god who listened to their complaints and always found a way to help them. "The First Night of Sleep" is based on a West African myth.

Objective: To motivate participation by everyone at the same time

Suggestions for the Teacher

Explain that when you raise your right hand, the children should make a sound (S). When you raise your left hand, they should make a motion (M).

Read the story aloud, pausing for the sounds and motions, when they are indicated.

*THE FIRST NIGHT OF SLEEP**

A long, long time ago before there was a moon, before there were stars, before there was the quiet of night to help you sleep, there was only daylight in West Africa.

Since there was daylight all the time, plants and vegetables grew quickly. Too quickly. As fast as the bananas grew, the people of the Abure tribe picked them from the tree, so they would not spoil. (M) As fast as the yams grew in the rich, red soil, the people dug up the sweet yellow potatoes, so they would not spoil. (M) People never stopped working. But when their baskets were full of food, they were so heavy that the people had to struggle to lift them even a finger from the ground. (M) Although there was plenty to eat, the people were not happy. For the more they worked, the more tired they became. Soon everybody was yawning. (S)

One day when Ananse the Spider visited earth, he heard all the people yawning at the same time. (S) When they saw him, they bowed their heads sleepily before him. (M)

Intikuma, the chief of an Abure village, rushed to welcome Ananse and led him to a tall mahogany tree.

"Ananse," he began, "please help us. What good is the sky god's gift of food, if my people are too tired to eat? All day they work in the fields, but day never ends. As soon as one crop is picked,

* Joanna H. Kraus, *Sound and Motion Stories* (Rowayton, Conn.: New Plays, 1971), p. 12.

another is ready. There is never time to rest. Look," he whispered and pointed to a young boy.

The boy peeled a fresh banana. (M) He opened his mouth to eat it. (M) He raised the banana to his lips. (M) Suddenly he shut his eyes with the banana still in his hand. (M) He was sound asleep.

"You see," the Chief said slowly, "He was too tired to eat the sweet banana fresh from the tree. My people will starve if they do not have time for sleep."

Ananse nodded in agreement. (M) Nyame the sky god had created man, but he had done it much too quickly.

Ananse sat on the branch of a tree and thought. (M) The plants seemed to grow before him, and the people rubbed their eyes sleepily as they worked. (M)

Finally Ananse spoke, "If there were darkness, the plants could not grow. If there were darkness, you could not work. If there were darkness, then you could rest."

"But how is that possible?" asked the Chief.

"Leave that to me," said Ananse. "But first you must do as I say. Ask all the men, women and children to bend their heads to the ground, yawn into the earth and sprinkle that earth on my wings as I pass by."

The Chief beat his drum three times to call his people together. (S) Sleep-ily they listened as he explained. Then they all bent their heads to the ground and yawned into the earth. (M & S) As Ananse went around the circle, each person sprinkled a drop of dirt on his wings. (M) Then Ananse flew up to the sky god Nyame and bowed low before him. (M)

But before Ananse could say a word the sky god growled, "You have earth dirt on your wings. Remove it. And never come before me again with it on."

Obediently Ananse brushed it away. (M) But as he did Nyame heard the sound of hundreds of yawns coming from the dirt. "Oh-h-h, Oh-h-h," they cried. (S)

"What is that terrible noise?" Nyame asked. "Stop it at once! What ungrateful animal did I create that complains so with that dreadful noise?"

"Oh mighty sky god," Ananse said, "it is the men, women and children below who make that sound, and only you are powerful enough to catch a yawn."

"What a lot of trouble they are!" said Nyame angrily. "What more do they want? How dare they disturb me and complain, after all I have done for them. I have given them food to eat, water to drink and daylight to work in. . . ."

"But great Nyame," Ananse interrupted, "they need darkness to rest in. They are not great like the gods. After all," he reminded him, "they are only people created in a hurry, not great like Nyame. People yawn when they are tired. The more tired they are, the more they yawn. That is the way it is with people. But if you would give them a dark time to rest the sound would stop," promised Ananse.

"Anything to stop that sound," said Nyame, and he ordered the other gods to weave a great, dark cloth to hide the daylight. The gods wove and wove. (M) Then they sewed. (M) And when all the pieces of cloth were sewn together, it was the largest, darkest cloth any of the gods had ever seen.

But the first time the cloth was lowered, the people and the animals were frightened.

For suddenly there was no daylight.

The snakes hissed. (S)

The crocodiles in the rivers roared. (S)

In the dark the trees of the jungle looked like strange beasts. When the people tried to walk, the vines of the jungle wound around their toes and legs. Some people were caught all night in the vines which wound through the tree branches. It was so dark that when they stretched their hands in front of their noses, they could not find their hands again. (M)

That first night none rested. People cried instead of resting. (S) Some cried out, "Nyame, Nyame, why are you punishing us?" The noise was so great, it wakened the great Nyame, who was fast asleep on a floating cloud.

Angrily he called for Ananse. "This howling is worse than the yawns, and just listen to them! All I hear are complaints. Cries and complaints! Their noise woke me up, and now it won't let me sleep. Ananse, you shall be punished for disturbing my dreams!" He lifted his powerful arm as though he were going to strike him. (M)

"Oh, mighty Nyame," Ananse said quickly, "before you strike, hear me first." (M)

Nyame lowered his arm. (M) "It is very simple," Ananse explained. "You have made a cloth for the gods, not for man. It is too perfect. When men weave cloth, there is room for light. If this great cloth had a few holes in it, it would not scare them so, and they would stop howling. And if the cloth were lowered more slowly, people could see their way through the jungle. Then they would not get caught in the jungle vines and cry all night."

The powerful Nyame turned, and Ananse hurried to make the holes in the cloth. He bit pieces here and pieces there. (M) It was hard work, and as the hours went by, he rushed to finish. Finally the great cloth was full of holes, but Ananse had been careless as he rushed. Some holes were much larger than others.

That night Ananse slowly lowered the great cloth, full of holes. (M)

Slowly the sunlight disappeared behind the mahogany trees of the jungle. It warned people to go home, and they all looked in amazement at the beautiful sunset. (M) That night people saw the first bits of light in the great cloth. They saw the moon appear as they reached their round mud houses with roofs of dried grass. They fell asleep counting the many different sized stars.

The next morning each woke up after his rest and stretched happily. (M)

The Chief beat the drum three times to call his people together. (S) Everyone ran to the square. (S)

No one felt sleepy.

As they reached the square, the Chief heard a noise above him on the branch of the tree. (S) He looked up and saw Ananse sitting there.

"Ananse," the Chief called, "it was you who gave us a dark time to rest. We thank you. It is you who are the friend of man."

"Shh," Ananse whispered. "That is our secret! The gift of night is yours as long as you never let Nyame hear you yawn again." And that is how Ananse tricked Nyame the sky god into giving man the moon and the stars and a time to sleep.

ACTIVITY 4.2

IMAGINATION AND PANTOMIME

Objective: To teach children that it is their imagination that makes an object what it is, and, therefore, we treat it as such

Suggestions for the Teacher

Seat five or six children in a small semicircle in the front or center of the room. The others watch but know that all will have turns.

Hand a small, nondescript object, such as a blackboard eraser, to the first player in the group. Say that it is a diamond bracelet, the most beautiful piece of jewelry any of them has ever seen. Then ask each player in turn to:

1. Handle it
2. Look at it
3. React to it
4. Pass it to the next person

When each child has had a chance to handle and react to the object, tell the group that it is now a kitten with very soft fur. The same group again takes it and reacts to it. The next time, it may be a wallet—dirty and torn—with nothing in it. The fourth time it is passed, it becomes a knife or a glass of water filled to the brim or perhaps an old valuable

Using our senses. (Courtesy of Carol Sterling, ARTS Partners, New York City Board of Education, Community School District #12)

manuscript. Each time the object is handed around, the group invests it with more of the qualities of the suggested object.

The observers usually are as interested as the players in the growing reality that develops. Depending on the time at their disposal, repeat the exercise with another group.

Questions for the Observers

1. How did we know it was a bracelet?

   "One player held it so that the diamonds sparkled in the light." "John held it as if it were very expensive." "Linda tried it on." "Charles looked for the price tag."

2. Why did we know it was a kitten the second time it was passed?

   "One stroked its head." "Another girl put it close to her cheek as if it were alive." "Barbara held its legs carefully when she gave it to Lois." "They all held it as if it were soft and round."

Questions for the Players

1. What did the wallet look like to you?

   "It was dark green leather." "It was old and torn." "There was a faded snapshot in the front." "It had a hole in the bottom." "It was muddy because it had been lost in the yard."

2. You were careful not to let any of the objects drop, but you handled them differently. Why?

   "The bracelet was valuable." "I didn't want it to get broken." "The kitten was alive, and that made it different from all the others."

Questions like these push the players to stronger visual images and greater power of observation.

Another exercise that serves to excite the imagination and let the players express it through pantomime is the suggestion that a table in the middle of the room is covered with a variety of small objects. Each participant must pick out one thing and show, by the way he or she handles it, what it is. The activity can be done by several persons at once, so that the attention is not focused on a single player. If the rest of the class members are seated in a semicircle, some will watch one player and some another. This is fun for all, and what self-consciousness may have existed in the beginning will soon be gone.

ACTIVITY 4.3

PERFORMING AN ACTION IN PANTOMIME

Objective: To help players sustain attention and organize ideas as they carry pantomime beyond a simple exercise into a complete activity

Suggestions for the Teacher

Have the children push back their chairs in order to create a playing space in the center of the room. Suggest the following activities, to be done by individuals.

1. Setting a table
2. Baking a cake
3. Feeding your dog or cat or gerbil
4. Getting dressed
5. Doing your homework
6. Turning on your favorite television program
7. Buying a pizza and taking it home
8. Riding on a crowded bus

When working with children in inner-city neighborhoods, use activities most common to those environments. Washing clothes rather than going fishing in a brook is familiar to these children and can, therefore, be more easily imagined and acted. This, incidentally, also helps children to regard their own experiences more positively.

ACTIVITY 4.4

TELLING A STORY IN PANTOMIME

***Objective:** To carry Activity 4.3 further by creating a simple story*

Suggestions for the Teacher

Have the children push back their chairs in order to create a playing space in the center of the room. Suggest the following situations, to be done by two or three children. They will need some planning, so give each group a few minutes in which to work on details.

1. You and your sister or brother are getting ready for a birthday party for your mother and must set the table. What are you going to put on the table? Are there any decorations? a cake with candles? presents? Is it to be a surprise? Perhaps your mother comes into the room just as you finish.
2. You are three friends on your way home from school one day when you see a wallet on the ground near the sidewalk. You wonder what to do with it. Finally, you decide to open it. You find what looks like foreign money. You touch it, and it feels different from any money you have ever seen or handled. You hear footsteps as someone comes running down the street; it is a stranger. You cannot speak each other's language, but you must find out whether it is his wallet. What do you do? Does he reward you? Perhaps it is not his, after all.
3. You are going on a treasure hunt in the park. Your instructions are to follow a path from the starting point and look for a piece of blue paper. Next, you are to look for a birdhouse about 10 steps to the left. (The bird calls will help you locate it.) Then, you must look for a popcorn man with a cart. (The smell of the popcorn will guide you to it.) A little farther down the path, you will see a stone wall covered with ivy. In the wall, there will be a smooth stone. Find it. Under the stone on the ground, you will discover your last direction: take 6 steps to the right, and the prize will be somewhere near you. What is it?

All three of these situations are fun for younger children but also help to strengthen their power of concentration, imagination, use of the senses, and ability to organize ideas. Knowing the interests and ability of the class, you can create other situations and simple stories that both entertain and teach.

ACTIVITY 4.5

EXPRESSING FEELINGS IN PANTOMIME

Objective: To express feelings in pantomime

Suggestions for the Teacher

Have the chairs and desks moved irregularly about the room. Read the directions slowly, so that the class hears and understands what it is going to do. The following situations may involve two, three, or several children. How many try them will depend on how well they work together, for the more children in a group, the more difficult it is to avoid confusion.

1. You are a group of friends taking a hike in the woods. It is a beautiful day, and you find strawberries and wildflowers. You stop to have your lunch, but when you are ready to move on, you discover that you have wandered from the path and are lost. Your happy mood changes to panic. Where are you? Should you go on or turn back? Is there any familiar landmark to guide you? Suddenly one of the girls finds a broken flower lying on the ground. As she picks it up, she realizes that it is on the path, and she must have dropped it when she looked for a picnic spot. Panic turns to relief as the group starts for home.

2. A group of boys discovers a cave (or the basement of an empty building). They go in, curious about what they may find. One of them stumbles over a box. The boys open it and find money and jewels. Excitement grows as they realize they have found hidden treasure. Then they hear voices; men are approaching. Terrified, the boys hide. The men go past, not seeing them. The boys run, escaping from danger.

3. You are going on a field trip to which you have looked forward for a long time. You get in the bus, but the bus will not start. After a few minutes, the driver lets you know that he cannot make it go, and so your trip must be postponed. Disappointed, you get out. Suddenly, the engine starts. You turn around and see the driver motioning for you to get back in. Your happiness is great because you can now go after all.

ACTIVITY 4.6

LA MER

Objective: To stimulate imagery through the use of music

Suggestions for the Teacher

Play a recording of Claude Debussy's *La Mer* (or other descriptive music). You may want to play it, or portions of it, twice. Then ask the children what it makes them think of, how it makes them feel, and what they see.

When it is played again, ask them to move to the music. (The length of time you spend on this will depend on the age of the group and its ability to become involved.)

Have the children sit down and talk. They moved in certain ways—why? Did they see persons in the music? Or were they "being" the sea? (This may lead into a very simple story. If the children are not ready to carry the idea that far, wait until another time.)

The next time it is played, the piece will be familiar to the group, and the children may want to do more with it, such as having something happen or seeing characters. You are now on the road to the creation of an original drama suggested by *La Mer*.

ACTIVITY 4.7

GREENSLEEVES

Children in the third grade probably know the melody and perhaps the words of "Greensleeves." If so, the work is half done, although familiarity sometimes inhibits a creative response.

Objective: To see what reaction a familiar folk song elicits

Suggestions for the Teacher

If the class likes "Greensleeves," have them sing it and then respond to it in movement, either as an entire class or in small groups.

Any folk songs or familiar songs may be used for the simple pantomime they suggest. Let the children try their favorites in this way.

ACTIVITY 4.8

BEING INANIMATE OBJECTS IN PANTOMIME

Objective: To depict inanimate objects through movement and sound, not words.

Suggestions for the Teacher

Move the chairs in order to make plenty of playing space. Then explain that you want to see how the children can show, without words or explanation, the following objects. The objects are inanimate, and the problem is to *be* the object, not to *use* or *handle* it. Children can work alone or in pairs.

1. You are toys in a toy shop. At midnight, you come to life. First, let's decide who each of you wants to be: a pretty doll, a rag doll, a dancing doll, a Cabbage Patch Kid, a teddy bear, a toy soldier, a jack-in-the-box, a top, a little car. When the drum is struck, it is midnight. When the drum is struck again, it is daybreak, and you must go back to where you were in the beginning.
2. You are puppets. Try to imagine what it feels like to be controlled by strings. Imagine that you are being held up and then dropped by the puppeteer. (While there is some characterization involved, it is the feeling of being manipulated by another that is the challenge.)
3. You are a mechanical appliance: a pencil sharpener, an eggbeater, a lawn mower, a hair dryer, a record player. Imagine what your parts are and how you move. (This is a challenging exercise, guaranteed to break down all inhibitions.)
4. Mirror images are great fun. Two of you face each other, one being yourself and the other your mirror image. Watch each other carefully. Whatever you do, your partner must also do. After a while, reverse roles.

Although these exercises rarely go beyond a single playing, they have value in the quality of imagination they invoke. All depend on close observation, memory of how things work, and inventiveness; if for no other reasons, they are worth doing occasionally. The mirror exercise, in addition, brings the inanimate (the image) and the animate (the human being) together. Its further value is in strengthening children's ability to work together. It is enjoyed by players of all ages, both the experienced and the beginner.

ACTIVITY 4.9

CREATING SILHOUETTES IN PANTOMIME

"Creating Silhouettes in Pantomime" is an activity that can develop into an art form. Most children have experimented with throwing shadows on a wall and have discovered the different effects that distance makes.

Objective: To be inventive in a new medium and lose the "self" in the shadow

Suggestions for the Teacher

It requires very little explanation to start the activity. Hang a sheet at one end of the room and place a strong light behind it. A floor lamp or a table lamp about 4 feet from the sheet works best. Have the children move between the light and the sheet and pantomime something to see what happens. The magic quality of a silhouette never fails to stimulate an immediate desire to try out ideas.

When all have had a turn, divide the class into small groups of manageable size (two or three) and suggest short, well-known situations or such rhymes as "Jack and Jill," "Jack, Be Nimble," and "Little Miss Muffet." Everyone will be eager to try out his or her idea, so the skits should move quickly. Later on, more time can be taken for more complicated and longer stories, but not with more than two persons performing at a time.

This activity, incidentally, is excellent for the timid child, who feels less exposed behind the sheet than out in the open. The emphasis should always be on the effect, not the child. Ask the children questions: What happens when the player is close to the sheet? far from the sheet? How is humor achieved? Can you make a figure larger? scary? distorted?

5

IMPROVISATION: CHARACTERS MOVE AND SPEAK

I hear; I forget—I see; I remember—I do; I understand.

—CHINESE PROVERB

Improvisation is difficult at first. Dialogue does not flow easily, even when it has been preceded by much work in pantomime and a thorough understanding of the situation or story. With practice, however, words do begin to come, and young players discover the possibilities of character development when oral language is added. Dialogue is apt to be brief and scanty at first, but usually begins to flow rapidly once children become accustomed to it. Players age 7 and older enjoy the opportunity of using words to further a story and more fully describe the characters they are portraying. It is a good idea to begin with simple situations in order to get accustomed to using dialogue before attempting more ambitious material.

Many of the situations suggested in Chapter 4 can be used for improvisation, although they were designed with movement in mind. Frequently, children begin to add dialogue of their own free will, as they feel the need to express ideas in words. When this happens, the leader accepts it as a natural progression from one step to the next. Young children, players for whom English is a second language, or older students who lack self-confidence usually wait until they are urged to try adding dialogue. The teacher should not expect too much in the beginning and accept whatever is offered, knowing that more will be forthcoming the next time.

IMPROVISATIONS BASED ON SITUATIONS AND OBJECTS

Even the simplest stories present complications for the beginner, so some preliminary exercises are suggested. The purpose is to give emphasis to dialogue rather than to the memorization of plot. Just one scene of a story sometimes can be improvised to advantage. The teacher should feel his or her way and, if interest is sustained better with excerpts from favorite stories, may prefer them to the situations suggested in Activities 5.1 to 5.7.

Sounds, incidentally, can stimulate imagination and lead the listener to the creation of an improvisation. For example, the teacher can beat a drum or tambourine, knock, ring bells, or make any other kind of sound. This works particularly well with younger children.

Similar to the use of objects or props, and equally effective in stimulating ideas, is the use of articles of clothing. Such garments as hats, capes, aprons, shawls, tail coats, and jewelry suggest different kinds of characters. Innumerable situations have grown from characters developed this way. For example, to one boy, a tail coat suggested a musician who was down on his luck and playing his violin on a street corner for pennies. A feathered hat helped a little girl create a lady of fashionable pretensions and become a comic character in her extravagant dress and poor taste. A shawl suggested witches, grandmothers, people in disguise, or a scene set in very cold weather.

It is wise to keep a supply of simple and sturdy costumes available for this kind of use. If children experience difficulty in getting into character, a piece of a costume may sometimes be all that is needed to provide the necessary incentive. Costume used in this way is not dressing the part, but is an aid to imaginative thinking.

IMPROVISATION IN SMALL GROUPS

While it is generally better for younger children to work in large groups, third graders and sometimes second graders can work in pairs. Teachers should try to avoid "featuring" children, but as they become more used to acting and role playing, they are able to handle situations involving only two characters.

SILLINESS

Every group leader has experienced times when "silliness" seems to be the order of the day. This is to be expected, not only with beginners, but even with experienced older players. While silliness is often due to self-consciousness, it may also be a result of exuberance, the letting off of steam after sitting still for a long time, or simply delight in the ridiculous. If teachers can bring a sense of humor to the situation, they can use silliness positively, turning the silly idea into a "what if." After all, most of our best-known fairy tales and myths deal with the impossible, but because we are familiar with them, we find them acceptable and use them without anxiety.

All new experiences and experiments are unpredictable—that is the hazard and the fun of them. Of course, silliness can be carried too far and go on too long. When that happens, a sudden change of activity, usually physical movement, diverts the attention. The use of a signal like "Freeze!" which is understood by all, will stop the behavior, giving the teacher a chance to turn the energy or irrelevant response into another channel. Do not be discouraged; one disappointing lesson does not mean failure. Remember that every scientist and artist works a long time—trying first one way, then another—before reaching a satisfactory solution to a problem. Why, therefore, should we expect every lesson to turn out as we had envisioned it the first time? A failed lesson may be a highly successful effort in terms of breaking down inhibitions, releasing imagination, or bringing out one shy child. Also, no two groups are the same. What goes well with one, may not even get off the ground with another. So do not give up.

CREATIVE DRAMA CORRELATED WITH SUBJECT AREA

While the subject of this book is drama as aesthetic education, the teaching of material in a variety of subject areas can be accomplished at the same time. The language arts are the most obvious related subject area, for when children enact prose pieces and poems, they are introduced to good literature and gain a deeper appreciation of it. Reading and speech are directly involved in any form of drama, as is physical education. Social studies provide a wealth of material involving history, geography, people of other lands, appreciation of other cultures, humane and environmental education, and social problems, all of which can be taught through discussion and improvisation. Activities 5.7 and 5.8, which relate to the community, present a few possibilities.

ROLE PLAYING

Although role playing as therapy is not the job of the creative-drama teacher or the classroom teacher using creative-drama techniques, some teachers have tried it with reported success. The purpose is educative rather than therapeutic, and the situations examined are common to all. Human conflicts and the ways in which problems are solved can promote social growth. Family scenes, school situations, and playground incidents (Activity 5.9) give opportunity for interaction and group discussion. Discussion is the most important aspect of role playing, according to some teachers, for it is during these periods that various points of view are presented and attitudes clarified. The teacher must accept all ideas, giving the boys and girls a chance to express themselves without fear of disapproval, and pose such questions as: How do you think the father felt? the brother? the mother? What did the man next door think when you broke his window? How do you think he felt the third time it happened? If you were he, how would you feel?

Peter Slade, an English educator and the author of *Child Drama*, summarizes the use of role playing: "I would go so far as to say that one of the most important reasons for developing child drama in schools generally is not actually a therapeutic one but the even more constructive one of prevention."[1]

It must be pointed out that playing the part of a fictional character also demands identification with the character and his or her problems. Exchange of parts gives all the players a chance to experience both sides of a conflict. Obviously, the real-life conflict that the group itself experiences is stronger than the fictional one, and the solution, if found, is of practical benefit.

IMPROVISATIONS BASED ON STORIES

The most popular and, in many ways, most satisfactory form of improvisation for children is based on good stories. While making up original stories is a creative exercise, a group endeavor rarely achieves the excellence of a story that has stood the test of time or was written by a fine author. Improvising from a story is a way of introducing literature, and when a story is well chosen, it offers good opportunities for acting. Chapter 6 discusses the ways in which both simple and more complicated stories may be approached.

Good stories on any level should have literary quality, worthwhile

[1] Peter Slade, *Child Drama* (London: University of London Press, 1954), p. 119.

Improvising the fable "The Tortoise and the Hare." (Courtesy of New Canaan Country School)

ideas, correct information, and dramatic value. Children up to the ages of 10 and 11 like fairy tales and legends. Older children may still enjoy these but tend to prefer adventures, biographies, and stories of real life. Frequently, the last, because of their length, have to be cut or the incidents rearranged. This is a learning experience that, if the group has had some experience, should not be too difficult.

Groups sometimes want to act plays that they have seen. This can be a worthwhile activity, although the tendency is to try to do it exactly as it was presented on the stage. Nevertheless, working on a reenactment of a play can be a valuable period of time spent with a good piece of literature and is to be preferred to the reproduction of television shows or enactment of stories from comic books.

In order to present the right story, the leader must, above all, know the group well. One leader, who was later to achieve remarkable success, told of her first experience as a young teacher at a settlement house in an inner-city area. Nothing she brought to the children in her drama group captured their interest. Improvisation seemed an impossible goal, although group members were alert and lively when she saw them on the street. Finally, she hit on the idea of asking them to tell her stories they knew. Hesitantly at first, then willingly, legends and family anecdotes came. She tried enacting them. Not only was the material a success, but the group doubled in size. Parents began to look in. Before the end of the year, an activity that had seemed doomed to failure became the most popular in the settlement. Some years later, the settlement drama department was to achieve nationwide recognition as an arts center. The search for material had led to the children themselves. Their cultural heritage and their creative use of it under intelligent and sensitive guidance was the first step.

Dramatic Structure

While it is not necessary for children in the first three grades to know the terminology and technical aspects of playwriting, it is a help for the teacher to be acquainted with the fundamental elements of a play as well as with a few of the commonly used terms. With knowledge of the ways in which plays differ from other forms of literature, the teacher will be able to provide better guidance in dramatizing stories. Most important, a play is written to be played. It is not a play until it is given life on a stage. We can and do read plays, to be sure, but this is not the original purpose of the playwright.

The basic elements of any play, briefly defined, are:

Acts. The major divisions of a play; short plays do not need such divisions.

Characters. The persons in the play in whom we can believe, even if they are fantastic (witches, giants, fairies).

Climax. The high point of the story.

Conflict. The struggle between two persons, two elements, or good and bad.

Dialogue. The lines of the play; dialogue defines the characters and advances the plot.

Hero or heroine. The main character, whom the story is about and with whom we can identify.

Narrator. The storyteller, often found in children's plays to bridge time and place and give necessary information.

Plot. The story.

Scenes. The divisions within acts, used to indicate a change in time or place.

Theme. The idea on which the story is based.

Villain. The "bad guy," who is in conflict with the hero or heroine.

The story "Jack and the Beanstalk" contains all the elements of a play. Because it is so well known, it is used as an example for children who may ask about terms.

JACK AND THE BEANSTALK

There was once a poor widow who lived in a cottage with her only son, Jack. She worked hard for a living, but as time went on, they became so poor that they had nothing left but one cow.

"I shall have to sell the cow," said Jack's mother one morning, "for there is nothing in the house to eat but a few crusts of bread."

Now the poor woman had so spoiled Jack that he could not understand their poverty and only begged her to let him take the cow to market to see what a great price he could get. With misgivings, at last his mother gave in to his arguments. Warning him not to sell the cow to the first person who wanted to buy it, she gave the boy a rope and told him to take the cow to the market.

Jack had not gone far when he met a butcher. Now the butcher was a shrewd fellow, who knew that he could take advantage of a simple lad like Jack. He pulled a handful of brightly colored beans from his pocket and showed them to Jack. Jack was fascinated with the beans and asked the man what he would take for them. The butcher hesitated, then replied, "I will trade them for your cow."

"Oh, no," said Jack. "I couldn't do that. My mother told me not to sell her to the first person I met."

"But suppose he offers you the best bargain?" argued the butcher. "These beans are magic. You will never have another chance to buy beans like these."

Jack considered the statement. If the beans were indeed magic, perhaps he should accept the man's offer. At last he agreed to the bargain. He put the beans in his pocket and gave the cow to the butcher. When he reached home, his mother was anxiously waiting.

"You are back very soon. Did you get a good price?"

But when Jack showed her the beans and told her how he had obtained them, she was greatly upset. "Oh, you stupid boy," she said. "You have given away our only cow, and now we have nothing!" And she threw the beans angrily into the garden.

Improvisation in an outdoor setting. (Courtesy of Creative Theatre Unlimited, Princeton, New Jersey)

Jack tried to comfort her, but it was no use. Both went to bed without supper. The next morning, when he awoke, Jack was aware of an unusual darkness in the cottage. He ran out to the garden to see what was keeping the sunlight from entering the room. To his amazement, he discovered that a huge vine had grown up during the night on the very spot where his mother had thrown the brightly colored beans. The boy could not see the top of the beanstalk, but he was determined to climb it to see how high it had grown. His mother begged him to stay on the ground, but he was stubborn and refused. Up he went, and soon he disappeared from her sight.

When he finally reached the top of the beanstalk, he found himself in a strange land. There were no houses or barns, only a barren, dry field. Suddenly, he heard someone call his name. Jack was astonished that anyone should know him, and he looked about to see who it might be. In the distance, coming toward him, he saw a young woman. She asked him how he had come there, and Jack told her all about the cow and the beans and the beanstalk. Then she asked him a strange question, "Do you remember your father?"

Jack replied that he did not, for his father had died when he was only a baby. The woman, who had magic powers, told him that it was she who had made him take the beans in exchange for the cow. Years ago, she had known his father and mother. "Your father was a fine, brave man, who was betrayed by a cruel giant."

Jack listened in amazement as she told him how the giant had stolen everything his father had left to him and his mother. "You are now in the land of the giant," the young woman continued. "I will help you to conquer him, but first you must promise me that you will not tell any of this to your mother. Not until later. She would worry, and there is much to be done."

Jack promised and agreed to follow the young woman's directions. Then he said good-bye and started off down the road, as she had told him. At length, he reached a large house. He stepped up to the door and knocked boldly. A woman answered. Jack explained that he was hungry and would like something to eat and a place to stay the night. The woman agreed, but warned him that her husband was a giant who liked to eat human flesh. When he appeared for his dinner, Jack must hide quickly.

Then she fixed a plate of good things for Jack's supper. Scarcely had he finished when the heavy footsteps of the giant were heard on the path. The woman quickly hid Jack in a large copper kettle and set out her husband's dinner. As the door opened, the giant stopped and looked about. "I smell the blood of a boy," he roared.

"You can see that no one is here," said his wife, but the giant ignored her and strode about the room, looking in all the cupboards and corners. Not thinking to look in the kettle, he grumbled at his fruitless search and sat down to his supper.

The giant ate heartily, then leaned back in his chair and asked for his hen. The woman went out and returned a few minutes later with a huge white hen. "You may go now," the giant said rudely. Then he turned to the hen. "Lay," he commanded. To Jack's utter astonishment, the hen laid a bright golden egg. Again and again, the giant asked the hen to lay, and each time she obliged him, every egg as golden as the one before. Finally, tiring of this pastime, the giant lowered his head and closed his eyes.

When Jack was quite sure that the giant was asleep, he climbed out of the kettle and tiptoed over to the table. Picking up the hen, he put her under his arm and slipped out of the room. Then he ran for the beanstalk. He climbed down it as quickly as he could and landed on the ground with a bump right in his own garden. His mother was overjoyed to see him, for in truth, she had all but given him up for lost. Jack showed her the hen, who laid golden eggs for him just as she had done for the giant.

For several months, Jack and his mother lived well on the money they got from the eggs. Then one day, Jack decided it was time to return to the giant's castle. Again his mother begged him not to go, but he was determined to recover his father's possessions, and so once more he set out on his journey, careful to disguise himself in a different suit of clothing.

When he knocked at the giant's door, the wife appeared as she had before. She was nervous this time, however, and not eager to let the "stranger" come in. She explained that the last lad who had stopped for food and a bed for the night had robbed them of their hen. Nevertheless, she let Jack enter and proceeded to set out a plate of good things to eat. She warned Jack that should her husband appear, he must hide himself quickly, or he would surely be killed. Just as before, Jack had hardly finished eating when the giant's footsteps were heard. Jack slipped into the pantry and hid in a bin of sugar.

The giant was more ill-tempered this time than before and shouted at his wife to hurry up with his dinner. Then he stopped and sniffed the air. "Are you sure no human being is in this room? Let me look."

Jack was paralyzed with fear as the giant approached his hiding place. But again luck was with him. The giant did not open the bin. Walking heavily to the table, he sat down and ate his dinner without speaking. When he finished, he ordered his wife to bring his bags of gold and then leave him alone. Jack watched as the giant piled the gold coins on the table. Finally, he yawned and swept the coins back into the bags and tied them securely. Within a few minutes, he was sound asleep. Jack waited until he was sure it was safe to come out of the pantry, then lifted the heavy bags to his shoulders. It was harder to manage this load than the hen, but by morning, he had made his way safely down into the garden.

His mother was delighted to see her son appear and begged him never to climb the beanstalk again. Surely, she insisted, they had enough money to live on for the rest of their lives. They repaired the cottage and bought a new cow, some fine clothes, and good food.

A year later, Jack knew that he must pay one more visit to the land of the giant. In vain, his mother begged him to stay at home, but he left, assuring her that just as he had returned safely twice, so he should do again.

This time, however, the giant's wife almost refused to admit him. "Every time I have given food and shelter to a stranger, he has taken one of my husband's greatest treasures, and I have been beaten for it." Nevertheless, she took pity on the lad and allowed him to come into the kitchen. Once more when the giant came for his dinner, Jack suddenly had to find a hiding place. Once again, the giant swore that he smelled human flesh and went to search for it. At last, however, he sat down to the meal that had been prepared for him, washing it down with mugs of strong ale. Then he called for his harp, told his wife to go, and ordered the harp to play him to sleep.

"Yes, master," replied the harp. Whereupon Jack heard the sweetest music he had ever heard in his life. In no time at all, the giant was nodding his head. Jack waited until he was sure the giant was asleep, then just as he had done twice before, he crept from his hiding place and lifted the treasure from the table. But to his horror, the harp called out in a shrill voice, "Master, master, wake up! Someone is stealing me!"

Jack ran as fast as he could with the harp clutched in his arms. The giant was close behind him. When he reached the beanstalk, Jack slid down, the harp calling out all the while. As he hit the ground, he felt the beanstalk shaking above him. He called to his mother to bring an ax quickly. Then he cut the stalk. The giant, who was already on his way down after Jack, fell to the ground.

At this moment appeared the young woman whom Jack had encountered on his first trip up the beanstalk. "Now you may tell your mother the whole story," she said, "for your father's old enemy is destroyed, and you have recovered the treasures that are rightly yours."

Jack and his mother rejoiced: she, that their days of poverty were over forever; and Jack, that his father had at last been avenged.

1. Jack is clearly the *hero*.
2. The giant is the *villain*.
3. Jack and the giant are in *conflict*. They are the two main *characters*.
4. The *climax* of the play comes when Jack makes his escape from the giant's house.
5. The *plot* falls neatly into two *acts* as it moves from the first part (selling the cow for the beans) to the second part (climbing up the beanstalk to the giant's country). The end comes so quickly that it cannot be called an act, but because it moves to a different location (Jack's cottage again), it is a *scene*.
6. There could be a *narrator*, if desired, but it is not necessary.

A good story has believable characters, a theme, a climax, and a leading character or hero with whom children can identify. The job of making it into a play involves the creation of dialogue that tells the story in language appropriate to the characters; decisions about where or if the story should be divided into acts and scenes; and what parts, if any, should be omitted. Folk and fairy tales are often long, with more episodes than are desirable for creative drama. Children most need our help in selecting the necessary parts or scenes. Start planning by asking the following questions:

1. What characters in the story do we need for our play?
2. What scenes are most important? Can we omit any?
3. Are there any characters we can leave out?
4. Do we need any other characters in order to make the story clear?
5. Are there any characters we can add in order to give parts to more children in the class (villagers, townspeople, chorus)?

Third graders can usually work with these questions easily. First and second graders enjoy enacting simple situations without being burdened with form and structure.

SUMMARY

Improvisation is the creation of a situation in which characters speak spontaneously. There are many ways of introducing improvisation, but some groundwork in pantomime is the best preparation. Once the players have achieved a sense of security in movement, they are ready to add dialogue to their improvisations. Dialogue does not come easily at first, but continued practice with familiar material usually induces the flow. There are many points of departure, and some of the most successful are: improvisation from situations, objects, or properties; from sounds; from characters; and from ideas and stories. By using stories, teachers have an excellent opportunity to widen children's horizons and introduce them to good literature with dramatic content.

Role playing is a kind of improvisation that has as its specific objective the social growth of the individuals involved. There may well be a place for it in the school or club program, but it must not be confused with creative drama as art. Both, however, are participant centered and in that respect differ from theatre. When observed by others, improvised drama of any kind should be considered as demonstration and not as performance.

ACTIVITY 5.1

SIMPLE IMPROVISATIONS BASED ON SITUATIONS

Objective: To create scenes suggested by situations

Suggestions for the Teacher

1. Describe the situations listed below in your own words, answering all questions but taking care not to make suggestions or solve problems.
2. When you are sure that all the children understand, divide the class into groups of three or four. (As the children become used to this type of activity, groups can be larger.) Give the groups a few minutes to plan their improvisations.
3. When all groups agree that they are ready, have one group at a time come forward and share its scene. In the early stages, it's a good idea to accept all honest efforts, regardless of how short or inadequate a scene may be. The children are doing their best, and the next time, the results will be stronger.
4. Have a brief class discussion after each scene, making sure that all comments are positive. This can be achieved by your starting the discussion with a positive comment. Whatever criticism is offered must be constructive; this is your most important job at this stage.
5. The children may want to reenact their scenes either the same day or on another day. If so, the next step is to help the players develop them further, adding depth and detail.

The following improvisations may be done with children of various ages, although the backgrounds of the players will determine the appropriateness.

1. This is an extension of Activity 4.8, "Being Inanimate Objects in Pantomime." The scene is a toy shop on Christmas Eve. It is midnight, and the owner has just closed the door and gone home. At the stroke of twelve, the toys come alive and talk together. They may consist of a toy soldier, a rag doll, a beautiful doll, a clown, a teddy bear, and a jack-in-the-box. Let us know by your conversation and movements who you are and, if possible, why you were not sold.
2. You are a group of children in an apartment house. It is Valentine's Day, and you are gathered in the front hall to look at and count your valentines. You see one child in the building going to the mailbox, and you notice that she did not receive any. How do you feel about this? What is each one of you like? Do you decide to do anything about it? If so, what do you do?

3. You are a group of children who live near a very cross, elderly woman. She chases you away from her property whenever you come near it. This particular morning, you see that someone has broken her fence and ruined many of her flowers. For the first time you feel sorry for her. What do you do? How does she react to you? Do you all agree that you should help her? Do your actions change her attitude toward children?
4. A new child has entered your class at school. He or she does not speak English, and some of the children laugh. When recess comes, you all go out to the playground. How does each of you treat the newcomer? How does he or she react to you? You are all different, so you will each feel and behave differently. Do you finally take in the newcomer, or do you exclude him or her? Try changing roles so that different players have the experience of trying the part of the new child. Does the improvisation change as you all think more about the situation?

All the activities have value beyond the creation of characters and dialogue. Social situations are presented with positive and negative solutions. Children are fair, and while they may not always show sympathetic understanding in their own behavior, they are quick to see injustice when observing or enacting a situation in which it occurs. This may not be the intended lesson at the moment, but the social awareness that is aroused is a valuable fringe benefit. And when it is the intent to discuss social awareness, one of the most effective ways of presenting social problems is through drama.

ACTIVITY 5.2

IMPROVISATIONS SUGGESTED BY OBJECTS

Not only situations and stories motivate improvisation; some very imaginative results can be obtained by the use of objects or properties.

Objective: To create scenes suggested by objects

Suggestions for the Teacher

Put an object in the center of the circle where all the players can see it. Ask them to look at it, without speaking, for three or four minutes and try to think of a story about it: Where might it have come from? How did it get here? What does it make *you* think of? Each of you will have an original story to tell; tell it.

Any object can function as a springboard, and no two groups will see it in exactly the same way. Among the kinds of properties that suggest ideas are:

1. A beach ball
2. An artificial rose
3. An old toy
4. A feather duster
5. A bell
6. An old woman's hat with feathers or flowers
7. A cane
8. An old dog leash

Few first and second graders are able to make up a story with a well-defined plot. This should not be expected of them, but it is good practice and fun to try. By the time they reach the third grade and have had experience with creative drama, children can be expected to organize their ideas surprisingly well. It is, however, nearly always the fact that the play is based on familiar stories or characters, which enables the players to create dialogue and identify more easily with the characters. Respect for the child's background and acceptance of the ideas that come out of it not only make for comfort, but also bring forth ideas that the teacher probably would not have thought of. Children of foreign background have a wealth of material on which to draw, but it too often remains an untapped source because they have been made to feel that it is unworthy of consideration. Both the stories they have been told and the details of their everyday lives contain the basic ingredients of drama.

ACTIVITY 5.3

IMPROVISING FROM COSTUMES

Objective: To create a character in action from a costume

Suggestions for the Teacher

The larger the class, the more difficult it is to handle an improvisation; therefore, it is wise to divide the class into several smaller groups, with one group playing at a time and the others observing. Scenes will be short, but every group must be given its turn, preferably during the same class session.

Bring out a large supply of garments (aprons, scarves, hats, long skirts, shawls, work gloves, coats) and put them in the middle of the room. Explain that there are more than enough for everyone in the class and that each person may select something that appeals to his or her imagination.

Ask the children to go off to a corner of the room and put on what they have chosen. (Children of elementary school age do not demand complete costumes; they are quite content to dress up in one or two garments and imagine the rest of the outfit.) Decide who the characters are, according to the clothes they are wearing.

Then announce that it is a Saturday morning in a small town, and you are all going to market. The scene is the village square with shops all around it. Go into the marketplace as your characters, but first decide whether:

1. You are shopping or just looking around
2. You are rich or poor
3. You are young or old
4. You are alone or with a friend or member of your family
5. You are a merchant or a farmer

The ideas will flow; the characters the children create will be vivid, but the dialogue at this stage will be scanty. Do not be discouraged and feel that you have failed if the results are less than you had expected. Remember that these are very young players, capable of thought and feeling but lacking in experience and vocabulary. That will come later. Simply getting into the improvisation in character for even a few minutes is an achievement for them and for you. Third graders can carry this situation further and may ask to; if so, you have the beginning of a good group improvisation at hand.

ACTIVITY 5.4

IMPROVISATIONS FOR TWO CHILDREN

Objective: To help children work cooperatively in pairs

Suggestions for the Teacher

Suggest that the children imagine themselves in the following situations.

1. You have been warned not to go down a dark street by yourself at night. This evening, however, you are in a hurry and decide to go anyway because it is a shortcut. About halfway down the block, you hear footsteps behind you. You look over your shoulder and see someone hurrying toward you. You hurry also; so does the other person. You decide to slow down; so does the person who is following you. By this time, you are frightened, but it is too late to turn back. You start to run, and so does he. You run faster; so does he. Finally, you reach the corner, but the light has turned red. As you stand there alone waiting for it to change, a friend comes up. It was the friend who was following you, but neither of you recognized the other, and both of you had been running to get to the brightly lit corner. You have a good laugh when you discover each other.
2. You are trying on shoes to take to camp. The clerk does not have what you want and tries to sell you something else. What do you do?
3. You are moving to a new neighborhood today. Your best friend comes around to say good-bye to you. Although you are looking forward to your new home, you are sad to leave the old neighborhood. What do you say?
4. Your aunt, whom you have never met, has come for a visit. You answer the door. What is she like? What do you say to each other?
5. You have found a kitten that you want very much to keep, but your mother has said you cannot have a pet. You try to persuade her that the kitten needs a home.
6. You have been wanting ice skates for your birthday. Your grandmother, who always selects the right presents, comes to the door with a box in her hands. When you open it, you find that it contains stationery. What do you say to each other?
7. You wore your sister's bracelet to a picnic. When you get home, you discover that you have lost it. Now you must tell her what happened.

ACTIVITY 5.5

IMPROVISATIONS FOR THREE CHILDREN

Objective: To help children work cooperatively in groups of three

Suggestions for the Teacher

Suggest that the children imagine themselves in the following situations.

1. Your grandmother (or grandfather) takes you to a department store to buy your birthday present. What do you choose? You have trouble making up your mind—why? The three characters are you, your grandmother (or grandfather), and the clerk.
2. Three friends are going out to play ball but cannot find the ball. You know that it is somewhere in the room, so you all search for it. Finally, one of you finds it. Who will it be? Where was the ball?
3. You are two friends taking a picnic lunch to the park near your homes. Each of you has brought something. What did you bring? Just as you are starting to eat, a child whom neither of you knows comes along. He or she is hungry and looks at your picnic basket. Do you share your food? pay no attention? Does he or she ask you for a bite? What do you do?
4. You and your friend find a five-dollar bill on the sidewalk. You want to keep it, but at this moment, a woman comes down the street looking for something. You are certain that she has lost the money. What do you do?
5. Your mother has just given your old rag doll to your younger cousin, who is visiting you. Neither of them knows how much the doll means to you. You try to pretend that it is all right.

ACTIVITY 5.6

"YOU-END-IT" IMPROVISATIONS

Objective: To create original endings for familiar stories or open-ended situations

Suggestions for the Teacher

The "you-end-it" improvisations are open-ended. They are to be played as regular improvisations until the end, when someone or the group must make an important decision. In adding endings to the stories, players may use details they observe, information they gather, or intuition; there is no right answer because each time the situation is improvised, it will be done differently, and the variations will affect the stories' conclusions.

1. Take a well-known story and instead of ending it as written, stop before the final action and end it differently. For example, in "Rumplestiltskin," imagine that the miller's daughter does not spin straw into gold. How would you end the story?
2. Do the same thing with "Goldilocks and the Three Bears." Suppose the bears come home while Goldilocks is eating her supper?
3. A small group of people is hiking in a national park. It is a beautiful day, and the hikers go farther into the forest than they had intended. Suddenly they realize that it is growing dark. They turn to go back, but discover that there are two paths and they cannot remember which one they had been following to arrive at their present location. A decision must be made quickly: one path will lead them back to their campsite; the other may be fraught with danger, and they will be hopelessly lost. What will they decide to do? Why do they make this decision?

The leader can make up other situations if the group enjoys the open-ended format. If the group is composed of very young children, simpler situations can be created for them, including nursery rhymes. For example, suppose you stopped "Humpty Dumpty" before the last line:

Humpty Dumpty sat on a wall,
Humpty Dumpty had a great fall;
All the king's horses and all the king's men . . .

Can they put him together again? If so, how do they do it? The players make the decision.

ACTIVITY 5.7

FIRE FIGHTERS

A field trip to a local fire station is a good first step, particularly for first and second graders. The trip stimulates discussion of the persons and equipment they have seen.

Objective: To learn about fire fighters, using creative drama as a teaching technique

Suggestions for the Teacher

Suggest that the class members might want to play fire fighters, performing the jobs they do and their response to alarms. This can lead to discussion of volunteer fire fighters, forest fires, fire prevention, and the plight of families whose homes are destroyed by fire.

A third-grade class can do a great deal with the topic, using creative drama as a way of learning and integrating important information about fire—its values and its dangers.

ACTIVITY 5.8

HUMANE EDUCATION

Objective: To raise children's consciousness of the needs of animals and give information about their care and protection

Suggestions for the Teacher

Post pictures of house pets. After the children have had an opportunity for free discussion, ask how many children have pets. What is the role of the pet in family life?

What are the animal's needs? food? care? Explain that animals know fear, pain, happiness, loneliness, shame, and pride. Have children act out how they think a pet feels when it is:

1. Lost
2. Hungry
3. Sleepy
4. Alone
5. In pain
6. Afraid
7. Playful
8. Happy

Perhaps invite a veterinarian to the class to discuss how he or she helps animals. Instead of or in addition to the veterinarian, invite a representative from the local A.S.P.C.A. to explain local animal laws and people's responsibilities toward animals. Most communities have laws that guarantee the safety and protection of both animals and human beings.

Dramatize stories about animals. Many good ones promote understanding and sympathetic treatment of domestic animals as well as knowledge of wild animals.

ACTIVITY 5.9

ROLE PLAYING

Objective: To create an understanding of the feelings of others and change an attitude of prejudice to one of friendliness and acceptance

Suggestions for the Teacher

The first step will depend on the group, the situation, and the right moment to step in. A discussion of newcomers in a neighborhood may be the starting point. Or an actual episode involving a youngster may necessitate bringing it up. Possibly, a story can be used as a springboard.

Once the subject has been introduced, suggest an improvisation for several players: a group of friends meet a new foreign child in the playground at recess. They exchange words, leading to cruelty. (The newcomer may ask to play with them, and they taunt him or her about not knowing the rules of the game, about appearance, or about language; the newcomer even may be threatened by the group.) At this point, the teacher stops the drama and changes parts.

One of the group of friends (a ringleader, if possible) takes the part of the newcomer, and the newcomer takes that child's place in the group. Play the situation through again; then stop it.

A serious discussion follows. This usually elicits some remarkable insights as the children realize what they have been doing. While it is true that they have consciously been cruel, they rarely have a real understanding of the *feelings* of the victim.

6

MAKING PLAYS FROM STORIES

PLAYMAKING AS A CLASSROOM ACTIVITY

When the group has had experience with pantomime and improvisation and knows something about structure, it will be ready to attempt to dramatize a story. Children often have suggestions of their own regarding favorite stories that they want to dramatize. Regardless of how well they know the story, there is still some preliminary work to be done before improvisation begins. The teacher, well acquainted with the group by this time, knows the kind of material that will have an appeal and present the fewest difficulties. Success is important to future work, so the teacher will want to select a story that he or she is relatively sure the group can handle.

There is a wealth of good literature readily available, which both group and teacher can enjoy and find worthy of their efforts. The stories in this chapter and the poems in Chapter 7 are illustrative of the kinds of material that groups in the early grades have used successfully. Suggestions are offered as to ways in which material may be presented and handled. It should not be inferred that these are the only or even the best ways of using the material; they are merely examples of the thinking done by some groups.

Folk tales, legends, and fables are recommended material for use on all levels, although different age groups will view them according to their own maturity and experience. For young children, stories should be simplified in the telling, whereas in working with older children, greater emphasis can be given to characterization. Meanings and insights come with experience as well as age; hence a really good story spans many age levels.

When the teacher has decided on an appropriate story, he or she must decide whether it is better told or read. In general, telling the story is preferable because it establishes a closer rapport with the class and gives the teller a chance to observe reactions and to clarify any points that appear to puzzle the audience. This means being thoroughly familiar with the material; in fact, the beginning teacher will do well to practice telling the story aloud before presenting it to the group.

After the story has been told and all questions have been answered, the children are ready to begin planning how they will dramatize it. A discussion should include a review of the plot and descriptions of the characters. Then the class is ready to try playing it. Asking for volunteers is a good way to start. This gives the stronger class members a chance to try it first and the more timid an opportunity to become better acquainted with it before taking their turns. Casting is done on a voluntary basis the first two or three times. Later on, the leader may suggest that other children try various parts. For instance, he might say, "Lynne hasn't had a chance yet. How would you like to try the princess this time, Lynne?" Or, "John has been the cobbler. Let's give Alan a chance to play it. And you, John, be one of the townsfolk." Or, "I know David has a strong voice. How about letting him be the giant?" In other words, the teacher must be concerned with the development of each participant. Later on, when the group is ready to play the story for the last time, the leader might suggest those children who have brought the greatest reality to each part, but this is as close as the teacher comes to typecasting.

The situation may be played any number of times, but the replaying should not be interpreted as rehearsal. It is hoped, of course, that with each playing, the story will gain in substance and depth; there will be deeper insights; and the participants will develop greater freedom and self-confidence. The discussions preceding and following each playing are important aspects of creative drama, for it is during these periods that some of the most creative thinking takes place. Some questions that might precede the first playing are:

1. What do we want to tell?
2. Who are the people?
3. What are these people really like?
4. What are they doing when we first meet them?
5. Where does the first scene take place?
6. What kind of a house do they live in?

After the scene has been played once, more specific questions can guide the discussion:

1. Did the players tell the story?
2. What did you like about the opening scene?
3. Did the people show that they were excited (angry, unhappy, and so on)?
4. When we play it again, can you think of anything that would improve it?
5. Was anything important left out?

In the course of a year, there are often delightful results, and both the teacher and the group may want to share them with others. There is no reason why this should not be done, provided public performance was not the original intention. More often, however, the initial results will be crude and superficial. Dialogue will be scanty, despite the most careful planning. To the experienced leader, this does not represent failure. It is an early stage in the development of the group and may, at that point, indicate real progress. Acceptance of the effort does not mean that the teacher is satisfied to remain at this level but that the efforts have been recognized. In time, the teacher will become more selective in what he or she accepts, but in the beginning will accept all ideas because they have been offered.

PLAYS BASED ON STORIES

The first two stories have been chosen for inclusion because of their simplicity. Most groups are familiar with them and like them and need only be refreshed as to the details.

Fables

Fables are popular with some groups, although the obvious moral does not appeal to others. One advantage of a fable is its brevity. There is action as well as a quick and satisfying ending. Even though there is little opportunity for character development, some groups will fill in the plot with delightful and imaginative dialogue. Activities 6.3 and 6.4 present well-known fables.

"The Sun and the Wind" and "The Country Mouse and the City Mouse" are favorite fables with many children. They also provide excellent opportunities for pantomime, as well as ideas for discussion. A group of fables, incidentally, makes a good program without taxing either teacher or players.

The fable in Activity 6.5 is longer than Aesop's fables, but it has the same advantages of a simple story line based on an amusing or intriguing idea.

Folk Tales and Legends

After a group has mastered the fable, it is ready to take on a longer and more detailed story, such as the folk tale. A word is in order regarding the use of folk and fairy tales in creative drama. At one time, they were the exclusive fare for dramatization and children's theatre. The reaction against them was based in part on a need for more diversified material and contemporary themes and in part on a question as to whether modern children were interested in fantasy. Bruno Bettelheim's *Uses of Enchantment*[1] has caused us to take a second look at traditional material. Yes, we do want to introduce new stories, but in seeking them, we must take care not to discard the rich resources of the past. The psychological values of the fairy tale and the cultural insights offered by the folk tale are important aspects of a child's experience. In addition, both genres offer imaginative possibilities for dramatization.

An effort has been made to present stories from a variety of ethnic and racial groups. Many of our folk and fairy tales originated in the British Isles and Germany. Most children and teachers are unfamiliar with folk tales and legends from other parts of Europe and of peoples of our own hemisphere. Activity 6.6 presents an Italian folk tale and Activity 6.7, a Spanish one, which I learned from a Spanish student. The Western Hemisphere is represented by an American Indian legend (Activity 6.8) and a Bahamian story (Activity 6.9), to which I was introduced by a Bahamian teacher in New York City, who is collecting stories that she heard as a child. The islands of the Caribbean are, I suspect, a rich source of material for creative drama, as yet unexplored in textbooks and anthologies of children's literature.

It is hoped that the leader, in planning a unit or season, will offer material from both the old and the new, the fantastic and the real, the amusing and the serious. Variety and quality capture and hold the interest. Fantasy is not necessarily escape from reality; it can also be an instrument for the analysis of reality.

SUMMARY

The stories in this chapter were selected for inclusion because of their simplicity and successful use with beginning groups of all ages. There are many excellent stories just as suitable for creative playing, and the interested leader will have no difficulty finding them. Tastes and inter-

[1] Bruno Bettelheim, *The Uses of Enchantment* (New York: Knopf, 1976).

ests of the group will guide the selection, although one of the values in creative drama is the opportunity it offers for introducing new material and good literature. One thing the leader will discover is that no two groups ever handle a story in quite the same way.

The procedure suggested is as follows:

1. Presentation of the story (read or told)
2. Organization of the material
3. Improvisation
4. Evaluation
5. Replaying

Remember that dialogue will be brief and the scenes shorter than planned. Less conditioned to the conventions of the proscenium stage than adults, children are freer in their use of space, planning scenes in various parts of the room simultaneously. When a class is held in a room with a platform at one end, the children are likely to use it as a particular place—a mountaintop or a distant land—rather than as the central playing area. For every age group, there are fewer inhibitions if a large room, instead of a stage, is used. Playing in the round reduces self-consciousness and is conducive to freer movement, since the scattered observers do not seem like an audience.

Evaluation is an important aspect of creative drama and leads into the replaying, which should acquire new depth and richer detail. Changing parts, with each participant playing, may not always make for a "better" performance, but it does give each a chance to play the part of his or her choice.

Finally, teachers must keep in mind that

1. Children want to succeed. In the creative-drama class, where there is no right or wrong, success is possible.

2. Children want to relate to others, although they may not know how to go about it. In the creative-drama class, which is a communal art, cooperation is an essential element. Therefore, establishing a relationship with others is implicit.

3. Children want to learn, although they may resist being taught. In the creative-drama class, players are learning constantly while enjoying participation in our oldest art form.

Y 6.1

OR SALE

"Caps for Sale," or "The Peddler and His Caps," is popular with younger children but equally interesting to older children and even adults because of the underlying theme. Very young children enjoy being monkeys and like to take turns acting the Peddler. Older children see the parallel between the behavior of humans and of monkeys and hence find in this tale a meaning worthy of their thought and effort.

Objective:* *To enact a simple story in which the entire class can take part

Suggestions for the Teacher

Tell the story first. Be sure the children know it well. When the story has been told, review the plot to make certain that it is clearly understood. From here on, there are many ways of proceeding. You may ask where the story begins and how many scenes the group sees in it. The children may suggest two, three, four, and even five, although they usually come to the conclusion that three main scenes are necessary:

1. The Peddler starts out on his travels
2. He arrives in the village
3. He stops to rest in the forest

"The Peddler and His Caps" (Courtesy of Tamara Hunt, University of Hawaii at Manoa)

Some groups imagine a road running all around the room, with the three scenes laid in different areas. This enables the Peddler to move from one place to another and gives him an opportunity to talk to himself as he walks along. Since no scenery is used in creative drama, such an arrangement is perfectly feasible. Incidentally, one advantage of a large room in dramatizing this story is the amount of freedom it provides the players: they are not limited by the rows of seats or the traditional stage area. When the group is playing in an auditorium, however, the succession of scenes will follow a more conventional pattern, unless there is an apron (area in front of the curtain) to accommodate some of the action.

In discussing how the Peddler's occupation might be introduced, one group may suggest that he have a wife with whom he can talk over his plans for the day at breakfast. Another group may give him a helper; another, a son; and still another may insist that he lives alone and so talks to himself.

Whether or not his trip down the road is considered a separate scene depends on the importance the group attaches to it, but the next major scene is certainly the village in which the Peddler stops to sell his caps. One of the advantages of a story of this sort is the opportunity for characterization afforded by the villagers. Since any number of villagers may be included, there is an opportunity for many children to take part. The mayor is always a favorite, although other delightful characters may be created: a shoemaker, a mother, a small boy, a farmer, a young girl, and a milliner are examples. The playing of this scene will be long or short, depending on the characterizations and the fun the children have with it. Again, if a road is used to suggest the Peddler's travels, he will move along to a place designated as a part of the forest. If the group is small, the same children who were villagers can be monkeys. If the group is large, however, there is ample opportunity for others to play the monkeys. One of the best features of this particular story is the flexibility of the cast: whatever the size of the cast, the entire group can take part in the play.

Regardless of age, children always respond to the monkeys, and the activity demanded by their antics is conducive to bodily freedom. There is such great opportunity for pantomime in the final scene that the leader might do well to begin with it, as a means of relaxing the group. By the time all the class members have been monkeys, they are better prepared to begin on the story.

In this and, indeed, any story selected for dramatization, it is a good idea to work on small portions first, rather than attempt the entire story at once. No matter how well the children may know the material, it is quite another thing to improvise the scenes. Therefore, working on short bits, not necessarily in sequence, makes for more successful playing. In this respect, it is similar to rehearsing a play; the director does not attempt to run through the complete script until the actors have rehearsed each scene.

CAPS FOR SALE

There was once a little old man who made caps. All year long, he worked at them: red caps, pink caps, yellow caps, blue, green, and purple caps, caps with feathers and caps without. Every so often, when he had made a large enough number of caps to sell, he would put them in his pack and take them around to the villages. This particular morning, he decided that he had plenty of caps to peddle, and since it was a very fine summer day, he took himself off. His cries of "Caps for sale" roused the townsfolk, and soon many of them were trying on caps and selecting the ones they wanted to buy. Butchers, bakers, shoemakers, mothers, children, and even the mayor himself gathered around the little Peddler, trying on caps and admiring their appearances. Finally, the mayor, who had found nothing to his liking, took off his cap and tossed it back to the Peddler, suggesting that he come again some other day. "Not today, Peddler. Come back another time."

Reluctantly, all the townsfolk followed his example, echoing the mayor's words that he return another day. Realizing that he could sell no caps in this village, the little Peddler departed. Before long, he passed by the edge of a woods and, feeling very sleepy, decided to lie down and rest. Soon, however, he fell fast asleep, his hats lying on the grass beside him. Now it happened that this part of the woods was inhabited by a band of monkeys. Monkeys are curious little fellows, and finding the Peddler asleep under a tree, they decided to investigate the contents of his pack. First one, then another, cautiously approached. When they saw that the Peddler was wearing a cap on his head, the monkeys tried the caps on their own little heads. Then they scampered a distance away, chattering excitedly, for they were very much pleased with themselves. The sound of the chattering soon awakened the Peddler. He reached for his pack and was astonished to find it empty. Greatly puzzled, he looked about him to see where the caps might have gone. Suddenly, he saw the monkeys. He called to them, pleasantly at first, and asked them to give back his caps. They only chattered, "Chee, chee, chee," pleasantly, in reply.

Then he shook his fist at them and demanded his caps, but they just shook their fists back. Angrily, he stamped his foot at them, but they only stamped their little monkey feet at him in return. He begged, and they begged; he moved a few steps away, and they moved a few steps away. Suddenly, it occurred to him that the monkeys were doing everything he did. With a sweeping gesture, he removed his own cap and tossed it to the ground at his feet. Immediately, all the monkeys removed their caps and threw them down to the Peddler. He gathered his caps up as quickly as possible, then made a low bow and thanked the monkeys for returning them. Chattering happily, the monkeys also bowed; each was pleased with the trick he thought he had played on the other.

ACTIVITY 6.2

BREAD AND HONEY

"Bread and Honey" is a delightful little story for small children. They probably will enjoy hearing it read several times before wanting to act it.

Suggestions for the Teacher

Except for Ben, all the parts are short. It is suggested that several children play Ben, shifting with each encounter. The number of characters can be increased almost indefinitely to accommodate the size of the group. Children identify easily with Ben and enjoy the story for its own sake.

If the children are very young, the teacher may have the entire class play each animal before trying it individually. Older children might want to play it for younger ones, in which case props will enhance the humor.

*BREAD AND HONEY**

FRANK ASCH

One morning when Ben was getting ready for school, his mother took a loaf of fresh bread out of the oven.

"Can I have a piece?" asked Ben.

"The bread is too hot now," said his mother. "But you can have some when you get home."

"With honey on top?" asked Ben.

"Yes," said his mother, "with lots of honey on top."

"Okay," said Ben, and he hurried off to school.

That day, Ben painted a picture of his mother. When the bell rang, he decided to take it home. On the way, he stopped to show the picture to Owl.

"I love it," said Owl. "But you made the eyes too small."

"I have my paintbox with me," said Ben. "Maybe I can fix that."

"Fine work!" said the Owl when he had finished.

At the riverbank, Ben showed the picture to Alligator.

"I just love it!" said Alligator. "But the mouth needs to be much, much bigger!"

"How's that?" asked Ben.

"Much better!" said Alligator.

A little way down the path, Ben met Rabbit and showed her the picture. "I love it!" said Rabbit. "But the ears are too short."

* Frank Asch, *Bread and Honey* (New York: Parents Magazine Press, 1981).

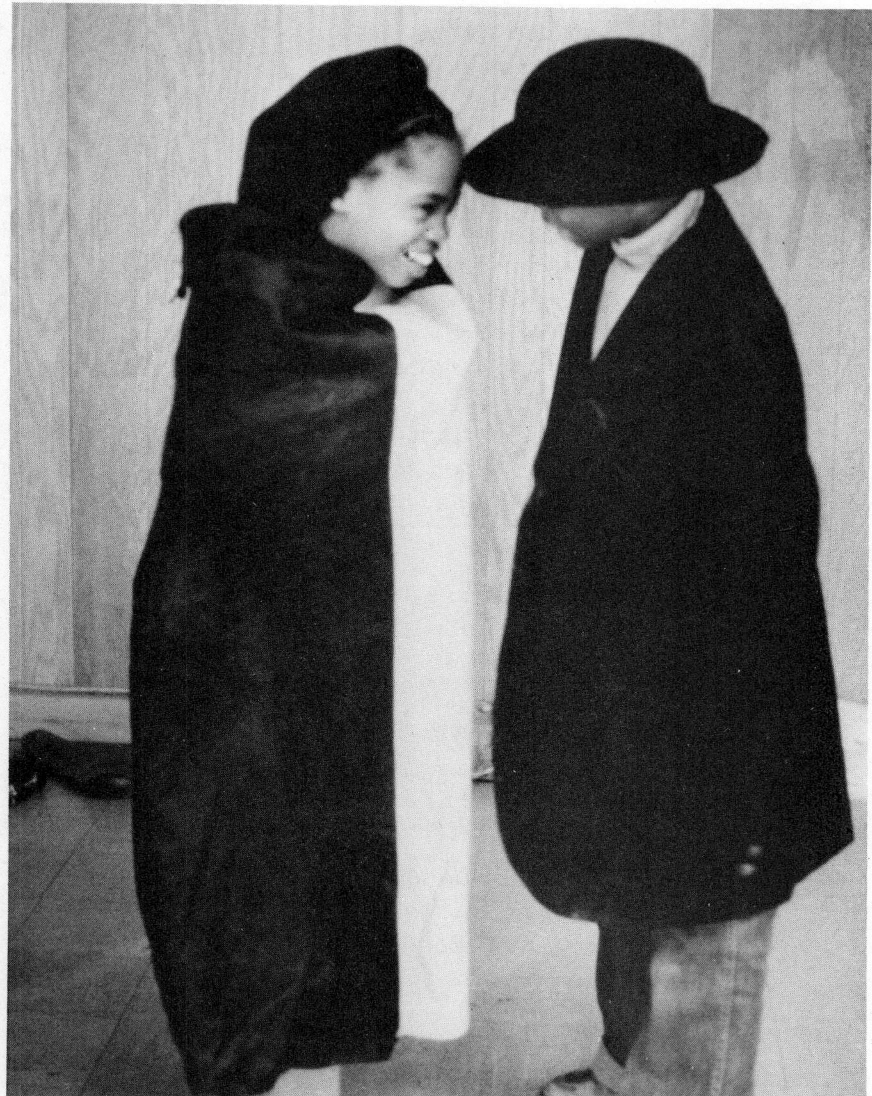

Making plans. (Courtesy of Creative Arts Team, New York University)

"Oh, that's easy to fix," said Ben.

"How's that?" asked Ben.

"Wonderful," said Rabbit.

When Ben showed Elephant his picture, Elephant said, "I love it, but the nose is too small."

Once again, Ben took out his paints.

"How's that?" asked Ben.

"Unforgettable!" said Elephant.

Then Ben showed his picture to Lion. "I love it," said Lion, "but you forgot a fluffy mane."

"How's that?" asked Ben, when he had added the mane.

"A picture to be proud of," said Lion.

When Ben was almost home, he saw Giraffe and showed him his picture. "I just love it," said Giraffe. "But the neck is too short."

"How's that?" asked Ben.

"Perfect," said Giraffe.

Ben ran the rest of the way home. When he got there he said to his mother, "Look what I made—a picture of you!"

"I love it!" said his mother.

"Just the way it is?" asked Ben.

"Just the way it is," said his mother. And she hung it on the refrigerator. Then she gave Ben a thick slice of homemade bread with lots of honey on top.

ACTIVITY 6.3

THE BOY WHO CRIED WOLF

Objective: To dramatize a short, simple story, recognizing the moral it teaches

Suggestions for the Teacher

1. Discuss fables and what distinguishes them from other kinds of stories. (short and simple; often making use of animals and elements of nature as characters; always pointing a moral)
2. Read a fable aloud. *The Boy Who Cried Wolf* is a good one to start with because the whole class can take part. The townsfolk offer opportunities for creating a variety of persons.
   a. Who are they?
   b. What is each doing when he hears the boy's cries, and what is his reaction when he discovers the trick?
   c. Who starts up the mountainside first?
   d. How would an old man feel if he climbed up a steep hillside for nothing?
   e. How does each one respond the second day?
   f. What does each say to his neighbor on the third morning?

   Such questions as these help the group create individual characters of the crowd.
3. This probably needs no planning time. Because the fable is so short, every child can have a chance to try the part of the shepherd.
   a. What is he like?
   b. How do we know that he is lonely and restless?
   c. Where are his sheep?
   d. How does he hit on the trick he plays?
   e. How does he feel when he sees the wolf?
   f. What does he do when the people fail to come to his rescue?
   g. Does he learn a lesson?
4. Time should always be given to a discussion of the moral and how it applies to them. Most children like to discuss the meaning of fables and find application to their own lives.

If there is a stage in the room, it may be used as the mountain where the sheep are grazing. If there is no stage, the boy can be at one end of the room in order to suggest the distance between him and the village. There is excitement in this story and the kind of action that appeals to younger children. The lesson, incidentally, is one that all are able to understand and appreciate.

THE BOY WHO CRIED WOLF

There was once a shepherd lad who went out to the fields each day with his flock. One day, growing tired of his lonely life, he decided to create some excitement. And so, when he was a distance from the village, he cried, "Wolf! Wolf!" The townsfolk, hearing his cries, dropped their chores and ran up the mountainside to help him. When they got there, however, the shepherd boy only laughed, and they realized the trick that had been played on them.

The following morning, the boy did the same thing, and again the townsfolk ran to his rescue. Discovering that he had fooled them a second time, they returned to their work, angrily vowing that they would not be taken in by this trick again. On the third morning, when the boy was high up on the mountain, he heard a disturbance among the sheep. Seeing a wolf attacking them, he called out in terror, "Wolf! Wolf!" No one came. Again he called "Wolf! Wolf! A wolf is attacking my sheep!"

The townsfolk heard his cries, but thinking it to be only a joke, did not go to his aid. The shepherd lad learned a lesson that day: If one cries "Wolf!" too often, no one comes when there really is danger.

ACTIVITY 6.4

THE TORTOISE AND THE HARE

"The Tortoise and the Hare" is another fable that has great appeal and that may be played without much time spent in preparation. Although the characters are animals, children enjoy discovering what they can do to suggest their characteristics and give them reality.

Suggestions for the Teacher

After the leader has told the fable, begin with total group participation: all can be hares and then tortoises. After some preliminary pantomime, the story can be played in its entirety. Younger children particularly enjoy the physical movement. A large room lends itself to the race, which may be run in a wide circle or in repeated circling of the space. Unless the group is very large, each child may have a turn playing one of the two parts, with the rest of the class participating as other animals watching the contest. This is a highly satisfying story for use in a single period or as a change from a more ambitious undertaking. Discussion brings out the moral, which children beginning at ages 8 to 10 comprehend easily.

THE TORTOISE AND THE HARE

There was once a Hare who was forever boasting of his great speed. In fact, whenever more than two animals gathered together in the forest, he would appear and then take the opportunity of telling them that he could outstrip the best of them. Stretching his long legs proudly, he would declare, "No one has ever beaten me. When I race at full speed, there is no one who can pass me."

The other animals said nothing, for there was no one who wished to dispute him. One day, the Tortoise, who had been listening quietly, replied, "I accept your challenge. I will race you."

"That is a good joke," laughed the Hare. "I could go to the goal post and back before you had passed the first marker."

"Save your breath until you've won," said the Tortoise. "I'm willing to race you."

The other animals, who were mighty tired of listening to the Hare's boasts, were only too glad to hear someone speak up, although they secretly wished it had been an animal with a greater chance of winning. Nevertheless, they cheered the little Tortoise on and helped draw up a course. Then they lined up on each side, and the Cock called the start of the race: "1–2–3–GO!"

The Hare was gone and out of sight in a flash as his white cottontail disappeared through the bushes. The Tortoise kept his eyes straight ahead and never varied his pace. Presently, the Hare returned and danced around him, laughing at his slow progress. The Tortoise didn't say a word. Then, to show his scorn for the Tortoise, the Hare lay down under a tree. He yawned, shut his eyes, and finally curled up and took his afternoon nap. The Tortoise only smiled and plodded on. After a while, the Hare awoke from his sleep. He opened his eyes just in time to see the Tortoise crawl past the winning post. As fast as he could make his legs go, he could not get there in time to save the race. The Tortoise, slow as he was, had crawled steadily forward, while the Hare had spent his time running in circles and taking a nap. "I've learned a lesson today," said the Hare, ashamed of himself for having made so much fun of his opponent. "It's hard work, and not speed, that wins the race."

ACTIVITY 6.5

THE TWO FOOLISH CATS

"The Two Foolish Cats" is a Japanese fable. It can be enjoyed by children of all ages, although it has particular appeal for younger children. The idea of fair play is well understood by even the youngest, and the trickster is always a popular character. The simplicity of the story precludes depth so far as study is concerned, but there is a lesson in it, if the leader wants to pursue it. "The Two Foolish Cats" is fun and, for that reason alone, worth doing.

Suggestions for the Teacher

A discussion of greed and fair play is bound to follow the telling of the fable. A small group will be able to play all three parts because of the brevity of the story. After playing and replaying the monkey, most children are ready to talk about his way of handling the problem. The humor must not be sacrificed to the moral, however; the value of the fable is its ability to convey a lesson in a humorous anecdote, usually told through animals.

THE TWO FOOLISH CATS

There were once two cats who lived together in peace and harmony. They were good friends, sharing food and shelter. One day, however, each of them came upon a fresh, sweet rice cake on a path leading into a woods. Delighted with their discoveries, they showed their cakes to each other, comparing them for size and freshness. Now it happened that the larger of the two cats had picked up the smaller rice cake. "This is not fair," he said. "I am larger than you, and therefore I should have the larger cake. Come, let us trade."

But the smaller cat refused, "No, I am smaller than you, and I need more food so I can grow to your size. I wouldn't think of trading."

Well, this led to an argument, each cat insisting that he should have the larger of the two cakes. They accused each other of greediness, and as they grew angrier, they began to growl and spit. The argument went on for some time, neither one willing to give in to the other. Finally the bigger cat said, "Let us stop. We will get nowhere fighting like this. Let us go find the wise monkey who lives in the forest. If we ask him to divide our cakes equally, we shall each have our fair share and our argument will be over."

The smaller cat agreed, for he was hungry and wanted to eat his cake. So the two took themselves off to the forest to find the wise monkey. They looked in the bushes and treetops, around rocks and behind the trunks of the trees, until at last they found him. They explained what they wanted, but the old monkey replied that he must hear each side of the argument. The bigger cat began. Then the wise monkey said, "Stop. Let me hear the other."

The smaller cat spoke up. When he had finished, the old monkey nodded his head gravely. "I think I can solve your problem. Give me the rice cakes."

The cats handed them over eagerly. The monkey took one in each hand and weighed them with care. "Yes," he said, "this one is heavier. Let me take a bite out of it. Then they will be the same size."

But he took a very big bite, and what had been the larger cake now became the smaller. "Dear, dear," said the monkey, "I shall have to take a bite out of *this* cake to even things up."

As you can imagine, he again took a large bite, and the first cake became the larger. Paying no attention to the cats, who were anxiously watching their cakes disappear, the old monkey went from one to the other until both cakes were gone.

"Well," he said, "you asked me to solve your problem, and I have done it. Without the cakes you have nothing to quarrel about." Whereupon he went off, leaving the two cats hungry and feeling very foolish indeed. But never did they quarrel again!

ACTIVITY 6.6

THE SHINING FISH

"The Shining Fish," an Italian folk tale, is particularly appealing to children in the third and fourth grades. While it is brief, it has more substance than many other simple stories of magic.

Suggestions for the Teacher

The three main parts can be alternated in order to give everyone in the group a chance to play them; meanwhile, the rest of the class can be the sailors so that they also are involved in the action.

THE SHINING FISH

An old peasant went out into the woods one morning to gather firewood. He was very poor, and he wondered how much longer he and his wife could manage to keep soul and body together. He was growing too old to do the hard work of his younger days, and they had no children to help them eke out an existence. They had no near neighbors and saw no one but the fishermen who passed their cottage each night with the day's catch. Rarely did the old couple have the price of a fish for their dinner. It was on this particular morning, as the old man stopped to pick up some twigs, that a stranger came toward him. He said that he knew of the old couple's poverty and wanted to help them. So saying, he handed the old man a purse containing one hundred ducats. Before the peasant could pull his wits together, the stranger disappeared as suddenly as he had appeared.

Now the old man was afraid that his wife might spend the money foolishly if he told her about it, so he hid it under a bale of straw behind their hut. The following evening, when he came home with his armful of twigs, he found a sumptuous meal spread out on the table.

"Where did you get the money to pay for all this?" he asked.

"I sold the bale of straw," replied his wife, "and I was paid a good price for it."

Well, the old man was mightily upset when he heard what had happened to the hundred ducats, but there was nothing to be done about it now. The next day, when he went into the forest to gather more wood, the stranger appeared again. "I know what happened," he said sympathetically, "but don't fret, for here is another purse. Mind what you do with it."

The old man thanked him and hurried home. "Where shall I hide them this time?" he said to himself. "I know—at the bottom of the ash pile. She will never think of going there."

Hats can help make stories into plays. (Courtesy of Creative Theatre Unlimited, Princeton, New Jersey)

But, alas, when he came home the next night, what did he behold but another feast on the table. "Where did this come from?" he demanded of his wife.

"You will be pleased," she replied. "I sold the ash pile for enough money to buy us a meal. Fish and cakes!"

"Oh, what have I done!" groaned her husband, and he proceeded to tell her about the stranger and the two bags of ducats.

The following day, when he went into the forest, he once more met the stranger. This time, however, his benefactor said, "I will give you no more money. What I will give you instead is a bag of frogs. Sell them and buy yourself the biggest fish you can find. Hang it by your window each night and see what happens."

Obediently, the old man did as he was told. That night, when he hung up the fish, he saw that it gleamed like a lantern in the darkness. When the fishermen at sea saw it, they used its light to guide them safely to shore. To show their gratitude, they gave the old peasants half their catch. What is more, the fishermen made a bargain with him; if the old man would hang the fish by the window every evening at dusk, they would always divide their night's catch. And so, from then on, the fishermen found their way safely to shore, and the old couple never knew hunger again.

ACTIVITY 6.7

THE CARLANCO AND THE GOATS

Objective: To enact a folk tale that probably is unfamiliar to American children

Suggestions for the Teacher

Bring in pictures of the Spanish countryside and peasant cottages. For most city children, pictures of goats and their kids will be helpful as well.

Tell the tale "The Carlanco and the Goats"; then talk about it. What meaning does it have for the children, in addition to the story itself?

Ask the children which scenes they would like to try first. It is a good idea to have all or several try being

1. The kids
2. The Carlanco
3. The wasp

All characters call for body movement, and the class will enjoy moving around the room as the different characters.

When the children seem to be ready to do more with the story, have them try portions of it. It is quite possible that they may never want to dramatize the whole story, but they will know it and will have grasped the moral.

THE CARLANCO AND THE GOATS

There was once in Spain a mother goat with three little kids. One day when she was up on the mountain, she saw a wasp drowning in a stream nearby. Quickly, she grabbed a branch in her mouth and held it out. The wasp managed to climb up on it, and the goat pulled her to shore.

"What a close call that was!" said the wasp. "You have saved my life. If you ever need help from me, go to that old wall yonder. I live there as Abbess of our convent of wasps. We are very poor, but if you will go there and ask for the Abbess, someone will call me to come at once. Adios, my friend."

So saying, the wasp flew away, her wet wings now quite dry.

One morning a few days later, the goat said to her children, "I must go up to the mountain this morning to gather wood. I will shut you in the house, and you must bar the door from inside. Do not open it for anyone. The wicked ogre, the Carlanco, may be about. If he sees me going away, he may try to get in."

"How will we know it is you when you come home?" asked the kids.

"First I will knock. Then you will hear me say:

'You may open the door for me but no other;
Three knocks will tell you that I am your mother'."

The goat went away, and the kids, who were very good and always did just what she told them, barred the door. It was not long, however, before they heard someone outside the house.

"Who is there?" called the oldest kid.

"It is only I, the Carlanco, my dear.
Open the door, you have nothing to fear."

But the kid, remembering what their mother had told them, called back, "No, I will not, for we promised our mother we would open it for her, but not for another."

This put the Carlanco in a great rage, and he tried first to push the door open, then to break it, but it would not budge. At last he went away, vowing to return.

When the mother goat came back with her load of wood, she called out, just as she had said she would, to her three little kids,

"You may open the door for me but no other;
Three knocks will tell you that I am your mother."

The kids slid open the bar, and the goat came inside. What she did not know was that the Carlanco was hiding in the forest nearby and had heard every word she had said.

The next morning, the mother goat went out as usual. The Carlanco was waiting outside. When he thought she was far enough away, he went to the door and in a soft voice, as much like the goat's as possible, called out:

"You may open the door for me but no other;
Three knocks will tell you that I am your mother."

Hearing this, the little kids believed that it was their mother, returning sooner than usual. So they went to the door and slid open the bar. When they saw that it was the Carlanco, they turned and scampered up the ladder to the roof, where the Carlanco, who was clever and strong, could neither reach nor follow them. He was so angry that he stamped about, roaring and kicking his feet.

When their mother came home with her load of wood, she called out as usual:

"You may open the door for me but no other;
Three knocks will tell you that I am your mother."

When the little kids heard her, they cried down from the roof that the Carlanco was in the house. The goat dropped her load of wood and flew to the convent of wasps and knocked at the door.

"Who is it?" asked the doorkeeper.

"I am a simple goat," replied the mother goat.

"What can we do for you? We are only wasps."

"Please call the Abbess," said the goat. "I need her help, and she told me to call in time of trouble."

"Very well," replied the doorkeeper, who was puzzled at the strange request.

The Abbess came at once when she was told that the goat was at the door. "Do not fear, dear goat," said the Abbess when she heard of the terrible thing that had happened. "Your kids are safe on the roof of your house, and in no time, I shall chase the Carlanco away."

When they reached the goat's house, the wasp crawled in through the keyhole. She flew at the Carlanco, stinging him first on the nose, then on the eyes. He did not know what was happening and ran around the room, howling, trying to escape from the sharp needles that seemed to be following him at every turn. Finally, giving up, he opened the door and ran off into the forest, never to return. As for the family of goats, they lived happily in their little cottage at the edge of the forest forever after.

ACTIVITY 6.8

A LEGEND OF SPRING

A "Legend of Spring" has proved to be extremely successful for creative playing because of its simplicity and opportunity for the entire class to take part in movement and mime. Players of all ages find it appealing and develop it in proportion to their experience and the amount of time that is given them.

Objective:* *To tell an American Indian legend in movement and words

Suggestions for the Teacher

First, be sure that the players are thoroughly acquainted with the story. Then, have them try in dance, movement, and mime to express the people's need for rain, wind, and sun. Young children often invent charming movements without the all-too-frequent stereotypes that older children offer. Hunting, fishing, planting, eating, and moving camp are activities that can be expressed in pantomime. Children love to think of as many ways as possible to show how the Indians lived and expressed their needs. While the story can be played without words, most groups will want to invent some dialogue. Some groups see the story in a single scene; others may break it into several. A drum is a valuable property for the leader at first, but later can be passed along to one of the children. A drum and plenty of space in which to move freely are the only requirements.

Involving the entire class in the story allows it to be played any number of times. Change parts with each playing, however, so that all participants have a chance to take major as well as group roles. The fact that study of the American Indian is so frequently in the curriculum of the early grades makes this legend a valuable inclusion for several reasons.

A LEGEND OF SPRING

The Indians of the Great Plains had suffered through a long winter, but this year, no sign of spring had appeared. Neither sun nor wind nor warm rains had come to awaken the seeds or bring the wild animals out of their winter hiding. One day, the Chief of the tribe called all the braves and squaws together. He explained to them that unless food were found soon, they would have to abandon their village and seek a home elsewhere. There was silence. The people looked up at the cold, gray sky, and down at the hard frozen earth. They knew the Chief was right, yet no one wanted to leave the pleasant valley in which they had dwelt for so many years. Finally White Cloud, youngest and strongest of the braves, spoke out. "I will go into the forest in search of food. With my strong bow and arrows, surely I can find food to bring back to my people."

"I will go with you," cried a second, then a third, and a fourth. Others rose from the campfire, where they had been sitting, and joined him. The old Chief smiled. "Go," he said. "Perhaps if you hunt deep enough in the forest, you will find the deer and rabbits to provide food until the spring comes to our land. While you are absent, we shall pray to the Great Spirit to make the sun shine again and the clouds empty warm rain on our fields."

The young men ran out as the drums beat a farewell. Then the old Chief called to the Great Spirit for help. The people danced around the fire, asking for sun, rain, and wind for their planting, and game for their hunters. When they finally dropped to their knees, exhausted, there was a rustle in the bushes. Looking up, they beheld a large golden bird flying toward the clearing. Scarcely had it appeared when White Cloud and his band of hunters broke through the underbrush. Two or three of the men had already raised their bows when White Cloud spoke.

"Do not shoot the golden bird. Perhaps it has come from the Great Spirit. It may be a sign for us if we wait to see what it wants. Hold your arrows. Do not shoot!"

The braves put down their bows and waited. Then the golden bird, seeing that the people meant her no harm, glided gracefully into their midst. Suddenly, she was transformed into a lovely young maiden with a golden bow and arrow.

"I have come from the Great Spirit," she said. "Listen to me carefully. Here is an arrow, which one of you must shoot straight into the dark cloud overhead. If the cloud is pierced, the rains will begin, and winter will leave your valley. If he who shoots the arrow does not succeed, you must prepare to leave your homes, for spring will not come this year."

So saying, she handed the bow to the Chief, asking him to select the brave who could shoot the straightest arrow. "You choose, golden maiden," he said. "It is your arrow. You choose the one who will send it from the bow."

Slowly the maiden circled the campfire, first looking at one, then another. Finally she stopped before White Cloud and handed him the golden bow and arrow. He took it from her silently, aimed at the cloud, and released the arrow. Up and up it went until it was lost from sight. Then, suddenly, a crack appeared in the sky. The sun came out, and the warm spring rain began to fall. The drum beat joyously as the people danced again, this time in thanks to the Great Spirit, who had answered their prayers.

ACTIVITY 6.9

HOW THE SOLDIER CRAB GOT HIS NAME

***Objective:** To enjoy a new story from a culture that is unfamiliar to most American children and learn about a group of islands off our eastern coast through the enactment of one of its folk tales*

Suggestions for the Teacher

The homeland of "How the Soldier Crab Got His Name," so near and yet so little known, is probably the least familiar of the countries represented by the folk tales. Collect pictures of the Bahamas, showing its geography, climatic conditions, and people. Photos are easily obtained because of the popularity of the Bahamas as a vacation spot.

Then have a discussion of the Caribbean islands. It is possible that some children may have visited them, but the majority will not have.

When you feel that the children are ready, tell or read the story. Because it is so long, scenes from it should be played first. Remember, it is never necessary to play a complete story. Younger children have their favorite parts and are often quite satisfied to play those scenes only, without any of the connecting material.

Some children may want to paint pictures of the little crab or the islands. Any extension of the activity furthers the learning and the appreciation.

New Words

Antennae. A pair of jointed sense organs on the head of an insect or crab; feelers.

Biter-claws. Claws that seize, cut, or bite.

Conch shell. The large, spiral-shaped shell of a sea mollusk.

Flamingo. Tropical bird with long legs, long neck, webbed feet, and bright red or pink feathers.

*HOW THE SOLDIER CRAB GOT HIS NAME**

KITTY KIRBY

Under the hot Bahama sun there lived a little gray crab. He was a very small creature, and he didn't even have a shell of his own. But he pushed his body into shells that he found on the beach. Now the little gray crab was really a remarkable fellow. He had two antennae on his head and six legs and one big biter. To see him marching along the beach with a snail's shell on his back was indeed quite a sight!

* Permission of Kitty Kirby (unpublished).

One day as he was out marching by the water and looking at all the new shells, he saw a big pink conch shell. And he said, "Good morning, Mr. Conch Shell. You look very pink and bright today!"

The shell answered, "Thank you, but I don't feel very well. For in a few moments, I know that I'll be sold to some tourist. You, Mr. Crab, you can always travel and move from shell to shell, changing yourself along the way. I think it's quite adventurous and exciting!"

"At least they want you. But I'm so small, no one wants me or even notices me," replied the crab. Suddenly a large wave crashed over the beach, and the little crab's antennae began to twitch. Through the vibrations he heard news of a special meeting that was to be held by the Lord of the Forest that afternoon. Only the most important creatures were to attend. Upon hearing this news, the little crab said good-bye to the conch shell, but he felt very sad because he had not been invited. "I'm going to go anyway," he said to himself. "At least I can listen, and I'm so small they won't even notice me."

The creatures all came—the green lizard, who scuttled through the grasses and rocks to be on time; the speckled frog, who hopped briskly along; the turtle, who crawled to the meeting. Also present were the wild pigs, who had no manners at all; the cackling chickens, who refused to stop making noises (to the great annoyance of the whistling ducks, who also wanted attention); and the parrots, who made fun of everybody by repeating the sounds uttered by their fellow creatures. No one noticed the little gray crab entering ever so quietly.

Then the Lord of the Forest spoke. He was the flamingo, with his pointed beak, his coat of pink feathers, his long graceful neck, and his spindly legs that seemed to stretch up forever. He flapped his majestic coral wings in order to gain the animals' attention.

"Quiet! Please! We want to discuss ways to protect ourselves from the strong winds and rains. Look what the storms have done to our homes, our nests, our ponds, and our trees! If someone can suggest a way to warn us when a storm is brewing, we can prepare for it and run for safety. I promise that whoever can help will be crowned with one of my most royal feathers."

"How can I tell when a storm is brewing?" asked the lizard. "I don't have a chance to know when a storm is brewing or which way the wind blows. Anyway, I have the rocks to protect me!"

The speckled frog spoke up. "I agree with you, Mr. Lizard. As for me, when a storm comes, I hide in the mud. Storms don't bother mud."

"Is that so?" asked the parrot. "From up on top I have seen many storms coming, while some of your family, Mr. Frog, have been washed away into the ocean. It is impossible to protect our nests and our little ones in a storm. Trees uprooted! Our nests blown away! Something has to be done!"

"What about me? What about me?" asked the turtle. "My poor hard shell just can't take all those branches falling on it anymore!"

The whistling ducks then said, "Well, lately it's been very bad for us in a storm. We think the chickens and the pigs will agree, for we've lost many of our young, who could not manage for themselves."

"It's true! It's true!" all the animals agreed. "But what are we going to do? How can we know when a storm is brewing? How can we prepare for one?"

Suddenly, the little gray crab crawled out from behind a tree into the center of the meeting. The animals all laughed when they saw him coming, with his tiny body and biter-claw crawling through the grass.

"Oh, Mr. Lord of the Forest," the little crab said, "I know I haven't been invited to your meeting, and I know I'm small and insignificant. But listen to me. I just might be able to help you."

"You!" snapped the turtle. "You don't even have a home of your own. You have to borrow a poor old snail's shell to live in!"

"What do you know about protecting us from a storm?" asked the cack-ling chickens and the whistling ducks.

"What do you know about protecting us from a storm?" echoed the parrots. Then all the creatures burst into laughter.

Finally, the Lord of the Forest raised his wing to hush them. "Let us listen to him. Let us listen to what he has to say. After all, any suggestion might be of help."

Then the little crab spoke again. "When a storm comes, my family and I start crawling from the beach up toward the hill where the pink sands lie. There is a little red house there that will shelter you. In it you will be safe, for this will be the worst storm in the history of the island!"

"But still you have not told us," said the Lord of the Forest. "How do you know when a storm is coming?"

"My two antennae begin to vibrate and I can sense danger in the wind, the clouds, and the sky," answered the crab. "It's all these together that tell me when a storm is brewing. And there's something else, something extra which I can't explain, something magic. When the air is thick and still, and there is a big black cloud in the sky and my biter begins to itch, this means that a terrible storm is brewing. I warn all the crabs, and we start marching from the shore up to the hill, hundreds of us, until we reach the old red house. There we pile one upon another, until we have formed a giant ball."

"Can you imagine such a story!" cackled the chickens and the ducks.

"It hurts my shell, I'm laughing so hard!" exclaimed the turtle.

The Lord of the Forest quieted them. "Now that's enough! After all, the little crab was only trying to help us. And no one else has come up with any better ideas. Go back to your homes and think about it. We shall all meet here at the same time tomorrow."

The next day all the animals met again. It was a beautiful afternoon, and the sun was shining brightly. The turtle had taken his bath in the pond, and his shell was shining like a bell. The whistling ducks and the cackling chickens had preened their feathers especially for the meeting. The speckled frog puffed up his chest and cleared his throat several times, to let everyone know he had an idea, since he was hopping and ready to go.

And so they met. All, that is, except the little gray crab. The Lord of the Forest flapped his pink flamingo wings. "I see that you are all here today and on time. Does anyone else have a solution to our problem about the storm?"

There was silence. The animals all looked at each other. No one had a suggestion. At that moment, a big black cloud appeared in the sky. Suddenly thunder roared and lightning flashed. The wind began to blow, and the rain came down upon the forest.

Trying to steady himself, his wings flapping wildly, the Lord of the Forest shouted, "Look! Up there! Marching . . . hundreds of them! The little crab is leading his family up the hill. We must run! All of you. Run and fly to the house on the hill and lock yourselves in as the little crab told you!"

The lizard moved fast, the frog even faster. The chickens flew. And the parrots flew quickest of all. The pigs barely made it, and the poor little turtle with his shiny shell said, "Oh, Mr. Lord of the Forest, I hope I can make the crawl."

"I shall help you," said the Lord of the Forest. And so all the animals made it to the top of the hill and went inside the house and closed the door.

By this time the last of the crabs had reached the top of the hill. And one by one they piled upon one another until they looked like a giant ball protecting the house where the animals huddled.

The winds howled, and the rains came down like rocks upon the forest. The house swayed back and forth. Never had there been such a violent storm. The waters came up from the ocean right to the top of the hill. But the ball of crabs stood firm.

Suddenly, everything stopped. The wind died away, and the waters of the ocean retreated. The skies cleared, and the sun came out. Opening the door slowly, the Lord of the Forest peeped out into the sunlight. He leaped back in amazement, and all the creatures trembled with fear.

Then slowly he looked out again, and there in front of the door he saw the most magnificent sight! He couldn't believe his eyes. He gathered all the creatures together to see the giant ball.

While the creatures watched, the ball began slowly to come apart, as one by one the crabs let go. Last to leave was the little gray crab.

"Oh, it's the little gray crab!" cried all the creatures in surprise. "He saved us from the storm."

"Yes," said the Lord of the Forest. "By marching like a soldier from the shore to the hill, he gave us a warning that a storm was brewing. He is our Soldier Crab."

"Soldier . . . crab! . . . Soldier . . . crab!" cheered all the creatures.

"Soldier . . . crab! . . . Soldier . . . crab!" parroted the parrot.

Plucking a royal pink feather from his wing, the Lord of the Forest spoke. "You have saved us all, little friend. And now I have the honor of presenting you with this royal coral feather."

All the animals voiced their approval. The ducks and parrots flapped their wings, and the chickens cackled. The pigs grunted, and the lizard's tongue flitted, while the frog hopped around the turtle.

But the little crab said, "Why, thank you, My Lord. This is a great gift, to be sure, but I cannot accept it. I am happy that I was able to protect all of you from the storm, and I shall be happy to do it again, whenever I'm needed. But I am so small—what would I do with a royal feather?"

"Surely we must thank you in some way," said the Lord of the Forest.

"Well, just to be invited to your meetings, to be a part of your family, that would make me most happy."

"Of course. That is so little to ask, for you are our best friend, our counselor in times of storms. I dub you 'Soldier Crab of Our Islands.'"

And all the animals agreed, shouting, "Hail to our Soldier Crab!"

7

THE POSSIBILITIES IN POETRY

Children like poetry. They are sensitive to the rhythm of it and enjoy the repetition of sounds, words, and phrases. The direct approach of the poet is not unlike their own; hence poetry, unless it has been spoiled for them, has a special appeal. The music and language, as well as the ideas, feelings, and images of poetry, reach younger children particularly, capturing and stimulating their imagination. For this reason, poetry can be used in creative dramatics with highly successful results.

Many teachers find poetry a more satisfactory springboard than prose for introducing creative playing to a group. This is probably an individual matter, depending as much on the teacher as on the participants. If teachers enjoy poetry themselves, they will find that it provides a rich source of material that can be used at all levels of experience and with all ages. For children, poetry and play go together quite naturally.

What kinds of poems are usable? How can poetry and movement be combined? Has choral speaking any place in creative dramatics? For the answers to these questions, the teacher has only to go to the children themselves as they engage in their play. Many of their games are accompanied by chants, which are a form of choral speaking. Rhythm is basic in action games, while some games are played to verse, with the players often making up their own stanzas. If we listen, we note the enjoyment of repetition, refrain, and the sounds of words. Only very much later does poetry become a literary form to be taken seriously, and when it does, the element of play, unfortunately, is too often lost.

CHORAL SPEAKING

Because poetry lends itself so well to group enjoyment, let us begin with a consideration of choral speaking, its purposes and procedures. Choral reading or speaking is simply reading or reciting in unison under the direction of a leader. It is not a new technique, for people have engaged in it for centuries. It antedated the theatre in the presentation of ideas and became an important element of the Greek drama. Evidences of choral speaking have been found in the religious ceremonies and festivals of primitive peoples, and it is still used for ritualistic purposes in church services and on patriotic occasions. In the early twentieth century, moreover, it was recognized as one of the most effective methods of teaching the language arts and of improving speech habits. Choral speaking has three major purposes:

1. Learning (when the purpose is process and, therefore, is participant centered)
2. Performance (when the purpose is program and, therefore, is audience centered)
3. Enjoyment

As with creative drama, it does not necessarily follow that the practice of choral speaking must result in performance. Practice has values of its own, whether or not the product is shared with an audience.

VALUES

One of the values of choral speaking is that it can be used successfully regardless of space or class size. While a group of 20 or so is more desirable than one of 40 or 50, the larger number need not be a deterrent.

Many teachers consider the greatest value of choral speaking to be the opportunity it provides for speech improvement. Pitch, volume, rate, and tone quality are important to the effective interpretation of material. The need for clear diction is apparent when a group is reading aloud, whereas the practicing of speech sounds alone is often a tedious and unrelated exercise. During discussion, even young children will make suggestions as to how a poem should be recited. Vocal expression and clear enunciation of speech sounds are often acquired more easily and with greater motivation when the group works together on meaning.

A third value, which choral speaking shares with creative drama, is the opportunity it provides for cooperation. Choral speaking is a group activity, and thus directs each individual to a common goal. The child with the strident voice learns to soften his tone, whereas the shy child can work for more volume without feeling self-conscious. Even the speech-handicapped child may recite without embarrassment, because she is not speaking alone and, therefore, is not conspicuous.

A fourth value of choral speaking is its suitability to any age level. It may be introduced in the kindergarten, but it is equally effective when used in high-school or college classes. Not all material is adaptable to choral work, but much is, and the major criterion is probably that it be enjoyed by the speakers themselves.

Procedures

There are many ways of beginning choral speaking, but with younger children, it probably will spring from their own enjoyment of a poem and their desire to say it aloud or to speak while acting a poem. Discussion of the meaning and of the various ways of interpreting the material in order to bring out the meaning gives pupils a part in planning the group reading. A second reading will reveal further meaning, as well as difficulties in phrasing and diction. For children in the early grades, speaking rather than reading is the obvious preference. Older children, whose ability to read aloud is well developed, can rehearse the performance and are able to handle longer and more difficult material. Young children should be given poetry that they can memorize easily and speak; otherwise, the teacher should read it, suggesting to the children that they repeat a refrain in unison.

Although a structured activity, choral speaking offers a real opportunity for creative thinking, as each group works out its own presentation. The amount of time spent on a poem will vary, but it is more important to keep the enthusiasm alive than to work for perfection. With practice, the participants will grow increasingly sensitive to the demands of different kinds of material, and their results will improve in proportion to their understanding and enjoyment.

Most authorities on choral speaking suggest dividing the group into light and dark voices. This is not quite the same as a division into high and low, or soprano and alto, voices but has to do with quality and resonance as well as pitch. Some leaders, however, believe that a division in which there are both light and dark voices in each group makes for more interesting quality. However it is done, some division is necessary for any class of more than 10 children. Some poems can be read by three groups if the class is very large. These may include middle voices; although, again, it is the material that will suggest the groupings, rather than an arbitrary division.

Ways of Reading

Unison. In unisonous choral speaking, the whole group speaks together. Although the simplest technique in one sense, reciting in unison is the most difficult, since using all voices limits variation. It takes practice to achieve clear diction and make the reading interesting. Some poems, particularly short ones, are most effective when read or spoken by the entire class.

Antiphony. In antiphonal speaking, each one of two groups takes certain parts. Many poems are more effective when recited in antiphony than in unison. The poem will dictate the way it may be read.

Cumulative. The cumulative technique is used to build toward a climax, or certain high points in the poem. As the term suggests, cumulative choral speaking is the accumulation of voices, either of individuals or of groups.

Solo. Lines or stanzas often call for individual speaking. Solo choral speaking can be an effective technique, as well as a way of giving an opportunity for individual participation.

Line-around. Line-around choral speaking is solo work, in which each line is taken by a different person. Children enjoy this technique and are alert to the lines they have been assigned.

As the group progresses and attempts longer and more difficult material, it may suggest using several or all of these techniques in one poem. The results can be remarkably effective, encouraging attentiveness, self-discipline, and imaginative planning. Occasionally, sound effects can be added. Music, bells, drums, and vocal sounds, produced by the children themselves, provide an opportunity for further inventiveness.

Because our primary concern is creative drama, only those poems that suggest movement or pantomime are included in this chapter. The poems and nursery rhymes in Activities 7.1 to 7.8 have been used successfully with groups, combining choral speaking and activities suggested by the content or sounds of the poems.

While the poems in Activities 7.9 and 7.10 may be used for choral speaking, they are too long for memorization and are better used for improvisation. If the teacher reads them aloud slowly, either first or while the children improvise movement, they will inspire a creative approach. They suggest many interpretations.

As the teacher works on choral speaking, values in addition to the ones mentioned earlier soon become apparent. First of all, for most children, it is fun. In addition,

1. Choral speaking offers the timid child and the slow reader an opportunity to overcome his or her fear by being in a group, yet occasionally having a line to say alone.
2. It moves the aggressive child into the background within an acceptable structure.
3. It introduces children to new material and offers them an opportunity to repeat old and familiar works.

One word of caution: Avoid excessive practice. Drilling for perfection can destroy the values of choral work and have a lasting negative effect.

POETRY AND DANCE

Poetry grew out of dance and song, and so they are natural companions. Inviting a dancer to the class—the dance teacher or perhaps an older student who has had more dance experience than the class—adds another dimension when working with poems. Dance offers an abstract expression rather than the more literal interpretation of mime and improvisation. Dividing the class, with half moving to the cadence and meaning of the poem and half speaking it, calls for imagination and cooperation. This approach is not suggested for older students only; younger children, although lacking performance skills, are often freer than are older children in interpreting poetry through movement.

Working on poetry first in mime and then in dance helps students to experience it more fully. Lyric verse lends itself best to nonverbal interpretation, whereas narrative and dramatic verse stimulate the improvisation of dialogue. Some groups respond to poetry more readily than others, but most will enjoy it if the leader's approach is positive and enthusiastic.

A poet or a professional children's-theatre company that performs poetry may inspire children. One such company (Periwinkle Productions, of Monticello, New York) began playing poetry programs over 20 years ago and retains poetry performance as an important emphasis in an expanding theatrical repertory. In addition to poetry reading and performances, the company works in schools with teachers to encourage creative writing, principally poetry. Special classes as well as English classes have responded to the stimulation and have achieved some remarkable results.

SUMMARY

Poetry is an effective springboard for improvisation. The directness of verse motivates the players to a direct and imaginative response. For this reason, poetry is a good starting point for the beginner, although it can be used at any time with even the most advanced players. Because the sounds of poetry have as great an appeal as the content and mood, it is suggested that poetry be spoken as well as acted.

Choral speaking is a group art and can, therefore, be combined with creative drama if the teacher so wishes. Some of the reasons for using choral speaking are as follows:

1. It can be done with groups of any size and age.
2. It emphasizes group rather than individual effort.
3. It provides an opportunity to introduce poetry.
4. It offers the shy or disabled child an opportunity to speak.
5. It promotes good habits of speech through enjoyable exercise, rather than drill.
6. It is satisfying in itself.
7. It can be combined successfully with rhythmic movement and pantomime.

Chants and the repetition of words have a natural appeal to children. Thus poetry and nonsense verse may prove a successful method of introducing creative drama. Skill in movement, rhythms, and pantomime are increased as all children are given opportunities to participate.

ACTIVITY 7.1

HAPPY NEW YEAR

In England, children used to go caroling from house to house on New Year's Day. Their listeners gave them money, much as we give candy and apples for trick or treat on Hallowe'en. Whether or not they received a contribution, they sang or spoke, and this old rhyme has been handed down.

Objective: To combine speaking in unison with movement

Suggestions for the Teacher

The group can say the verse together, with one child acting the part of the caroler; or half the group can speak, with the other half playing the carolers. Perhaps one child will want to speak and the rest perform the actions. There are various possibilities in even so short a rhyme as this.

HAPPY NEW YEAR

Happy New Year! Happy New Year!
I've come to wish you a Happy New Year.
I've got a little pocket, and it is very thin.
Please give me a penny to put some money in.
If you haven't got a penny, a halfpenny* will do.
If you haven't got a halfpenny, well—
God bless you!

* Pronounced *hā pə nē.*

ACTIVITY 7.2

TICK-TOCK

Objective: To combine sound effects with group speaking

Suggestions for the Teacher

The verse "Tick-Tock" suggests the use of sound effects rather than action. Part of the group might say the first and third lines, with the others taking the second and fourth. Or if two clocks are suggested, a solo voice might take the refrain and the total group, the other lines. Even so simple a poem as this provides some opportunity for inventiveness. Try saying it this way:

TICK-TOCK

All Slowly ticks the big clock:
Solo Tick-tock; tick-tock!
All But cuckoo clock ticks a double quick:
Solo Tick-a-tock-a, tick-a-tock-a,
Tick-a-tock-a, tick!

ACTIVITY 7.3

MERRY-GO-ROUND

Objective: Speaking in unison while moving to verse

Suggestions for the Teacher

Begin with a discussion of merry-go-rounds. All children love them, so you have an appealing image at once.

The poem "Merry-Go-Round" is fun for children in the early grades because of the action. As with many verses, it can be spoken by half the group while the other half acts the merry-go-round. If the group is small, everyone can do the action, with the teacher repeating the lines. It is such a simple poem that in no time, the class will have memorized it without trying.

Sometimes a group likes to imagine the merry-go-round running down until it comes to a complete stop. This can obviously lead to a new beginning, with a different group of riders getting on.

*MERRY-GO-ROUND**

DOROTHY BARUCH

I climbed up on the merry-go-round,
And it went round and round.
I climbed up on a big brown horse,
And it went up and down.

Around and round and up and down.
Around and round and up and down.

I sat high up on a big brown horse,
And rode around on the merry-go-round,
And rode around on the merry-go-round.
I rode around on the merry-go-round
Around
And round
And
Round.

* Dorothy Baruch, "Merry-Go-Round." In *I Like Machinery,* 1933. Permission granted by Bertha Klausner International Literary Agency, Inc.

ACTIVITY 7.4

NURSERY RHYMES

Both younger and older pupils enjoy inventing different ways of sharing nursery rhymes. These five rhymes can be interpreted in more than one way: literally, telling the story; and abstractly, miming the characters caught in amusing or nonsensical situations.

Objective: To discover the possibilities in simple nursery rhymes

Suggestions for the Teacher

Since children know the rhymes, you can begin with part of the class saying the words, and the other part miming or moving to the story. This is an opportunity to divide the class into two groups, one with light and one with dark voices. While one does not use the word *dance* here, I have had more than one group move to the rhymes in delightful dance-like movements.

SIMPLE SIMON

Light voices

Simple Simon met a pieman,
  Going to the fair;
Says Simple Simon to the pieman,
  Let me taste your ware.

Dark voices

Says the pieman to Simple Simon,
  Show me first your penny;
Says Simple Simon to the pieman,
  Indeed I have not any.

Light voices

Simple Simon went a-fishing,
  For to catch a whale;
All the water he had got
  Was in his mother's pail.

Dark voices

Simple Simon went to look
  If plums grew on a thistle;
He pricked his finger very much,
  Which made poor Simon whistle.

Try three groups

THE QUEEN OF HEARTS

First group

The Queen of Hearts
She made some tarts
All on a summer's day;

Second group

The Knave of Hearts
He stole the tarts,
And took them clean away.

Third group

The King of Hearts
Called for the tarts,
And beat the Knave full sore;

Second group

The Knave of Hearts
Brought back the tarts,
And vowed he'd steal no more.

Unison and Line-Around

OLD MOTHER HUBBARD

All voices

Old Mother Hubbard
Went to the cupboard
To fetch her poor dog a bone.
When she got there, the
cupboard was bare,
And so the poor dog had
none.

Solo

She went to the tailor's
To buy him a coat;
But when she came back
He was riding a goat.

Solo

She went to the barber's
To buy him a wig;
But when she came back
He was dancing a jig.

Solo

She went to the hatter's
To buy him a hat;
But when she came back
He was feeding the cat.

Solo

She went to the grocer's
To buy him some fruit;
But when she got back
He was playing the flute.

Solo	She went to the cobbler's To buy him some shoes; But when she got back He was reading the news.
All voices (except for "Your servant" and "Bow wow," which are solos)	The dame made a curtsy, The dog made a bow; The same said, "Your servant," The dog said, "Bow wow."

LITTLE MISS MUFFET

Light voices	Little Miss Muffet Sat on a tuffet, Eating her curds and whey;
Dark voices	Along came a spider, Who sat down beside her And frightened Miss Muffet away.

Cumulative

HUMPTY DUMPTY

Part of group	Humpty Dumpty sat on a wall,
Add more	Humpty Dumpty had a great fall;
Add more	All the king's horses and all the king's men
All of group	Couldn't put Humpty together again.

ACTIVITY 7.5

ECHO

Objective:* *To create original stories or dramatic activities from a poem

Suggestions for the Teacher

"Echo" is a variation on "Nursery Rhymes." Because the poem probably is unfamiliar, you will have to read it aloud first, and then spend a little time talking about echoes and where one hears them.

Echoes are fascinating, and this anonymous poem may prompt a group to make up an original story. It lends itself so well to choral reading, however, that it is suggested that the class try it one way first, and then discuss whether something else might be done with it. The lines in which the Echo speaks are good solo lines that stimulate speculation as to who the Echo is, what he is like, where he is hiding, and whether he is ever discovered. Some groups have made up delightful stories about him after reading the poem together.

ECHO

I sometimes wonder where he lives,
This Echo that I never see.

I heard his voice now in the hedge,
Then down behind the willow tree.

And when I call, "Oh, please come out,"
"Come out," he always quick replies.
"Hello, hello," again I say;
"Hello, hello," he softly cries.

He must be jolly, Echo must,
For when I laugh, "Ho, ho, ho, ho,"
He answers me with "Ho, ho, ho."

I think perhaps he'd like to play;
I know some splendid things to do.
He must be lonely hiding there;
I wouldn't like it. Now, would you?

ACTIVITY 7.6

HALLOWE'EN

Although choral speaking is an effective way to begin pantomime, it is not the only way of using poetry. Often a poem can be introduced by the teacher, either before or after improvisation. The poem may serve as a springboard to action in which the whole class participates. One short poem that has proved highly successful with many groups is "Hallowe'en."

Suggestions for the Teacher

The period might start with a discussion of what we think of when we hear the word *Hallowe'en.* Most groups suggest pumpkins, witches, orange and black, elves, broomsticks, cats, night, ghosts, trick or treat, and masks. Some pantomime to music can be introduced here, with the whole class becoming witches, cats, or ghosts. After the children are thoroughly in the spirit of Hallowe'en, read the poem two or three times until they are very familiar with it. On the third reading, they probably will be saying "Sh! Hst!" with you.

When the group is small, all the members may be eerie creatures, witches, and ghosts. When the group is large, it can be divided into several parts, with each one choosing one idea to pantomime. Pumpkins have been suggested in a variety of ways: rolling about on the floor in rounded shapes, squatting with big smiles, and moving in circles to music. Music is helpful, although not necessary. This poem never fails to arouse a response, and on one occasion led to an informal program of Hallowe'en poems and improvisations.

HALLOWE'EN

GERALDINE BRAIN SIKS

All	Sh! Hst! Hsst! Shsssh! It's Hallowe'en.
Light voices	Eerie creatures now are seen. Black, bent witches fly Like ugly shadows through the sky. White, stiff ghosts do float Silently, like mystery smoke.
Dark voices	Lighted pumpkins glow With crooked eyes and grins to show It's Hallowe'en.
All	Hsst! Shssh! Sh! Hst!

ACTIVITY 7.7

SING A SONG OF SEASONS

"Sing a Song of Seasons" has been most successful with children in the first three grades. The universality of its theme appeals to everyone and stimulates an imaginative response at any time of the year.

Suggestions for the Teacher

Before reading the poem, the children can do pantomimes of simple sports and games. Flying kites, skating, tossing a ball, jumping rope, and playing games are familiar activities that serve to get the group moving. After perhaps 15 minutes of this kind of activity, read the poem. Discussion about games and sports appropriate to each season directs the thinking and often brings some unexpected suggestions. After everyone has had a chance to offer ideas, ask how the poem might be played.

If the class is separated into four groups, each group can take a season, showing various games and sports associated with it. Some groups create situations for each season, such as going to the beach in summer, with sunbathing, swimming, picnicking, and the like. More than one group has created a scene with characters for each season, using the poem only as a springboard for an original situation. It is urged that this be done in the round, rather than in the front of a room, so as to allow for as much movement as possible and easy passage into the center without breaking the mood.

*SING A SONG OF SEASONS**

ALICE ELLISON BRAIN

Divide class into four groups, each saying one verse; entire class says refrain

It's spring.
Such a happity, hippity, hoppity
First spring day.
Let's play! Let's play! Let's play!

It's summer!
Such a swingy, swazy, lazy
First hot day.
Let's play! Let's play! Let's play!

It's fall!
Such a brisky, frisky, crispy
First fall day.
Let's play! Let's play! Let's play!

It's winter!
Such a blowy, snowy, joy
First winter day.
Let's play! Let's play! Let's play!

* Geraldine Brain Siks, ed., *Children's Literature for Dramatization: An Anthology* (New York: Harper & Row, 1964), p. 8. Reprinted by permission of Alice Ellison Brain.

ACTIVITY 7.8

IMAGININGS

A poem such as "Imaginings" lends itself to all kinds of improvisation. Every child will find an answer to the following question: What lies behind the little red door?

Suggestions for the Teacher

It is a good idea to read the poem aloud two or three times before asking what the group sees in it. If the class is not too large, every child may be given a chance to describe what he or she sees. Younger children find buried treasure, a forbidden city, thieves, a ghost town. Some may describe a place they know, with friends or neighbors inhabiting it. This poem is a wonderful springboard for the imagination, since it leads the listeners to the threshold, and then leaves them free to follow their own ideas.

Some groups have been stimulated to plan an original play, involving several characters. If many good suggestions come out of the discussion, you may want to break the class into groups of three or four children, who will, in turn, dramatize their ideas. Occasionally, if a group is very small or if you want to plan an individual lesson, each child may pantomime what he or she sees and does behind the red door. The poem can hold a group for two or three sessions, depending on the children's readiness to use the material and the interest it arouses.

This poem may be done as choral speaking, but is probably better if you read it and the children act it.

IMAGININGS

J. Paget-Fredericks

Imagine!
A little red door that leads under a hill
Beneath roots and bright stones and pebbly rill.

Imagine!
A quaint little knocker and shoe scraper, too—
A curious carved key
Is waiting for you.

Imagine!
Tiptoe on doormat, you're turning the key.
The red door would open
And there you'd be.

Imagine!
Shut the door tightly, so no one could see.
And no one would know then
Where you would be.
Imagine, if you can.

ACTIVITY 7.9

SOME ONE

"Some One" has the same power as does "Imaginings" to evoke an imaginative response. Although the poem is short, it creates an atmosphere of mystery and wonder: Who can be knocking? How large is the "wee, small door"? Who am "I"? Do I ever find out who my mysterious visitor was? How do I react?

Suggestions for the Teacher

Groups of all ages enjoy imagining this situation, and you may expect a variety of responses and interpretations. Some children have insisted that the door can be no more than a few inches high, which of course leads into the question of whose house it is. Fairies, elves, friendly insects, and mice have been suggested. Other children have seen it as a cottage door—small compared with the doors of city buildings. Visitors, in this case, vary from mysterious strangers with magic powers to actual persons. Indians have been suggested, investigating an early settler's cabin. Because the poet does not say who knocked, the players are entirely free to create their own situations, and some delightful stories have been inspired as a result. Try it different ways.

*SOME ONE**
WALTER DE LA MARE

Some one came knocking
  At my wee, small door;
Some one came knocking,
  I'm sure—sure—sure;
I listened, I opened,
  I looked to left and right,
But naught there was a-stirring
  In the still dark night;
Only the busy beetle
  Tap-tapping in the wall,
Only from the forest
  The screech owl's call
Only the cricket whistling
  While the dewdrops fall,
So I know not who came knocking
  At all, at all, at all.

ACTIVITY 7.10

TWO STEVENSON POEMS

The poems of Robert Louis Stevenson have long appealed to children, and both their content and the suggestions for action make them especially appropriate for creative drama. "My Shadow" and "The Wind" can be used with first graders, who may be familiar with them.

Objective: To create movement suggested by poems

Suggestions for the Teacher

The idea of a shadow offers all kinds of possibilities. The group might try acting this one together—half being children; half, shadows—while you read it aloud.

MY SHADOW

ROBERT LOUIS STEVENSON

I have a little shadow that goes in and out with me,
And what can be the use of him is more than I can see.
He is very, very like me from the heels up to the head;
And I see him jump before me, when I jump into my bed.

The funniest thing about him is the way he likes to grow—
Not at all like proper children, which is always very slow;
For he sometimes shoots up taller like an India-rubber ball;
And he sometimes gets so little that there's none of him at all.

He hasn't got a notion of how children ought to play,
And can only make a fool of me in every sort of way.
He stays so close beside me, he's a coward, you can see;
I'd think shame to stick to nursie as that shadow sticks to me!

One morning, very early, before the sun was up,
I rose and found the shining dew on every buttercup;
But my lazy little shadow, like an arrant sleepy-head,
Had stayed at home behind me and was fast asleep in bed.

Suggestions for the Teacher

"The Wind" also offers a wonderful opportunity for strong movement. The group can divide in many ways, being everything that is mentioned: the wind, the birds, the kites, the skirts, and other things that the children may suggest. Wind is a good topic for discussion, often suggesting the creation of original stories as well as the search for other stories, such as Aesop's fable "The Sun and the Wind." A whole unit could be developed on the subject or on the natural elements: wind, sun, rain, hail, clouds, and rainbows.

THE WIND

ROBERT LOUIS STEVENSON

Teacher reads each verse	I saw you toss the kites on high And blow the birds about the sky; And all around I heard you pass, Like ladies' skirts across the grass—
All say refrain	O wind a-blowing all day long, O wind, that sings so loud a song.
	I saw the different things you did, But always you yourself you hid. I felt you push, I heard you call, I could not see yourself at all—
All say refrain	O wind a-blowing all day long, O wind, that sings so loud a song.
	O you that are so strong and cold, O blower, are you young or old? Are you a beast of field and tree Or just a stranger child than me?
All say refrain	O wind a-blowing all day long, O wind, that sings so loud a song.

ACTIVITY 7.11

MOBILE

Most children at one time or another have made a mobile. Perhaps there is one in the classroom. The poem "Mobile" describes one, suggesting how it moves and how it seems to be alive. Can the poem be used as a springboard to suggest movement and dramatic action? See what it suggests to the class when you read it aloud.

Objective: To create movement and action suggested by a poem

Suggestions for the Teacher

Birds, fish, and sailboats often are used as subjects for mobiles, because they move, dip, turn, and swirl as the air circulates around them. There is almost a magic in the way a mobile moves, even when there appears to be no breeze stirring. Have the class, without using words, move as a mobile:

1. Moving as separate parts of the mobile
2. Putting the parts together in a formation
3. Moving without touching the other parts of the mobile

Now break the class into small groups, each suggesting in movement the images described in the verse. Try adding the images to the moving mobile.

This may lead to the making of a mobile or the creating of a verse. Or it may lead to an entirely different way of suggesting a mobile. See what it makes the class feel, see, and do.

MOBILE *

DAVID MCCORD

Our little mobile hangs and swings
And likes a draft and drafty things:

Half-open doors; wide-window breeze,
All people when they cough or sneeze;

Hot dishes giving off their heat;
Big barking dogs, small running feet.

Our mobile's red and made to look
Like fish about to bite a hook:

Six fishes with a hook in front
Of each. They range in size—the runt,

* David McCord, *All Day Long* (Boston: Little, Brown, 1966).

Or baby, up to papa fish,
With hooks to watch and make them wish

That they could reach the nice blue worms
A-dangle there with swirly squirms;

Six fishy mouths all open wide,
Six sets of teeth all sharp inside,

Six fishy holes where eyes should be,
Six fish to swim on airy sea.

I'm eating breakfast now and they are watching me.
And I must say

That every time I take a bite
I see and feel their sorry plight.

8

PUPPETS AND MASKS

Puppetry is both a delightful art form and a versatile educational tool. It has many uses in the elementary-school classroom:

1. It encourages the use of the imagination.
2. It develops listening skills.
3. It develops communication skills.
4. It permits the expression of feelings that some children inhibit in their creative drama and dramatic play.
5. It helps the teacher diagnose social and learning problems.
6. It teaches subject matter in every area of the curriculum.
7. It combines both the visual and the performing arts on a small scale, possible in any space or situation.
8. It costs nothing, yet provides a wealth of opportunities for learning and fun.

The mask, closely related to the puppet, shares some of these uses and values. One could say that puppetry starts with dramatic play, when dolls and toys are manipulated to perform various roles and actions, whereas the young child's game of peek-a-boo, with the hands hiding the face, illustrates an early concept of the mask. As children grow older, they assign both mask and puppet more specific functions and handle them with greater dexterity. Children's first awareness of the mask as a mask, however, probably occurs at about the age of 4 or 5, when they wear it as part of a Hallowe'en costume. Children of that age put on masks, confident that they are hidden from view and disguised as ghosts, witches, or monsters. Puppets and masks have much in common; in fact, they sometimes are indistinguishable from each other. In this chapter, some of the ways in which both can be made and combined with creative drama will be discussed. Although each form merits a book in itself, the limitations of space and content preclude more than the most elementary discussion. There are, however, a number of excellent texts concerning both forms, and it is hoped that teachers interested in incorporating puppets and masks into their curricula will investigate those texts listed in the Bibliography.

PUPPETS

Many persons associate puppetry with the field of entertainment, although it is equally at home in the classroom. Today, with the popularity of the Muppets and other puppet characters on television, children learn about puppets at an early age and become acquainted with some of the techniques of handling them. This familiarity suggests to the teacher ways to include puppets either as special craft projects or as tools for teaching subjects other than arts and crafts. A further, and particularly valuable, use is the social or therapeutic one: through the puppet, a shy or troubled child is often able to express what she cannot state as herself. Best of all, perhaps, because these engaging little creatures are such fun to make and manipulate, they capture the child's attention and hold it in a variety of situations.

Puppets as Teaching Aids

Because of their power to hold and sustain the attention of a class, puppets facilitate learning. Unlike some curricular materials, puppets are not limited to any one area of study. They can be used to teach any subject, ranging from the language arts to science and math. They can be combined with other teaching materials, and they can be used alone. The value of puppets lies in their mobility, not in their beauty or complicated construction. Those made by teachers and children are usually more satisfactory than are commercial puppets. If puppets are purchased, however—and there are many on the market—they should be selected for their durability, and the nonwashable and fragile should be avoided.

The degree of sophistication of puppets that students create depends, of course, on the age and previous experience of the students. While the simple puppets of young children can be wonderfully effective, experienced older groups find a challenge in making more elaborate ones. It cannot be repeated often enough, however, that a good puppet is one that can be manipulated easily; the most beautiful puppet in the world is a failure if it does not move easily and well. Another consideration, and an important one, is the child's perception of his or her work. In other words, "it is not what the puppet looks like that counts but rather how the child feels about the puppet . . . a rabbit puppet made by a child does not have to look like a real rabbit—the child needs only to believe in it. . . . "[1]

Objects as Puppets

What is a puppet? Contrary to what many think, puppets are not dolls, although they often resemble them. Puppets are "actors" who come to life with the help of a puppeteer.

There are many different kinds of puppets. Some hang from strings; some are fastened to sticks called rods; and some slip over the hand like gloves. Some puppets are as tall as a person and must be pushed or moved from inside. Because the string puppet is the most complicated to make and manipulate, it is not recommended for the beginner or for the elementary-school classroom.

Almost any object can be a puppet: a toy, a tool, a hairbrush, a lollipop, a spoon, a broom. Even the hand can be a puppet, if the "puppeteer" moves it and speaks so that the hand appears to be doing the walking and talking. Just to prove it, try transforming a few common objects into puppets. Kneel behind a table and move an object along the edge of it. Keep moving. Here are a few things that can be used.

1. *A wooden spoon* Make it walk, run, jump, and disappear.
2. *A toy* A teddy bear or a rag doll, which are soft and move in different ways from the spoon, will do. Sometimes toys make fine puppets, but it is not a good idea to depend on them. The puppets you make yourself will almost always be better.
3. *A pencil, a ruler, a lollipop, an artificial flower* They will become different characters when you start moving them. Now try holding one in each hand. What happens when a pencil and ruler meet?
4. *Your own hands* What can they do that the other things cannot do? Hands make wonderful movements. Let them walk, dance, jump, fight, bow, and march off.

Look around for some other objects that have not been mentioned. Invent actions for them and decide what kinds of characters they seem to be. Remember that *you* make the puppet. It is not alive until you move it.

[1] Tamara Hunt and Nancy Renfro, *Puppetry in Early Childhood* (Austin, Tex.: Nancy Renfro Studios, 1982), p. 24.

Making Hand Puppets

The hand puppet, with its many variations, is the most satisfactory for any age level, and the classroom teacher will find it within his or her capabilities, regardless of previous experience. The hand puppet includes the bandana puppet, the finger puppet, the paper-bag puppet, the flat puppet, the shadow puppet, the sock puppet, and the glove puppet.

Materials. Just as a costume closet or box is handy to have for creative drama, so a supply of scrap materials is necessary for making puppets. You probably will not have to purchase anything because most of what you need will be in your own or the children's homes or in the school. Scraps of paper and fabric, boxes of all sizes, sticks, styrofoam, lollipops, apples, balls, and paper bags are usable. Ribbons, yarn, sewing materials, paper cups, paper napkins, discarded decorations, old socks, and gloves will find a use as somebody's puppet.

Bandana Puppets. The easiest puppet to begin with is the bandana puppet. Place a bandana or cloth over the hand. Let the first, middle, and ring fingers be the head of the puppet, and put a rubber band around them for the neck. The thumb and little finger are the arms. Put rubber bands around them in order to hold the cloth in place. Imagine that the hand is the actor. Have the puppet clap its hands, shake its head, and fall down.

There are many more things you can do in making a bandana puppet. For instance, try cutting a hole in the middle of the bandana and poking

Bandana puppet.

the first finger through it. Next, take a styrofoam ball with a hole scooped out for your finger and use it for a head. Heads can be made out of many things: a small paper cup, an apple (after cutting out the core), or a ball. The bandana puppet can be quickly made by the teacher, but making one is also within the capability of young children.

Finger Puppet. The finger puppet is the smallest of all puppets. It slips over the finger and can be played with as it is or used with larger hand puppets to show different-sized characters. For instance, a finger puppet might be an elf, with a hand puppet as a human being.

One way to make a finger puppet is to sew it of felt. First, make a pattern. Put the hand flat on a piece of paper and draw around the fingers with a pencil. Be sure to add a little extra material all the way around to allow for the sewing. Next, cut out the paper patterns and pin them on a piece of felt. You will have to cut two shapes for each puppet. Put the two shapes together and sew around the edges. Leave the bottom open for your finger.

Another way to make finger puppets is to cut the fingers off an old glove. White gloves are the best because puppet faces can be drawn on them. Slip the glove fingers over your own, and you will have five little puppets! Instead of drawing right on the puppet, you can cut paper circles and paint faces on them; when the paint is dry, the faces can be pasted on the puppets.

Paper-Bag Puppet. The paper-bag puppet is one of the best puppets with which to begin because bags come in all sizes and are easily obtained. Also, if you happen to tear the bag, there are many more around.

Paper-bag heads.

Adults, children, giants, and elves can be suggested with different sizes of paper bags. Small bags fit on the hands, whereas big bags will go over the head. If a bag is worn on the head, holes will have to be cut out for the eyes and mouth. Next, paint or draw a face on the bag.

Flat Puppet. The flat puppet is also often called the rod puppet. It is included here because it is easy to handle and can be used with other kinds of puppets. Flat puppets are a little like paper dolls. They can be cut out of lightweight cardboard, colored, and pasted onto tongue depressors or sticks. When the puppet is firmly attached to the stick, hold it in your hand just below the edge of the stage or table top. As it is moved, it will seem to be walking by itself. Animals make good flat puppets because you can draw only the side view.

If you would like to show your puppet moving in both directions, cut out two shapes and paste them together with the stick in between. Color both sides, and your person or animal can be moved from either left or right. One more advantage to flat puppets: they are easy to keep in good condition because they do not take up much space when put away in neat piles.

Shadow Puppet. Flat puppets can be used for shadow shows also. In order to give a shadow show, all you need are some flat puppets, a sheet, and a lamp placed behind the sheet. When the puppets are moved behind the sheet, they cast shadows on it. The closer they are to the sheet, the stronger the shadow, or silhouette.

Shadow puppets may be made more exciting if parts of them within the outside boundaries are cut out and backed by colored gelatins. Stores that handle stage-lighting equipment carry relatively inexpensive gelatins in a variety of colors. Older children love the challenge of mak-

Rod puppet.

Sock puppet.

ing these puppets, which in some ways resemble stained-glass windows. The strong light shining through the gelatin brings out the richness of the color and creates a magical effect. Plastic shopping bags in bright colors also can be used effectively. In the oriental theatre, where shadow plays originated, one can still see performances using puppets made of wood or hide decorated with elaborate openwork patterns. Older students enjoy making puppets of this kind with colored gelatin pasted over the open areas. The stylized result can be quite beautiful and effective.

Sock Puppet. A sock makes a very good puppet because it stretches, yet does not slip off the hand. You can do many things with a sock puppet, such as making it into a mouth. Put one of your own old socks over your hand, with your fingers in the toe and your thumb in the heel. You now have the upper and lower jaws of a mouth. Bring them together in a big bite. By adding eyes and other markings, you can create a bird, a wolf, a crocodile, or a dragon. You can make a puppet mouth more exciting by sewing a piece of red felt inside it and adding another piece for a tongue. So many children's stories have animal characters that the "mouth" is a useful puppet to have on hand.

Glove Puppets. The glove puppet requires more sewing than do the other types. It has to be cut out of two pieces of cloth and sewn together. It may also have a separate head. First, take a piece of strong cotton cloth and fold it in half. Felt is good because it does not ravel. Other fabrics will do, however, so use what you have on hand, provided they are sturdy.

Cut a pattern of newspaper for your puppet. There should be a head and two arms, and the pattern must be large enough to fit the hand.

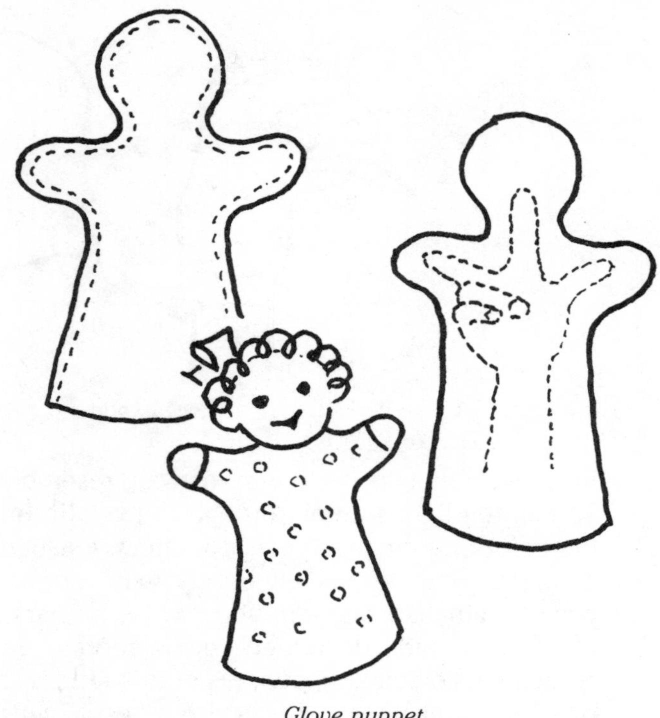

Glove puppet.

Pin the pattern to the material and trace around it. Then remove the pattern and cut out the puppet. Keep the two pieces of cloth together and sew around the edges, remembering to leave the bottom open to allow the puppet to fit over your hand. A felt puppet is ready to use as it is. If softer material is used, it should be turned inside out before sewing. Under any circumstances, allowance must be made for the seam.

Children will want to put a face on the puppet. Eyes, nose, and mouth can be drawn or embroidered on it. Buttons make excellent eyes, and yarn makes good hair. A little stuffing makes the head rounder. If you want to make a separate head, a lightweight material, such as styrofoam or papier-mâché, works well. After you have decorated the head, slip it over your first and second fingers, which are inside the puppet's body. Although it is harder to handle a puppet with a separate head than a puppet that is all in one piece, most children learn how to manage it with practice.

Holding the Puppet

There are different ways of holding puppets, so it is suggested that you use the one that works best for you. Because younger children have short fingers, they will have to experiment to find a comfortable way to hold the puppet. Some puppeteers put their first and second fingers in the neck, their fourth and fifth fingers in one arm, and their thumb in the other. Puppets can be held either in front of the body or over the head. Again, use whichever way is easier for you. If you are playing for a long time, it is usually more comfortable to work the puppet in front of your face. If you decide to hold your puppet that way, you will be seen by the aduience. This does not matter. The audience will soon forget that you are there.

If you want to hang a curtain between you and the puppets, you will need a stage. A dark, lightweight piece of cloth at the back of the stage will hide you and make the puppets stand out. If the cloth is semitransparent, you can see through it without being seen by the audience.

Some Basic Actions

Moving the puppet's head up and down means "yes." Shaking it from side to side means "no." When the puppet's hands point to itself, it means "me" or "mine." Moving one of its hands toward its body means "come here." Waving its hand many mean either "hello" or "goodbye."

Walking, running, and jumping can be suggested by the way you move the puppet across the stage. Try not to lift it in the air. You will soon get the knack of holding it down, so that it seems to be doing all the moving.

When two persons are puppeteering together, the chances are that each is holding a puppet. This is more difficult than playing alone, but it is also more fun. Each puppeteer has to make sure that the puppets do not bump into each other. Also, when one puppet is speaking, the other should remember to listen. Occasionally, there will be a scene for three puppets. This takes some doing, for three people will have to work together backstage, or one person will have to handle two puppets. It is a good idea at first to use stories that have no more than two characters on the stage at one time.

The Puppet Stage

It is not necessary to have a stage, for puppets can act anywhere. All that is needed is a smooth surface about 3 feet long. A table, a coffee table, a bench, or a box will do. A cloth stretched across a wide doorway will partially hide the puppeteers. Another idea for a stage is a cardboard box with openings cut in the front and back. This can be placed on the bench or table. The puppets can be manipulated through the back opening.

Puppets need no stage.

Scenery

Scenery is no more needed than is a stage, for the puppets can tell the audience where the story takes place. You may, however, want to use a piece or two of doll furniture, if it is the right size, or a small three-dimensional tree, securely fastened to the floor of the box, to suggest an indoor or outdoor location.

Stories for Puppet Plays

It is a good idea for children of any age to work without scripts because they have their hands full just moving the puppets. For children in the first, second, and third grades, this is a perfectly natural thing to do and a technique they have already used in playing with their toys. If they are very familiar with the story they are presenting, they can make up the dialogue as they go along, just as they do in creative drama. While many stories that are good for creative playing are also good for puppetry, not all work equally well. One thing must be kept in mind: there is very little room backstage (Activities 8.1, 8.2, and 8.3). The scenes often can be arranged so there will be no more than two, but, of course, some stories will lend themselves to puppet theatre better than others.

A flower garden of puppets.

Probably the most extensive use made of puppets as a teaching tool is in the area of the language arts. According to John Warren Stewig, "Children generate more verbal language during dramatic play than in any other situation."[2] In both creative drama and puppetry, extemporaneous speaking is involved; use of the puppet has the added advantage of shielding the speaker who is shy or weak in verbal skills, thus enabling him or her to communicate through the puppet. A skillful teacher makes use of the opportunity afforded by this communication to open up new areas of learning and tune into a student's thinking. Telling stories with puppets not only is fun, but also is a valuable activity on all levels. The move from storytelling to story dramatization is a natural next step, involving dialogue, character study, play structure, and growth in language competency. The use of puppets in the teaching of poetry has also proved successful in promoting the appreciation and composition of this form of literature (Activities 8.4 and 8.5).

Social studies provide a wealth of puppetry opportunities for the study of other people and other countries. Puppets provide exercise in bilingual education also; this can be done by way of dramatic sketches or taught directly by a familiar mascot puppet. The mascot, incidentally, is often able to hold the attention of the most restless group, a phenomenon observed by anyone who has ever used puppetry with children. In short, there is no area of the curriculum that cannot be enhanced by these appealing little creatures, which come alive in the most inexperienced hands, teaching and entertaining simultaneously. Their popularity with all kinds and ages of groups practically ensures success.

[2] John Warren Stewig, *Teaching Language Arts in Early Childhood* (New York: Holt, Rinehart and Winston, 1980), p. 123.

A child with an opossum puppet. (Courtesy of Nancy Renfro Studios, Austin, Texas; photograph by Debbie Sullivan)

Puppets as Therapeutic Tools

Puppets have been used effectively as both diagnostic and therapeutic instruments. It is understood that neither the classroom teacher nor the creative-drama specialist is a therapist; nevertheless, puppet theatre offers insights often undiscernible in other situations, and the sensitive teacher will take note of them. For the puppet becomes a nonthreatening little friend in whom a child can confide, entrusting his or her most private thoughts and feelings without fear of censure. This friend has access to the child's inner world and is able to speak to the outer world as an intermediary (Activity 8.6).

Puppetry provides socially accepted avenues for the discovery, expression, and release of emotions and attitudes. Therapists do not aim at well-rehearsed, finished performances; rather, they use puppets to encourage and help motivate patients and students in clinical and educational settings. Some professional puppeteers have engaged in special ongoing programs. George Latshaw, a well-known puppeteer,

A puppet joins the class. (Courtesy of Tamara Hunt, University of Hawaii at Manoa; puppet by Nancy Renfro)

worked with a group sponsored by the National Committee, Arts for the Handicapped, using puppets with severely handicapped children. Latshaw's puppets played and interacted with children in classrooms, often eliciting responses from those who had until then been detached from others or lacked verbal skills.[3] In their use of puppetry, the classroom teacher and the therapist share a similar goal. Thus the teacher will find puppetry an exceptionally effective way of drawing out children who are reluctant to participate in creative drama.

MASKS

Closely related to the art of puppetry is the art of mask making. Masks can be either part of a puppet project or an extension of creative drama (Activity 8.7). Some professional puppet companies combine masks and puppets for special effects. Children have no problem accepting this, for in their own play, they assume both animate and inanimate roles simultaneously. As for the mask, it is pure magic; it hides, changes, and transforms the wearer, suddenly suggesting a multitude of new possibilities.

Most children are fascinated with masks and enjoy inventing masks of their own. One of the most creative projects I have seen involved

[3] *Puppets—Art and Entertainment* (Washington, D.C.: Puppeteers of America, 1980), p. 9.

puppets and children wearing paper-bag masks, both made by a class studying North American Indians. Because the mask has been used by so many peoples at so many periods in history, it is a valuable resource for the teacher and a magic prop for the child who makes and wears it.

Types and Values of Masks

The mask may cover the entire head, the face, or the upper part of the face only, leaving the lower part exposed. The simple half-mask, worn on Hallowe'en or at masked balls, is a well-known example. The obvious advantage of the half-mask is its comfort. It is cooler than the mask that covers the entire face, and it makes speaking easier. Speaking through the mouth of a mask is difficult and distracting for the inexperienced performer.

Masks may be simple or elaborate, beautiful or grotesque; but except for the representation of animals, they are rarely realistic. The values of mask making are many and are implicit in this brief discussion. Masks provide an extension of the drama lesson; they reveal aspects of a culture in which the mask is an important artifact; and they release the wearer from all inhibitions. Many children feel freer when they are shielded from view by even a partial face covering. They project feelings and ideas through the mask, while they remain hidden. The mask serves the same purpose as the puppet in this respect. In fact, some interesting research has been done on the use of masks and make-up in therapy.

Teachers will be wise to avoid using the commercial masks sold in stores around Hallowe'en, just as they will avoid commercial puppets. One of the values of including the mask in the classroom is the opportunity it offers for imaginative construction and design. This is particularly valuable for a child who is shy about acting, but who has interest and ability in arts and crafts. In using the commercial mask or puppet, the teacher misses a rich opportunity for teaching.

Make-up is another form of mask. It is not the purpose of this text to go into its application for the stage; however, the make-up that persons create themselves provides valuable insights for the leader and drama therapist. Nancy Breitenbach, a therapist, describes her innovative work with make-up as "a form of free association," helping children through its use to discover who they are, whom they want others to believe they are, and whom they would like to be. In an article published in England, she lists the reactions of children of different ages to make-up and describes how it releases them into drama.[4] In her opinion, the eventual

[4] Nancy Breitenbach, "Secret Faces," *British Journal of Dramatherapy* 3, no. 2 (Autumn 1979):18–23.

removal of make-up, resulting in the reappearance of the child's familiar face, brings an affirmation of personal strength; strong feelings can be expressed, and yet the individual will return to his or her normal state with a greater degree of confidence and social well-being.

Grease paint applied to a child's face by an adult, on the contrary, tends to place the emphasis on the outer rather than the inner aspects of character. This is not to say that the formal, scripted play produced with costume and make-up is without value. It is simply not germane to creative drama; and the art of make-up is therefore left until the student is ready for formal play production.

Making Masks

Like puppets, masks can be made of a variety of materials.

Paper-Bag and Cardboard-Box Masks. For very young children, the paper-bag mask is by far the easiest and cheapest to make. It is also the most satisfying because it can be completed in a single class period. The brown paper bag from the grocery store slips comfortably over the head, and holes can be cut in it for the eyes and mouth. Younger children need help in locating the right places. Once the holes are cut out, the mask is ready for decoration. Strips of colored paper can be pasted on the bags for hair, moustaches, and even eyelashes. Paint, chalk, and crayons can be used to color them. Older children, studying a particular culture or tribal society, may paste or sew on feathers, cloth, jewelry, buttons, and so on. The paper-bag mask and the paper-bag puppet are identical. It is the intent that distinguishes one from the other. A mask, like a costume, is worn by a character, whereas a puppet *is* the character. In addition, a puppet leads to a performance, but a mask may be made for its decorative value alone.

Cardboard boxes can be used effectively to suggest robots and stylized characters. They are more difficult to work on than bags, and it often is hard to find boxes of the right size and shape. Because both bags and boxes cover the entire head, they muffle speech and limit freedom of movement.

As a follow-up activity, after a class has worked on material dramatically, masks have value in extending the learnings. When they are incorporated in a project that is further developed for an audience, they offer an added dimension for the observers.

Paper-Plate Mask. Masks made of plain, white paper plates are recommended for children in the second and third grades because of their shape, toughness, and availability. To make the mask appear three-

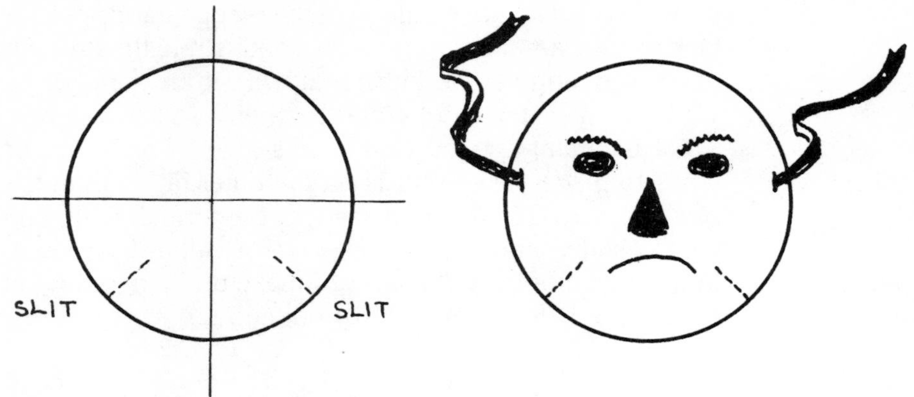

Paper-plate mask.

dimensional, cut two slits about 2 inches long and about 2 inches apart on the edge of the plate. Overlap the sides adjacent to each slit and staple them back together again, thus forming a chin and making the mask fit on the child's face. As with the paper-bag mask, holes for eyes, mouth, and nose must be cut in the appropriate places. A nose that protrudes from the face can be made of construction paper and pasted on the plate, further adding to the three-dimensional quality. From here on, experimentation with other materials is fun and will make each mask unique.

Papier-Mâché Mask. Papier-mâché is a substance made of pulped paper or paper strips moistened with thin wheat paste (wallpaper paste). The paper used may be newspaper, tissues, napkins, or toweling. Wheat paste may be secured from any hardware store (follow directions on the package).

Because papier-mâché masks are difficult and time-consuming to make, they are not recommended for children in the lower grades. With the guidance of an art teacher or a classroom teacher who is skilled in puppetry and mask making, they can be constructed by third graders, but the simpler forms are preferred and are quite satisfactory to young players.

SUMMARY

Puppetry and mask making provide an added dimension to creative drama as well as being arts in their own rights. Although it has been stated repeatedly throughout the chapter that the types of puppets and masks described are simple, requiring no previous experience or special course work in puppet and mask making, it is always wise to try out an assignment before giving it to a class. In this way, the teacher can foresee any problems that might arise and solve them in advance. Gathering materials and providing enough space for construction is important. As in creative drama, the encouragement of original ideas will help to prevent imitation of familiar television characters.

The teacher who includes puppets and masks in the curriculum will find them a rich resource. Regardless of the reasons for including them, the possibilities they offer are limitless. The major values may be summarized as follows:

1. Puppets and masks provide opportunities for developing motor skills. Tools and materials must be handled with care in order to construct puppets and masks that are sturdy and functional.
2. Dressing and decorating puppets require imagination. Each puppet must become a character, first through its costume, and then in the way in which it is decorated and painted.
3. Puppets require control. It takes controlled fingers to manipulate a puppet so that it can perform as the operator wishes.
4. Puppets and masks offer an avenue of expression. Through them, the puppeteer or wearer expresses the thoughts and feelings of characters.
5. Both puppets and masks have therapeutic power. Through them, timid or withdrawn children can find release, whereas aggressive children learn to subordinate themselves to the personality of the characters they are presenting.
6. Puppetry demands cooperation. Children learn to take turns and work together for a successful performance.
7. Puppetry and mask making are inexpensive. Delightful results may be obtained within the most limited budget. If there is no stage, a box will do until the teacher is able to construct something more permanent.
8. Puppets and masks may be ends in themselves or the means by which other ends are reached.

Given half a chance, the puppet engages the child as performer, playmate, teacher, and alter ego. The mask, although less versatile, is closely related, serving many of the same purposes.

LITTLE INDIAN TWO FEET'S HORSE

Objective: To dramatize stories with puppets the children have made

Suggestions for the Teacher

Tell or read the stories to the children. Then have them work on the stories and the characters until they are ready to show them to the class.

"Little Indian Two Feet's Horse" can be played just as it is, or it can be made longer by adding adventures. Since Little Indian Two Feet is a little boy who talks to himself, the audience knows what is happening. You can make the horse move by bending your hand so that the arm of the puppet becomes its front legs. Try out some movements until you find the ones that are right. The horse may be a flat puppet instead of a glove puppet, if you wish.

LITTLE INDIAN TWO FEET'S HORSE

Characters

Little Indian Two Feet

His horse

Little Indian Two Feet wants a horse more than anything else in the world. He often walks on the prairie, dreaming of the horse he will someday own. His father has told him that he can have a horse when he is older. That seems far away to a boy of 10! So one morning, Little Indian Two Feet decides to go out to see if he can find a horse. Perhaps if he hunts long enough, he'll see one on the prairie, a horse that no one owns. He walks and he walks. He calls and calls, but no horse answers. He climbs a hill, he looks over it, and he calls again. Still no horse comes to him.

He manages to cross a wide stream by a meadow. Two Feet walks in the tall grass until he is tired, but there are no horses grazing anywhere. Finally he decides to lie down and rest before starting home. In no time at all, Two Feet falls fast asleep. While he is sleeping, a pony appears. It is a colt, one of the wild ponies that run loose on the prairie. In fact, it is so young that it knows no fear. Since it has never seen a boy before, it steps up to look at him. The pony puts its soft nose against Two Feet's cheek and rubs against it. Two Feet awakens with a start! He can hardly believe his eyes. He sits up and touches the pony's shoulder. "Did you come to me?" he asks. "Do you want to go home with me?"

The pony nods its head as if to say "yes." Little Two Feet puts his arm on the pony's neck, and the two of them go off together. Little Indian Two Feet has found his horse at last.

ACTIVITY 8.2

THE FISHERMAN AND HIS WIFE

"The Fisherman and His Wife" is another good story for puppets to play. No scenery is needed. If you want to show the different houses, you can draw pictures of them and put them up behind the puppets.

Characters

The Fisherman

His wife

The Flounder

A poor Fisherman lived with his wife in a cottage by the sea. Every day, he went down to the shore to catch a fish for their supper. When his luck was good, he had enough fish to sell to their neighbors. One morning, the Fisherman went out as usual and sat down in his favorite fishing spot. Suddenly there was a tug on his line. He pulled and he pulled.

"What have I caught?" asked the Fisherman. He gave another tug on his line, and up came the biggest flounder he had ever seen.

Then, to his amazement, the fish spoke. "Please let me go. I have done you no harm."

The Fisherman couldn't believe his ears. "You can talk? I have never heard of a fish that could talk."

"I was once a prince," said the Flounder sadly. "An evil spell was put on me, and I am doomed to spend the rest of my life as a fish."

"I am sorry if I've hurt you," said the Fisherman, taking the hook from the fish. "Go back to your home in the sea."

"Oh, thank you," the Flounder said. "You have saved my life. If I can ever do anything for you, call on me. I'm never far away."

The Fisherman promised the Flounder that he would do so. Then, eager to tell his wife about his strange adventure, he packed up and went home. When he had finished his tale, his wife scolded him for his stupidity. "That's just like you! Why didn't you ask him for a nice house and some food for our dinner? He was a magic fish, and you let him go."

"I'm sorry, wife," said the Fisherman. "I didn't think of it."

"Well, go back down to the sea and ask for a house like our neighbor's, with enough food to last us a year."

"Very well," replied the Fisherman. So he went down to the place where he had caught the Flounder and called out:

"Oh, fish of the sea,
Come listen to me,

For my wife, my wife, the plague of my life,
Has sent me to ask a boon of thee."

Scarcely did he finish when the Flounder appeared.

"What can I do for you?" the fish asked politely.

The Fisherman told him.

"No sooner asked than granted," said the fish. "Go home, and you will find a house like your neighbor's."

The Fisherman hurried home, and there was a beautiful stone house where his little cottage had been. His wife appeared at the door, delighted with their good fortune.

For a time, the Fisherman and his wife lived happily. Then one morning, his wife, who was always discontented, said, "I don't know why you asked for this house. I should like a castle with servants to wait on me."

"This house is plenty good enough," said her husband.

"No," she replied, "Go back and tell the fish I must have a castle."

The Fisherman didn't want to do her bidding, but at last he agreed. He went down to the sea and again called out:

"Oh, fish of the sea,
Come listen to me,
For my wife, my wife, the plague of my life,
Has sent me to ask a boon of thee."

In a flash, the Flounder appeared. "Nothing easier," he said, after the Fisherman explained the matter to him. "Go home to your castle."

Then the Flounder disappeared, and the Fisherman returned home. Instead of the stone house, there was a great castle with towers and walls surrounding it. His wife was overjoyed. But after a time, she again became discontented.

She sent her husband back to the Flounder many times. She wanted to be the richest woman in the world. Then a queen. Next, an empress. And finally, Goddess of the Universe. Each time, her husband begged her to be content with what they had, but she would not listen. And each time, the fish granted her wish—until the last one.

"What is it now?" the Flounder asked the Fisherman.

"Oh, gracious Flounder," replied the Fisherman, "my wife wants to be Goddess of the Universe."

"Never!" declared the Flounder angrily. "I will grant no more wishes. Your wife can return to her cottage."

There was a loud noise like a clap of thunder, and the fish disappeared. Then the Fisherman went home, where he found his wife in the doorway of their humble cottage.

ACTIVITY 8.3

A MISTAKE

Objective: To tell a story with a surprise ending

Suggestions for the Teacher

Talk about storytelling. Then suggest to the children that they play "A Mistake." It is amusing, and they will enjoy the situation. Do not worry if the dialogue is scanty; it will be, and the play will be short. But the children will have been introduced to a play with a beginning, a middle, and an end enacted by puppets.

A MISTAKE

Characters

You

Your family (they talk offstage)

You come to breakfast early one morning, and no one is up yet. You call your mother, but she tells you to be quiet; she is trying to sleep. You find some food to eat; then you get your books and pack a lunch. You call to your family and tell them that they are all going to be late. You run out of the house, but a minute later, you come back in. Your father calls to ask who it is. You tell him that the school bus isn't there. He laughs and says, "Of course not. Did you forget? Daylight-saving time is over!"

ACTIVITY 8.4

SPACE TRAVELER

Objective:* *To add original endings to an unfinished story

Suggestions for the Teacher

A discussion of the situation probably should precede the acting of "Space Traveler." The extent, of course, will depend on the age and experience of the children, whether there has been recent exploration in space, and whether you have done any pantomimes about astronauts. Under any circumstances, you will have to precede the playing with some discussion, but all children love the idea of spaceships. The language arts are also involved, since the space traveler cannot speak English.

SPACE TRAVELER

Characters

You

A traveler from another planet

Imagine that you are walking in the country, when you meet a person from another planet. The spaceship has landed in a field nearby. The space traveler wants to know who you are, where you live, what you do, and what you eat. Then he (she) tells you all about him (her) self. Can you understand each other's language? How do you communicate?

ACTIVITY 8.5

GEORGE, THE TIMID GHOST

Suggestions for the Teacher

The open-ended story "George, the Timid Ghost" is fun to do any time, but is especially appropriate at Hallowe'en.

1. Tell or read the story aloud.
2. Have the children work on it in pairs, inventing their own endings.
3. When all are ready, have them show their puppet plays to the rest of the class.

GEORGE, THE TIMID GHOST

Characters

Father Ghost

George

There was once a timid ghost named George. He lived with his parents at the edge of a cemetery not far from town. He wanted very much to be able to scare people like a proper ghost, but every time someone approached him, he ran away. "Someday," he often said to himself, "I'll be as spooky as the rest of my family. Someday, but not today."

One night, George's father decided that it was time to teach his son a lesson. When it was quite dark, George's father showed him how to sneak up behind someone without being heard and to say "Boo." "Never hurt anyone," his father warned him. "Just give them a little scare."

George was eager to learn all of his father's tricks, so he practiced saying "Boo" in different tones of voice. He jumped out from behind trees, and he ran back and forth, waving his arms in the air.

"Good," said his father approvingly. "You're going to be the scariest ghost in town."

George strutted back and forth after his father went into the house. "I'm going to be the scariest ghost in town."

Suddenly he heard the sound of somebody running behind him. He froze in his tracks, determined this time not to run away. This is an unfinished story. What happened next? You make up the ending.

ACTIVITY 8.6

EXPRESSING EMOTIONS THROUGH PUPPETS

***Objective:** To express strong feelings through the puppet*

Suggestions for the Teacher

Have the children take their puppets and think how their puppets would act or look under the following circumstances.

1. Try to find ways of showing that your puppet feels:
   angry shy happy scared
   excited tired curious hungry
2. Next, see if you can put actions with a feeling:
   a. Curious—and looks into a box
   b. Angry—and hits someone
   c. Happy—and claps its hands for joy
   d. Thoughtful—and comes up with an idea

After everyone has had a chance to try out actions motivated by feelings, carry the idea a step further. Here are some simple situations in which the child is using the puppet as him- or herself.

1. Most of us get into trouble at one time or another. Do you remember a particular time when you got into trouble? Was it your fault? Did you think you were punished unfairly? How did you feel about it? Let your glove puppet be the other person in this story, and you be the finger puppet. Act it out.
2. Talking with your puppet is fun. Like a conversation with a person, it builds as it goes along.
   a. Imagine that your puppet is mischievous. You ask it to do something, and it refuses. It thinks of reasons why it won't do what you ask. How do you handle the puppet? Who wins in the end?
   b. Imagine that your puppet is angry, and try to find out what is wrong.
   c. Imagine that your puppet can't speak English. Try to make it understand you.
   d. Imagine that your puppet's feelings are hurt. Can you say or do anything to make it feel better?
3. The puppet is *you*. Talk to it, imagining that you are
   a. Your mother
   b. Your best friend
   c. The owner of a candy store in your neighborhood
   d. Your teacher
   e. A new child on the block

4. Try out the following verse as you look into your own inner world. Some children are amazingly perceptive in comparing their inner and outer selves.

*I HAVE TWO SELVES**

I have two Selves or so I'm told,
  My Outside and my In.
And if I take a thoughtful look
  I'll see myself within.

Although I know my Outside Self,
  I see it every day,
My Inside self seems hidden,
  So neatly tucked away.

It seems so strange I cannot touch
  Or taste or hear or see. . . .
I only *feel* all those things
  That are inside of me.

Both my Selves are special
  That's what I'm about.
Feeling on the *Inside*,
  Showing on the *Out*.

* Tamara Hunt, in Tamara Hunt and Nancy Renfro, *Puppetry in Early Childhood* (Austin, Tex.: Nancy Renfro Studios, 1982), p. 123.

ACTIVITY 8.7

ACTIVITIES FOR MASKS

While masks are fun to make just in themselves, they are even more fun and more satisfying when they serve a purpose; for instance, when they are worn in a play or a creative-drama class, or when they carry out a theme. Sometimes the mask will suggest an idea to the wearer!

A Circus

A circus calls for clowns, animals, a ringmaster, and any number of sideshow characters. Every person in the class can invent a different mask for a circus parade.

Holidays

Although Hallowe'en comes to mind first as an occasion for mask making, every holiday contains possibilities—for example, St. Valentine's Day, the Fourth of July, or St. Patrick's Day. What about your birthday? Every child in the class might try making a mask of himself or herself. It may look like you, or it may be simply your own invention.

9

DRAMA AS A TEACHING TOOL

DRAMA IN THE SCHOOL

The use of drama as a means of instruction is not new; historically, both drama and theatre have long been recognized as a potent means of education. The ways in which they are used today, however, are new, and they differ in a number of respects from the ways in which they were used in the past.

The United States has only recently discovered the relationship between theatre and school. Indeed, the twentieth century was well advanced before the arts began to have any real impact on public education in this country. Some schools offered opportunities in the arts, but usually as extracurricular activities or as minor subjects, rarely placed on a par with the so-called solids. On the secondary-school level, they were given even less emphasis. The arts tended to be what teachers made them; thus they reflected the teachers' backgrounds, interests, and attitudes.

Despite progress, however, the dispute regarding the importance and function of drama in education continues. Is it to be included in the curriculum as a means or as an end? Are we primarily concerned with its use as a teaching tool, or do we regard it as a discipline in its own right, to be taught for its own sake? Since the 1920s, many of the foremost leaders in the field of drama education have warned against the exploitation of drama and theatre to achieve other ends; that is, making it a "handmaiden" to other subject areas. This exploitation, incidentally, has been of concern to teachers of the other arts as well. Are the visual arts, for instance, to be respected as art, or are they to be utilized for the preparation of school decorations, posters, party invitations, stage sets, and the like? This concern is not to be confused with the inclusion of the arts in integrated projects, in which those same items might be made in ways that are related, often brilliantly, to a unit of study.

Drama as Art

When drama is taught as an art form, the goals are both aesthetic and intrinsic: aesthetic, because product is important; intrinsic, because the child is a major concern. Overall objectives in such teaching include range of perception, sincerity, and the deepening of feeling and thought; for arts education is "education of the senses, of the intuition, not necessarily a cognitive or explicit didactic education."[1]

Drama classes include work on movement and rhythms, pantomime, improvisation, character study, and speech. Teachers help students to develop greater awareness as they create dramatic situations and, later on, rehearse scenes and plays. The problems of structure, organization, unity, and plot are studied through guided improvisation and group discussion. Characters and their relationships to other characters in a situation or play are analyzed for insights into motivation for their actions. Students are encouraged to express their own ideas and interpretations and to offer suggestions to the group. Indeed, the teacher's first job is to create an atmosphere in which children feel comfortable and at ease with one another while working together.

Actually, there is less difference between drama/theatre as a tool for teaching and drama/theatre as aesthetic education than appears on the surface. Good material for creative drama, like good theatre, makes use of a wide variety of subject matter: literature, personal experience, and the ways of life of other persons and societies. A wise selection of material makes for rich content, and when young players are motivated to use their minds, bodies, and honest emotions, they are developing important techniques for living.

Drama as Tool

The 1970s, which brought new British concepts of drama and theatre education to this country, caused some far-reaching changes in our practices and a reexamination of our methods and goals. Classroom

[1] Robert Landy, *Handbook of Educational Drama and Theatre* (Westport, Conn.: Greenwood Press), 1982, p. 201.

teachers, more comfortable with the use of drama as a technique for teaching other subjects than with the production of plays (for which they had little or no background), discovered the English model to be an exciting and useful way of working. Proponents of these new techniques offered the suggestion that administrators might find drama and theatre to be more acceptable as an educational medium than as aesthetic education and would therefore be willing to lend it support. This argument would be further strengthened, they said, if research could prove that children's learning is enhanced when drama and theatre are used as teaching tools.

Professional children's-theatre companies, influenced by the shift in emphasis, took a look at their offerings, and many found that another dimension could be added without changing their work in any substantive way. As a result, many companies prepared study guides and teachers' packets; some offered workshops following their performances in order to extend the experience, thus making theatre more than an engaging hour of entertainment. Some of the newer companies took a frankly educational approach from the start. They developed their own pieces based on curricular units and social issues of concern to children and young people. They realized that scripts would have to hold the attention of an audience if they were to have impact and challenge thought.

Teachers who prepare their classes for attending plays through the use of materials sent in advance by producing companies and who welcome the suggested follow-up activities have found such theatre a stimulus to learning. In whichever context theatre is used—to heighten appreciation and give aesthetic pleasure, or to serve as an aid to learning—good theatre is a rich experience for children.

The name most frequently mentioned in regard to drama as a learning medium is Dorothy Heathcote, a British educator. She has given workshops and summer sessions in different parts of the United States and has been the subject of three films made at Northwestern University.

Her approach to drama has been particularly appealing to classroom teachers, who find in it techniques that they can use in their own teaching. She works, as she says, from the inside out; her concern is that children use drama to expand their understanding of life experiences, to reflect on a particular circumstance, and to make sense out of their world in a deeper way. Her goal is not the teaching of drama alone, but of other subjects as well. In fact, there is no area of the curriculum in which she has not used drama. She begins with process, and in time moves to a product that may take an audience into account, although this is not her major concern. Her intent is always the depth and breadth of learning, which excites the class and brings satisfaction to the

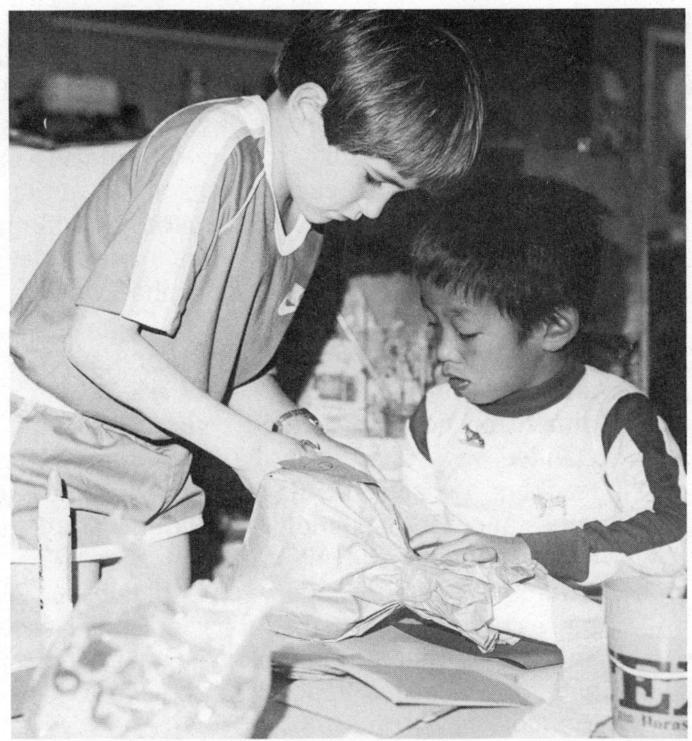

Children teach others. (Courtesy of Nancy Renfro Studios, Austin, Texas; photograph by Debbie Sullivan)

teacher. She consciously employs the elements of drama to educate, according to Betty Jane Wagner, and aims "to bring out what children already know but don't yet know they know."[2]

In lieu of putting on plays and dramatizing literature, Heathcote prefers to help children find the dramatic moment in an event or a unit of study. She believes in helping the teacher use drama to teach more effectively, not to exploit it to sugar-coat nondramatic material; and encourages the teacher to work with children as guides and resource persons. If there is a drama specialist in the school, Heathcote advocates having the classroom teacher, or generalist, follow up the lesson with the specialist's suggestions. If there is no specialist, the classroom teacher must learn how to discover the tension, conflict, or point of greatest interest in a topic; how to collect relevant source materials; and how to guide the class through an original piece of work. This process

[2] Betty Jane Wagner, *Dorothy Heathcote—Drama as a Learning Medium* (Washington, D.C.: NEA Press, 1976), p. 13.

may last for a few periods or for an entire semester, depending on the scope of the study and the age and interest of the children.

Dramatizing an event, Heathcote believes, makes it possible to isolate and study it. Like most creative-drama teachers, she starts with discussion. She uses the children's ideas and encourages their making decisions.

INTEGRATED PROJECTS

When substance becomes didactic or when creative drama is used to sugar-coat difficult material, it fails as education; likewise, when creative drama makes use of only trivial subject matter or an endless succession of theatre games, it fails as art. But the integrated project, one of the older methods of combining dramatic techniques with curricular material, has proved highly satisfactory.

Projects integrating drama, music, dance, creative writing, and the visual arts with social studies and literature have been popular since the early days of the progressive-education movement. Even the most traditional schools have found integrated projects an effective way of teaching and learning. Arts educators have generally endorsed such programs because they place the arts at the core of the curriculum rather than on the periphery. Accorded an importance equal to that of the academic subjects, the arts thus became a basic part of the educational system. Integrated projects continue to find popularity in schools where staff members are able and willing to work closely together. This is often more easily accomplished in small private schools, where the schedule allows for flexibility and where there is concern for student interest.

The integrated project usually starts in the social-studies or English class. With a unit of study as a base, various aspects of it are explored. In the first three grades, "Our Community" is a common theme. The students learn about schools; stores; service areas such as the fire and police departments and the transport systems (Activity 9.1); local myths and legends; and music and the arts. Map study and the American Indian are also units that offer rich possibilities for dramatization.

The classroom teacher brings in pictures, photographs, newspapers, and visual aids of all kinds and organizes field trips to local social agencies and organizations. If possible, representatives from the community are invited into the classroom to talk about their responsibilities to the community. Older persons with interesting stories to tell of historical happenings within their own or their family's lifetimes add another dimension.

One particularly interesting study in which I was involved as drama teacher was "The River." Rivers were shown in their importance to the

Drama—a dynamic way of learning. (Courtesy of Scott Regan, Bowling Green State University)

life of all creatures: as a source of drinking water, as a means of transportation and communication, and as an inspiration for music and dance. An exceptionally cooperative group of faculty members worked together to help an eager fourth-grade class explore these various aspects of the river. The study culminated in a "documentary" for a lower-school assembly. Although the value to the children was in the *doing* rather than in the *showing*, we agreed that so much good work had gone into it that the children's wish to share it with others should be supported. "The River" was a highlight of the year.

Language Arts and Creative Drama

Probably the most obvious value in creative drama is its application to speech. Improved speaking habits are a shared objective of educators and teachers of drama. When players feel the need to communicate orally with others, they seek the words they want and try to pronounce and articulate them clearly. This chapter suggests some speech-related activities that act as an incentive for improving oral expression.

The familiar activity "Show and Tell" is popular in the elementary classroom. Children enjoy it, and teachers find it a natural way to encourage oral communication, since holding and demonstrating with "props" tends to eliminate self-consciousness. Many other classroom activities also provide work on oral communication. One of the oldest and best is storytelling, a favorite pastime in itself as well as a primary step in the preparation of a dramatization.

Storytelling. Storytelling is an ancient art that continues to be loved in spite of, or perhaps because of, our technical advances in communication. Television brings a vast array of entertainment into the home, but it can no more replace the living storyteller than film can replace theatre. The reader–audience relationship depends on the rapport between the one telling and the others listening to the story—the listeners' involvement in the material and the way it is presented to them, which varies with each telling. The age, background, and interests of the listeners, the physical surroundings, and even the time of day affect the development of that rapport. Fortunate the boys and girls who are exposed to a good storyteller; fortunate, also, the one who possesses the skill to choose just the right story for the occasion and make it live again for his or her listeners.

Traditionally, stories were told for three purposes: to entertain, to teach, and to transmit the culture. These purposes have not changed essentially, although in an era of mass education, the storyteller primarily provides entertainment and aesthetic pleasure. Folk tales, myths, legends, fables, biography, and history offer a wealth of storytelling material. A lively tale, believable characters, and a worthwhile theme are the primary requisites.

Most teachers of young children have had training and practice in telling stories, and they tell them well. This is not only a value in itself, but also an enviable skill in helping children tell stories and act them out. Children take pleasure in sharing their favorites; at the same time, they are acquiring new skills in communication. Every child should be given a chance to tell a story of his or her own from time to time. If the class is large, each child may be given a portion of a story to tell, one way of ensuring equal participation for all. Besides practice in recall and organization, storytelling offers a splendid opportunity for work on vocabulary, syntax, and diction. Children love words and enjoy learning new ones, given half a chance and some encouragement. Vocabulary building is a never-ending opportunity and cannot begin too early.

Speech Improvement. There are times in every class when individual work is needed on certain sounds, depending on regional dialects or the language development of the children. Spanish-speaking children have difficulty with the *j*, for instance, whereas children whose primary language is German find the *v* and the *w* difficult. Oriental youngsters are able to articulate the *l* and the *r* but reverse them in words. Many children who are native speakers of English substitute *d* for *th* and distort some vowels and consonants. One way of avoiding the boredom of drill (with its questionable value) is to repeat jingles and tongue twisters in which the troublesome consonants and vowel sounds occur. Rather than singling out individual children for this, the teacher should have the whole class participate. Young children find amusing rhymes presented as choral speech, such as those in Activity 9.2, a challenge, if not a game.

Written Communication. Creative drama as an approach to writing is a relatively new technique used by some teachers. Children's playwright Aurand Harris introduced it in the Cleveland schools a few years ago; it was so successful that he has been invited back for several residencies. Harris works directly with the children in the classroom, stimulating them to write down their ideas for plays first created and developed orally.[3] His educational goals are an improvement in written communication and an ongoing interest in the dramatic form.

Children in the third and fourth grades are responsive to this way of teaching, although it can be used in the middle and upper grades as well. It is an effective technique because of the immediacy of drama, the naturalness of dialogue as a way of telling a story, and the eagerness of children to put down on paper what they have just improvised.

ARTISTS-IN-THE-SCHOOLS PROGRAM

Another approach to drama and theatre education is the artists-in-the-schools program, which brings performers into the classroom for a morning, a day, a week, or sometimes a much longer period of time. Actors perform, demonstrate, or work directly with the children. This provides an opportunity for teachers to learn new techniques that help them to continue on their own after the actors have gone. It also exposes children to the creative artist, whom they otherwise would probably never meet. Throughout the United States, actors, dancers, musicians, painters, puppeteers, and poets are brought into schools through funded programs. Information on available artists (both groups and individuals) is available through state arts councils and state departments of education. Although not every school has made use of either the program or the concept, many have, and children have had their education enriched as a result.

[3] *Aurand Harris Demonstrating Playwriting with Children* (Cleveland: Edward Feil Productions, 1983) is a 30-minute videotape for teachers, showing Harris at work.

Often available are student performers from local universities. Some theatre departments with child drama/theatre programs offer workshops following performances in schools. While they are not professional actors, these students often are sensitive to children and are familiar with the community and the background of the people who live in it. Some extend and enrich the children's experience by preparing study guides for teachers.

One further comment regarding drama as a teaching tool. In helping children overcome prejudice and reject stereotypes based on race, religion, sex, ethnic background, age, and handicapping conditions, *classroom practice* is as potent a force as subject matter. The way that teachers handle groups and challenge condescending attitudes is also a form of teaching. While the material we use is unquestionably important, the way in which we deal with students makes a lasting impression. Children tend to treat others as they have been treated; thus a fair and sensitive leader is a role model, affecting social attitudes and values. By our own behavior, we are able to create a climate of acceptance, with respect for all regardless of individual difference.

SUMMARY

The number of activities that can be incorporated into a curriculum to improve speech and teach the language arts is almost limitless. "Show and Tell," storytelling, sound and motion stories, group discussion, and improvisation are among the most popular. Speech is our most important means of communication, although the written language often receives the greater emphasis in schools. It is through the oral language, however, that our earliest learnings take place; through it, we are able to express our thoughts and feelings, our needs and desires.

The creative-drama class offers a rich opportunity for practice in both written and oral communication. Because drama deals with ideas and literature, vocabularies are enlarged, and the ability to express thoughts clearly is strengthened. Interpretation of characters brings color to the voice and melody to the speech, as players take a variety of roles.

The controversy regarding drama as means or end is not settled, and perhaps never will be. Compelling arguments on both sides press for a curriculum in which there is a place for each. Leading educators have declared drama and speech to be central to a language curriculum. They believe that drama can motivate writing and improve oral skills; they believe that it stimulates reading. Some insist that it can be used to teach any subject effectively.

There is agreement among many educators that study of the arts gives form and expression to human feeling and that attending the theatre as a spectator is a rich experience not found in film and television viewing. In the foreword to a publication released by the State University of New York in 1978, a strong stand is taken regarding the place of the arts in education:

> *The arts are a means of expressing and interpreting human experience. Quality education of individuals is complete only if the arts are an integral part of the daily teaching and learning process. The integration of the arts in the elementary, secondary and continuing education curriculum is a key to the humanistic development of students.*[4]

[4] *The Arts as Perception (A Way of Learning)*, Project Search, The University of the State of New York (Albany, N.Y.: The State Department, Division of Humanities and Arts Education, 1978), p. iii.

ACTIVITY 9.1

OUR PUBLIC TRANSPORTATION SYSTEM

Objective: To learn about the bus, train, or subway as a means of public transportation and to understand it in terms of location, people's needs, and historical development

Suggestions for the Teacher

Because this is an integrated project, it should be discussed beforehand by the teachers who would be involved—the classroom teacher, the music teacher, the physical education teacher, the art teacher, and the drama specialist, if there is one.

1. Post pictures of the bus, train, or subway at various stages of their development.
2. Have a class discussion of how the children and their families and neighbors travel from one part of the city or town to another.
3. Bring in pictures showing the history of the local transportation system, a map of the city, and any other materials that show where and why the system was designed and constructed as it was. This will bring about a discussion of the needs of the people. Methods of transportation vary according to the location and type of community—do you live in a large, densely populated city, a small town, a suburb, or a rural area? The need for school buses may also be part of the discussion.
4. If possible, show the class ground-breaking ceremonies that were held as the various routes were completed. It adds interest when ceremonies are used to illustrate important events in the development of a city. In addition, the children's families and neighbors may be able to remember these celebrations and thus relate the study to the children's own lives and surroundings.
5. Improvisations of these events and anecdotes deepen understanding and make them more real. A third-grade class may want to create a play or *docu-drama* (a dramatic documentary containing facts and story). This is an excellent time to try some playwriting, either having the children doing the writing or taking down the dialogue as the children create it orally.
6. Songs and dances of the period further enhance the study and help integrate learning.
7. The project may develop to the point that the class wants to share it with others: their parents or perhaps another third- or second-grade class.
8. If drawings or maps are made, you can mount them on bulletin boards to illustrate different aspects of the transportation system.

ACTIVITY 9.2

USING JINGLES FOR SPEECH IMPROVEMENT

Objective: To improve or correct poor articulation of particular sounds

Suggestions for the Teacher

First of all, do not use letter names. Use instead the sound for which the letter stands. Think of something that makes the sound you want to work on—for example, *s*. Ask what a radiator sounds like when air is escaping or what a teakettle sounds like when the water is boiling. The *s* comes out of a tiny hole, just the way it comes out of your mouth between your tongue and upper front teeth. Making the sound through imagery dissociates it from the letter with which the speaker has had difficulty. Here is a jingle for the *s* sound in the initial position:

Sal sat on a seesaw—
  A seesaw, a seesaw.
Sal sat on a seesaw
  All on a sunny day.

Sue sat on a seesaw—
  A seesaw, a seesaw.
Sue sat on a seesaw
  And sang a song so gay.

Sal fell off a seesaw—
  A seesaw, a seesaw.
Sal fell off a seesaw
  And down fell singing Sue.

More difficult is the *s* in combination with other sounds:

I hunted for my slipper,
  That sly and slippery slipper.
I couldn't find my slipper
  And I cried myself to sleep.

A scrawny old witch scrabbled out of a dream.
  We heard her screech, and we heard her scream,
Scratch and scrape in the chimney stark
  That scrawny old witch who rode in the dark.

And in the final position:

Miss Goose and Miss Mouse
  Ran a race around the house.
Said Miss Goose, "If I miss,
  I shall be hungry after this!"

S, *l*, and *r* are the most troublesome consonants for many children, and *i* and *o* as in *how* are diphthongs that some children find difficult.

*The Jingle Book for Speech Improvement and Speech Correction,** from which these jingles are taken, contains a wealth of useful rhymes, but you can also make up original ones to meet special needs. With sounds presented in this way, drudgery becomes play, and many problems disappear as if by magic.

* Alice L. Wood, *The Jingle Book for Speech Improvement and Speech Correction* (New York: Dutton, 1968), pp. 70, 80, 83.

10

CREATIVE DRAMA FOR THE SPECIAL CHILD

Let each become all that he was created capable of being; expand, if possible, to his full growth; and show himself at length in his own shape and stature, be these what they may.

—THOMAS CARLYLE

This chapter considers creative drama in one of the newer areas of education: special education, or the education of the exceptional child or the child with special needs. Special education may be defined as any program of teaching techniques designed to meet the needs of children whose abilities deviate markedly from those of the majority of boys and girls of their age. Included in this group are the intellectually gifted as well as the mentally retarded, the physically handicapped, the emotionally disturbed, the culturally and economically disadvantaged, the non-native speakers of English, and the underachiever, whose problems may not have been identified.

Until recently, very little was done to help these children, whose basic needs are the same as those of so-called normal children but whose individual needs require special educational services. A difference of opinion still exists as to when or to what extent these children should be integrated into regular classrooms; but there is recognition that their special needs must be met and that they should be helped to take their places with their peers in as many areas as possible and as soon as they are able to do so. One of the greatest obstacles to this goal has been the widespread notion that these children are "different" from normal children. Modern educators and psychologists have pointed out the values of getting these boys and girls into regular classrooms while they are receiving additional enrichments, remedial help, or therapy. The remediation should be an aid to their instruction, rather than a separate program of instruction.

MAINSTREAMING

Mainstreaming is the term used to define the integration of exceptional children with the so-called normal. The major objective is social: to assist both groups in working and living together. To this end, many practices may be followed.

Speech therapy, remedial reading, language classes for non-English-speaking children, psychological counseling, and special classes for the partially sighted, blind, or deaf may be included in the school day without removing a child from the group for more than a period or two at a time. Most schools do not have such extensive programs of special services, but many schools have set up some programs to meet the more urgent needs of the school or community. In some instances, special activities have been added as enrichment for the culturally disadvantaged as well as for the gifted. In all these programs, there is an opportunity to use creative drama as a therapeutic process. As used here, the term *therapeutic* does not imply psychodrama or sociodrama, but points to an aspect of an art form in which children find pleasure, emotional release, mental stimulation, personal satisfaction through success, and, most of all, a chance to use and stretch their imaginations.

SPECIAL CHILDREN

The Gifted Child

One group of children that has received very little attention, perhaps because they are able to move ahead on their own, is the intellectually gifted. Only recently have educators and parents taken constructive steps to enrich the curriculum so that these gifted boys and girls may receive the stimulation they need by participating in extra classes and following individual interests. One of the areas that has been used most successfully for enrichment is the arts. This is not to imply that *all* children should not have wide and continued exposure to the arts, but because this is an area with endless possibilities, it has been selected often for

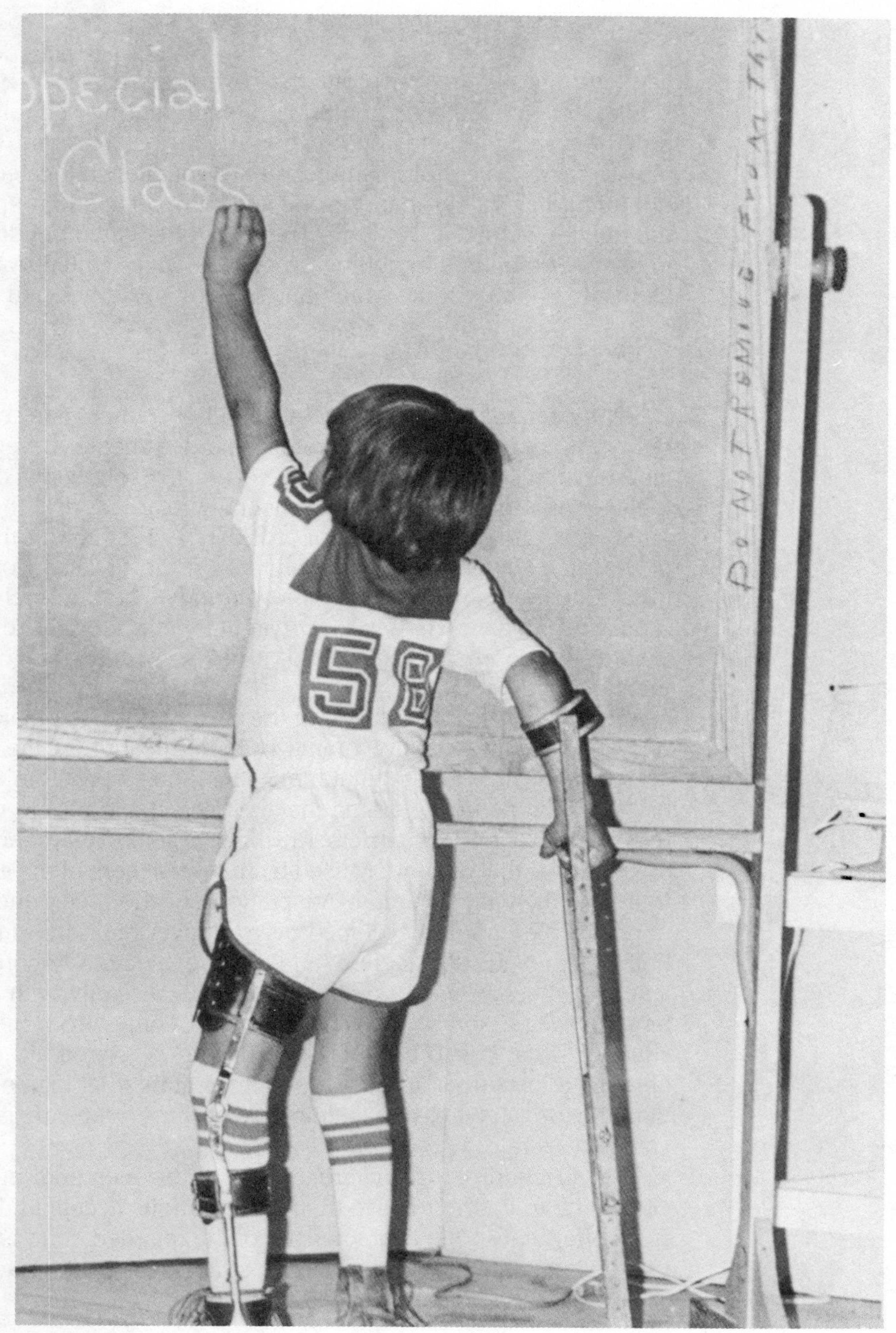

(Courtesy of Jody Johnston, The Rainbow Company of Las Vegas)

use with the gifted. Arts programs have been designed both as after-school activities and as additional classes during school time. Some programs include field trips to museums, theatres, and concerts, although funds given for this purpose are generally allocated for the use of all children rather than for one specially selected group. Classes in drama, dance, music, and the visual arts offer gifted children a chance to use their abilities in putting on plays—often written by the children themselves—and in designing and making costumes and scenery.

The Mentally Retarded Child

Mental retardation describes a condition rather than a disease. Although it can refer to any degree of retarded mental development, the classifications most commonly used are the following: the educable mentally retarded, the trainable mentally retarded, and the dependent mentally retarded. This discussion of creative drama in the education of the mentally retarded child centers on the first category. It is with this group that play can be most rewarding as both a teaching tool and a pleasure. Inasmuch as play constitutes an important role in the all-around development of the child, it has a special significance for the mentally retarded.

According to a survey taken in the early 1960s,[1] the major objectives of teachers using creative drama in the education of the mentally retarded child were to stimulate language and to promote social development. The nature of drama makes it a versatile tool in working with these handicapped youngsters. Rhythms, dramatic play, and pantomime are activities that are widely used by many teachers of the educable and trainable mentally retarded. Adaptations of the techniques used with normal children and developed over a longer period of time can bring both immediate satisfaction and lasting benefit. According to one teacher who has used creative drama successfully with mentally retarded groups, some of the best material comes from the very social situations that cause the retarded child to be stared at and shunned: entering a restaurant; ordering food and eating it; going on a bus, train, or plane trip; and dressing—simple daily activities that the average child easily masters.

Like all children, the retarded want to be members of a group, to contribute to it, and to have their contributions accepted. Drama offers this opportunity. One characteristic of the retarded child is slowness to use the imagination or to deal with abstract ideas. Some teachers believe

[1] Geraldine Brain Siks, *Children's Theatre and Creative Dramatics* (Seattle: University of Washington Press, 1961), chap. 17.

that the retarded child becomes more imaginative when placed in a class with normal children. Whether in a regular class or a special class, however, the pace is slow. Recognizing this handicap, the teacher can guide retarded children's dramatic play and stimulate their responses. Frequently, the leader errs in expecting too much too soon. Retarded children need more help and encouragement than do other children; they have to repeat experiences more often; and, finally, they must learn self-confidence and feel the satisfaction of having their contributions, however small, accepted. The game of pretending can help such children learn to use their imagination, to prepare for new experiences, and to lay a firmer foundation for oral communication. Experienced teachers state that dramatic activities help to develop the skills of listening and looking. In this way, attention is engaged.

Rhythms and movement games are excellent beginning exercises. They aid the development of large muscles while they motivate use of imagination. The acting out of simple stories comes much later. At first, retarded children will be more comfortable participating in a group than working individually. They probably have experienced frustration and the sense of being different; their need for praise and encouragement, therefore, will be greater than that of a normal child. When they show an interest in moving out of the group to become specific characters—someone other than themselves—they are ready for the next step. Now, instead of general group activities, individual roles may be undertaken. The teacher not only needs to provide stimulation at this stage, but also must give clear and simple direction: Who is the character? How does he walk? What is he doing? How does he do it? What does he say?

If social ease and a sense of security are the first consideration, oral expression is the second. Guided dramatic play is a way of introducing oral vocabulary and developing concepts that prepare the child for reading. A variety of experiences will help to provide a better understanding of the world, and acting out words that describe this world will give them meaning. Action words such as *jump, run, skip, skate,* and *throw* teach by doing. Nouns such as *farmer, mailman, mother,* and *grocer* can become the basis for dramatic play and pan-tomime. Mentally retarded children who have been guided carefully and slowly through dramatic play will eventually be ready to dramatize simple stories. By this time, they will have achieved some personal freedom and mastered a functional reading vocabulary. The procedure of planning, playing, and evaluating is the same as that followed in the normal classroom, except that with these children, the task and the process must be simpler and will take longer.

One particularly important point to remember is that adjustments in all activities for the retarded should be made on the basis of their interests and needs. Stories selected for dramatization should, in addition to being clear and simple, reflect the interests that give meaning to children's lives. As their interests widen, a greater variety of stories may be introduced, with new words to express and describe them.

Not only literature but other subjects as well can be taught through the medium of improvisation. For example, one teacher had the children in her arithmetic class be plus and minus signs and pieces of fruit; through acting out simple problems of subtraction and addition, the children were able to see the correct answers. So-called creative walks, on which children became trees, flowers, stones, birds, and animals, helped them to observe and recall what they had seen after they returned to the classroom. Such use of creative drama is not generally sanctioned; and, indeed, it was discouraged in Chapter 9. With retarded children, however, communication and social development are the primary goals; art is secondary. The potential in drama for motivating children and achieving these primary goals validates its use. In time, other objectives can be established, but these are not possible until children have developed a sense of security, have acquired some freedom of expression, and have mastered a working vocabulary that will enable them to take on the roles of others.

Participation by the retarded child in a formal play is to be discouraged. A continuing program of creative drama, on the contrary, offers an opportunity for social growth, emotional release, and a way of learning. As one teacher put it after using creative-drama techniques successfully for many years: "These children need to be crawled with first—then they can walk." When they have reached the walking stage, they often astonish us with what they have learned.

The Emotionally Disturbed Child

It is with emotionally disturbed children that the classroom teacher must exercise the greatest caution. We know so little about these children and the causes of their problems that the possibility of doing harm is greater than with any other group. Indeed, it is often difficult to distinguish between the emotionally disturbed child and the mentally retarded child because of the frequent similarity of behavior. Frequently repeated testing must be done in order to determine the nature of the condition. What might be a rewarding activity for the retarded child might not be good enough for the child who is disturbed. Psychodrama and play therapy are accepted techniques in the treatment of emotionally disturbed children, but they can be damaging in the hands of the lay person, regardless of his or her background and skill as a teacher of creative drama. The seriously disturbed child probably will not be found in the regular classroom, but will be enrolled in a special class or special school, in which services—which may or may not include psychiatric help and play therapy—are provided. Children in special schools often are referred to outside clinics or therapists, and drama may be part of the treatment.

Remedial Drama. *Remedial drama* is an umbrella term used here to cover several specific techniques. As was stated earlier, drama/theatre has historically been an essential part of human development. In preventive and therapeutic work, drama is primarily concerned with communication and therefore with helping individuals and groups develop and build better relationships. According to Sue Jennings, "[It] does not differ in content or technique from other types of drama, although great care must be taken in selecting and applying drama techniques to remedial work."[2] Her emphasis is on experience; and the goals of drama, used in this way, are *socialization, creativity,* and *insight*.

Eleanor Irwin, well-known drama therapist, draws a distinction between a therapeutic experience and therapy as a treatment. She says that "any experience which helps an individual to feel a greater sense of competence and well-being may be thought of as therapeutic."[3] This is the sense in which the word *therapy* is used by many persons and in which it would be most accurately applied to the work of most classroom teachers using drama with the children on a regular basis.

Drama therapy, role playing, psychodrama, and *sociodrama* are the terms most frequently heard with reference to remedial drama. They differ both as to technique and as to thrust. David Johnson of Yale University, a leader in this new field, defines drama therapy as "the intentional use of creative drama toward the psychotherapeutic goals of symptom relief, emotional and physical integration, and personal growth."[4] Drama therapy, like the other arts therapies, applies a creative medium and establishes an understanding or contract between the client and the therapist. Thus it is differentiated from creative drama in an educational setting.

The child who functions well enough to be in a class with normal children may derive great benefit from dramatic play and dramatization. Under these circumstances, engaging in creative drama may be both an emotional release and a socializing experience. Bear in mind, however, that because the child's language and speech are frequently poor,

[2] Sue Jennings, *Remedial Drama* (New York: Theatre Arts Books, 1974), p. 4.

[3] Eleanor Irwin, "Drama Therapy with the Handicapped," in *Drama/Theatre and the Handicapped,* ed. Ann Shaw and Cj Stevens (Washington, D.C.: American Theatre Association, 1979), p. 23.

[4] David Johnson, mimeographed material, 1978.

he or she is likely to meet with frustration and difficulty in the oral expression of ideas and the improvisation of dialogue. An inhibited child cannot be expected to function at as high a level as the other children and needs much more support and encouragement. An aggressive child, on the contrary, has to be restrained in a tendency to take over or to distract others. The attention span of children with emotional problems is likely to be shorter than that of other children. Activities 10.1 and 10.2 are designed to increase the attention span.

According to some experienced teachers, dramatic play, when first introduced to the child with emotional problems, should include situations based on reality rather than on fantasy. Highly imaginative situations may cause young children who are not in touch with reality to meld with the idea or to identify too closely with the characters played. All children tend to become deeply involved in the dramatic play. The normal child can suspend disbelief for the duration of the period, and then return to reality. The disturbed child may not be able to shake off the role so easily, however, and may continue to be the character long after the play period has ended. As said earlier, though, we are dealing here with the child who is able to be in a normal group and therefore may be helped by his or her more reality-oriented peers.

There is a general agreement that dance, rhythms, and ritual movement are excellent for disturbed children. Physical activity gives them a sense of the body; the large movements, such as skipping, galloping, stretching, and moving the arms, are wonderful exercises for those who are poorly coordinated. "Reaching for the sky or pushing away the clouds," "feeling big," "growing tall"—all are movements that contain an element of drama.

Although it is suggested that all groups benefit from starting a session with movement, it is essential for children with problems. Through ritual, they find security; through warm-ups, use of the body; through moving as a group, a lessening of self-consciousness. It is further suggested that dance involving physical touch is often helpful, and patterned dance, with its structure, is a better starting point for some children than are freer dance forms. Under any circumstances, rhythms that involve moving the whole body, clapping the hands, and making sounds to a beat are all good ways of getting and holding attention. Sue Jennings warns against involving children with problems in "end-of-session" discussions. She advises just letting it happen. The leader's first job is to establish trust and security. Verbalization may be slow, and any analytical discussion should be a future goal.

Both finger puppets and glove puppets have been found to work successfully with children who are too inhibited to assume roles themselves. Such children usually have a poor self-image; thus it takes longer to build interest and ego strength to the point where they are able to move out of the group to assume roles and sustain them through improvised situations. Again, we are speaking of children with knowledge of themselves and their reality. When they reach the point where they can enter into dramatic situations with relative ease, these emotionally disturbed children will begin to derive some of the same benefits gained by other children. In terms of objectives, interaction with the group, ability to concentrate, ability to express themselves orally, and ability to take the part of another come first on the list. After these objectives have been met, these children should be able to work with joy, accomplishing as much as and sometimes more than the others in the group. Their sensitivity, if properly guided, can be an asset to their understanding of a character and their creation of a characterization. Drama, because of its total involvement—physical, mental, emotional, and social—offers a wealth of activities, all of which have therapeutic value, if properly handled.

The Physically Handicapped Child

In many ways, physically handicapped children present fewer difficulties to the classroom teacher than do the emotionally disturbed or the mentally retarded. Their handicaps are visible, and their limitations, obvious. Problems are easier to identify, and depending on the seriousness of the disability, decisions have already been made as to whether they can function in a regular classroom. As with all exceptional children, the physically handicapped are thought to be better off integrated into a normal classroom rather than segregated; if the disability is so severe that special services are required, however, they may have to be enrolled, at least for a time, in a special school or in a hospital.

For our purposes, we shall consider the physically handicapped to include the deaf child, the partially sighted or blind child, and the child unable to function normally because of some other physical disability. Frequently, children with physical problems have emotional problems as well; to overcome both these handicaps, they need all the support and encouragement that the teacher can give as they struggle to reach their goals. Because of the conspicuousness of the handicaps, however, they are generally treated with more compassion and understanding than are their classmates with emotional problems whose behavior is inappropriate or immature. Persons whose psychological problems cause them to behave in a socially unacceptable manner are often criticized or ridiculed, prompting the comment, "Why must they act that way?" Persons on crutches never evoke this reaction, for we know that they are walking as well as they can. In spite of, or perhaps because of, their physical limitations, children who cannot hear, see, or speak clearly or who lack physical coordination or cannot walk need an opportunity to escape the walls of their prison on the wings of the imagination. Creative drama offers this opportunity, although admittedly the goals must be modified for physically handicapped children.

The Little Theatre of the Deaf, which achieved national prominence at the end of the 1960s, is a shining example of what can be done by actors for children who cannot hear. Because oral communication is emphasized in early education, deaf children are at a disadvantage when attending theatrical performances, just as they are in ordinary classroom situations. Pantomime is the obvious means of reaching the hard-of-hearing, and it is in this form that The Little Theatre of the Deaf has succeeded so brilliantly. A cue can be taken from this experiment: pantomime is an area of drama in which children with hearing loss can participate.

Again, movement is an ideal way to begin activities. Large physical movements come first, and then rhythms and dance. Small muscle movements follow. Sensitive to the deaf child's keen visual perception, the leader can move from dance into pantomime. There is motivation for speech in drama, but the easiest communication is through pantomime, in which the deaf child can achieve success. Stories may be told in this medium, giving pleasure to both player and observer. My observation of creative-drama classes in a school for the deaf revealed remarkable possibilities for learning and emotional release.

Blind or partially sighted children face different problems. They are at home with speech, so storytelling is an excellent beginning activity. Choral speaking, like music, is also an art in which they can excel and at the same time find pleasure. Original poetry composed by the group offers a chance to express feelings and personal responses. Free movement is more difficult for the blind child than for the sighted child, but it is not impossible. Carefully guided improvisation may be attempted, although the formal play, in which movement is predetermined and is not changed in rehearsal, is by its nature easier. One director who has had great success with a blind drama group stresses the fact that she never moves scenery or props once the placement has been established. A knowledge of where things are enables the players to move freely and easily about the stage. For the blind or partially sighted player, formal drama offers greater security than does improvisation.

Children with physical problems that prevent them from running, walking, or even using their arms or legs easily have also found drama to be within the range of their capabilities. Participation of the children while they are seated is an excellent way of involving everyone in pantomime, choral speech, and puppetry. In preparing a dramatization, the roles of narrator and storyteller are highly regarded and can be handled by a child who may not be able to engage in more active participation. The imaginative teacher can find a place for the disabled child in which he or she is able to add to the group endeavor, thus enhancing the self-image and giving a sense of achievement. The philosophy of all therapeutic recreation includes this sense of pride in a job well done and the joy of creative accomplishment.

Physically handicapped persons are able to do and enjoy a much wider range of dramatic activities than was formerly thought possible. Most obvious but little used in the past is puppetry. The puppeteer in a wheelchair is able to run, jump, dance, fly—in short, to perform every physical activity—through the puppet. And, in most cases, such a puppeteer is at no disadvantage.

There are a number of theatre groups for the handicapped across the nation. Robert Landy's *Handbook of Educational Drama and Theatre*[5] lists Theatre Unlimited in San Francisco; Process Theatre with the Handicapped of the Alan Short Center in Stockton, California; The San Diego Theatre for the Disabled; and The National Theatre Workshop of the Handicapped in New York City. One group that must be given special mention is The Rainbow Company in Las Vegas. The company holds classes in creative drama, mime, technical theatre, make-up, costuming, and playwriting for children from preschool through high school. The Rainbow Company has received national acclaim for the quality of its work with disabled performers; in 1982, it was selected as a model site for the fourth consecutive year by the National Committee: Arts for the Handicapped.[6]

The Kids' Project, a puppet troupe created in 1977 in response to the problems of mainstreaming, has become an effective and growing medium for reaching handicapped schoolchildren.[7] The puppets represent a variety of disabling conditions: blindness, deafness, cerebral palsy, mental retardation, and learning disabilities. Two nondisabled puppets are also included in the skits, in which they learn to accept the others. One segment of the performance is devoted to each of the handicapped puppets, followed by a question-and-answer period. Barbara Aiello, the originator of The Kids' Project, was a special-education teacher in Washington who realized that putting handicapped children into regular classrooms in compliance with the Education for All Handicapped Chil-

[5] Robert J. Landy, *A Handbook of Educational Drama and Theatre* (Westport, Conn.: Greenwood Press, 1982).

[6] A 1982 brochure of The Rainbow Company reports that "this designation has been made to only ten sites in the country and indicates 'exemplary programming in the arts by, with, and for the handicapped.'"

[7] "Puppets Depict Life of Disabled," *New York Times,* 10 July 1983, p. 39.

dren Act of 1975 demanded attitudinal changes, if true integration were to take place. After years of separation, both handicapped and nonhandicapped needed to understand each other.

Aiello used the puppets in her own program, "Kids on the Block," but she also made it possible for others to purchase them. Buyers pay a one-time fee—which includes puppets, props, and scripts—but they are restricted to nonprofit use. By 1983, 500 groups, including 50 in foreign countries, were reported to be using the puppets. New York State alone had 16 troupes funded at both state and local levels. Although the New York troupes use the same curriculum, they vary their styles to fit the area in which they are performing. For example, urban children experience problems on the street that are unknown among rural children.

Extensions of the project may be found in some high schools, and at the time of this writing are being planned for adults in the workplace. The values of puppets are described in Chapter 8, but the impact of this program demonstrates their effectiveness in reaching youngsters who have trouble relating to others and nondisabled persons who have trouble establishing a rapport with the disabled. One of the most remarkable aspects that I have discovered within the last few years is the ingenuity teachers and children's-theatre directors have shown in finding new ways of reaching young people and of including heretofore excluded populations. The Kids' Project is an example.

The Culturally and Economically Disadvantaged Child

Since the advent of the Head Start program, we have been hearing much about the culturally disadvantaged child, or the child in the disadvantaged urban area. This is not a new problem in our society but one that, for a variety of reasons, is now attracting wide attention, with government and private-foundation funds having been allocated for the establishment of educational and recreational programs. The arts, including dramatic play and creative drama, are emphasized in many of these programs. The values cited in Chapter 1 have tremendous implications for these children, who were born into an environment lacking books, playing space, supervision, the arts—and, in many cases, language itself. According to one group of leaders at a conference on the subject of creative drama in special education, the problems of these children are manifold. For example, poverty may preclude treatment of a physical handicap; the handicap causes feelings of inadequacy; and this results in emotional disturbance. Hence, the child suffers a combination of problems requiring understanding and skill beyond the qualifications of the average well-prepared teacher.

The need for special training is recognized, and many universities and organizations are offering courses in this area. Because this is a subject of specialized interest and content, it is beyond the scope of this book; but for those teachers and recreation leaders who are interested in working in disadvantaged areas, let it be said that creative drama and theatre are approved and exciting techniques.

Nevertheless, the classroom teacher can do much for ghetto children. Actually, the first work in children's drama in the United States was initiated in the settlement houses of our large cities at the turn of the century. It is significant that the first children's theatre in America was established at the Educational Alliance in New York City in 1903 for the children of immigrant families.

Since that time, the schools have taken up the challenge, although the social settlements have by no means abdicated their responsibilities. During the 1960s and 1970s, street theatre began to appear in our cities: free performances of drama, music, and dance in ghetto neighborhoods, where strength is drawn even as it is given. Some of these productions have been subsidized by state arts councils; some, by municipalities; others, by churches and universities. Some have been part of a two-pronged program, involving both participation and spectator enjoyment. Many school districts have reported pilot projects in the arts for culturally disadvantaged youngsters, and drama is a frequent inclusion.

The schools have been concerned in recent years with bilingual education and the teaching of English as a second language. Particularly in large urban areas has the need been felt for teachers with a knowledge of Spanish and the ability to teach English in the early grades to children who enter school speaking a foreign language. One technique used and discussed today involves movement and pantomime.

For over a century, body movement has been recognized as bearing a relationship to the acquisition of a second language. Indeed, several methods making use of mime, rhythm, and sign language have been devised for teaching foreign languages. Movement is, therefore, not a new technique; rather, it is now recognized as an integral part of the learning process. Movement plus oral activities offer a great variety of opportunities for learning on any level.

The child who is learning a second language is faced with a problem not unlike those faced by disabled children. It is therefore suggested that the procedures be much the same. Dance is recommended as a beginning because it forces more concentration than does pure verbal exercise. Folk dances involve a physical response to oral commands.

Pantomime makes the spectator guess what the performer is doing and thereby ties the word to the act. Choral speech has great value because it offers practice in talking, pronunciation, and interpretation. It is, in addition, an enjoyable exercise that does not single out the less able speaker.

Creative drama with bilingual children does not differ from creative drama with other groups except in the matter of vocabulary. The most common error in dealing with these children is underestimating their ability and overestimating their verbal skill. If given very short but interesting activities, they can be successful and thus improve their self-image.

One gifted young drama teacher, whose work with a bilingual sixth grade I observed recently, used television commercials as assignments. Each child wrote and performed a commercial for a well-known product. These skits were clear, brief, and, in some cases, humorous; in every instance, they were within the capabilities of the youngsters, who enjoyed creating and improvising them. An activity of this kind can be done on almost any level and can be assured of being understood. Incidentally, a few bilingual plays have been written and published. The play *¡Zas!* by Virginia A. Boyle incorporates English and Spanish in the dialogue.[8] This is an example of one approach to language learning through theatre.

A particularly interesting experiment, for nonachieving children in San Antonio, was originated by Jearnine Wagner of Trinity University. Called Learning about Learning, it is based on a philosophy of the consideration of the whole child—at school, at home, at church, in the neighborhood. Federally funded, a staff of 25 worked for two and a half years on a special curriculum directed primarily at the fourth, fifth, and sixth grades. Special books relating to the child's world were written and used to stimulate his or her interest in self, problems, and others. The first objective was to develop a more positive attitude. This accomplished, the child was free to learn, and an exciting program of community-oriented activities was set up. Creative activities, including drama, formed an important part of this curriculum, which was aimed at helping children to discover who they were and to value this discovery.

Because of the emphasis on the urban child, there has been less recognition of the disadvantaged rural child. In working with both urban and rural children, experienced teachers urge beginning with children's own experiences and interests rather than forcing preconceived ideas on them. Encouragement of their efforts helps build confidence and motivation to explore new ideas and new interests.

[8] Virginia A. Boyle, *¡Zas!* (Chicago: Coach House Press, 1980).

The Problem Group

Occasionally, a teacher has a group composed of hyperactive or simply tense, overstimulated children, who can pose a problem for the leader. These children may not be termed special, but they are difficult for the inexperienced teacher or the teacher who is used to an average class. What to do when your usual procedures do not work? when the group cannot be assembled? when the children lose interest quickly or cannot handle the freedom of creative drama? I am convinced that the best methods come through trial and error, which varies with the individual. But here are a few suggestions that I have found to work successfully with problem groups.

1. Find out all you can about the children. If the group numbers more than 12, see if it can be split into two groups, each meeting for half the allotted time. Sometimes the art or physical-education teacher is glad to help in this way.
2. Establish clear-cut boundaries of space and freedom. If you are meeting the class in a large or all-purpose room, set up boundary lines with chairs. These chairs are not to be moved.
3. Give children the magic command "Freeze!" whenever you want them to stop moving or talking and to listen. This works well with most groups, provided the word is not overused.
4. Keep your directions clear and to a minimum. Too much talk on your part will turn them off.
5. Have definite plans for the day, with alternative plans ready in case the first fail to capture the interest.

Now you are ready to start, and Activity 10.3 suggests a few methods to focus the children's attention.

SUMMARY

This chapter has dealt with the subject of the special, or exceptional, child in the most cursory way, and it is hoped that teachers of any handicapped group or of a class in which there is a child with a handicapping condition will avail themselves of the growing literature in the field. Each condition cited merits a book in itself. The purpose of discussing them here is to:

1. Raise the consciousness of the teacher in order to make him or her become more aware of the needs of the disabled or special child in the group.

2. Offer encouragement to try creative drama and puppetry with disabled children.
3. Give an introduction to some of the materials in the field.

A practical starting place for the beginner is with assessment—of oneself, of existing programs, and of the facilities that are available.

The exceptional child, regardless of the condition that sets him or her apart, suffers isolation and unhappiness. Life is said to be dependent on one's social network,[9] which in the case of the exceptional child is all too often lacking. Social isolation is defined as nonparticipation in activities that require interpersonal contact. Drama is an ideal way to meet and work with others and to establish interpersonal relationships through a shared interest.

The exceptional child merits individual attention, and each teacher knows the capabilities as well as the disabilities of the various children in the group. We are not discussing here the special-services school; we are, rather, concerned with the exceptional child in the regular classroom and the ways in which creative-drama techniques can be utilized to meet his or her needs and potential. Although unable to do everything that the normal child does, the exceptional child can do some things well, and from this experience can move forward, thus gaining pleasure and a sense of accomplishment. One successful teacher stresses *listening* as the first and most important element of the teaching process. What is the child trying to tell us? What is unspoken and why? Important cues are there to be picked up by a sensitive ear.

Every teacher recalls with clarity those disabled children and college students who have been able to meet the challenge of learning and succeed beyond all expectation. The child with muscular dystrophy who participated in the enactment of an Indian legend by sitting around an improvised campfire with the rest of the braves. The boy with the broken leg who beat a drum because he could not walk, yet was able to lead the group. The child labeled "slow" who memorized a lengthy part in a play although she was failing in her academic work; after that, she improved in all areas—was it, perhaps, because of increased self-confidence?

Not all will attain this degree of success, but all can achieve in some measure if we hold the belief articulated by Emily Gillies in an article describing the Institute of Physical Medicine and Rehabilitation in New York: "Here is a child's world where we can concentrate on the abilities, not the disabilities, which brought him here. Hopefully, if given enough

[9] Joseph Zubin, *Aging, Isolation and Resocialization* (New York; Van Nostrand–Reinhold, 1980), p. viii.

sense of accomplishment, he can come through to a discovery and recognition of himself as a person."[10]

The classroom teacher does not presume to be a therapist, but by knowing the exceptional children in the class—their problems and needs—the teacher may apply the techniques of drama to effect growth, strengthen abilities, and build a more positive self-concept. Moreover, the teacher can work with the therapists to their mutual benefit. These are our goals.

[10] Emily Pribble Gillies, "The Katherine Lilly Nursery School," *IMPR* 2, no. 3 (1962):11.

ACTIVITY 10.1

ADDING TO THE ACTION

A good exercise for any group of children but particularly good for the disturbed is "Adding to the Action."

Objective: To focus attention

Suggestions for the Teacher

One child begins a pantomime. This might be a person shoveling snow. Another child, who knows what the first child is doing, steps up and joins in. The second child may also shovel snow or do something that relates to it. The pantomime is kept up until the whole group has entered into the activity, one at a time. This is an excellent means of focusing attention and assisting each child to "join" the group in a natural and logical way. If the class is large, two smaller groups can be formed, each taking a turn at the same exercise.

Another suggestion is a variation on the old game of statues. One child comes into the center of the room and strikes a pose. She freezes as another person joins her. Each one stays in a pose until the entire group has come together, forming a large sculpture. This exercise is not drama therapy but is pantomime with possible therapeutic benefits, inasmuch as it encourages both observation of others and movement that relates to others.

ACTIVITY 10.2

MAKING A MACHINE

"Making a Machine" is the popular *machine theatre game,* which is particularly appropriate for the child who has difficulty focusing attention or is disturbed. It is more distanced than "Adding to the Action" because it does not involve human beings or human activities.

Objective: To focus and hold attention as the team constructs an entity

Suggestions for the Teacher

First, decide what kind of a machine to make—an ice-cream maker, a corn popper, a gum-ball machine.

Then one child goes into the center of the room and starts a motion in space. He or she is followed by another child, who adds an appropriate motion to it. Then a third child joins in.

This can continue until the machine is considered complete. If the class is large, it is a good idea to divide the group into subgroups of five or six, each of which has an idea for a machine.

ACTIVITY 10.3

PREPARING FOR GROUP WORK

Objective: ***To help children function as a group so that they can work on a project together***

Suggestions for the Teacher

Find out what most interests the children. Is it art? music? gym? This will help you in your selection of material.

Find a strategy to get and hold their attention. Until you do, you probably will not be able to conduct a lesson of any kind.

Start the session with movement—big, vigorous movement to stretch tense muscles. Then move quickly to another activity. If you play a guitar and sing, you can get the group to sing songs that they know and like; or, if a new song, something they will respond to and find easy to learn.

Some leaders start with a game: Simon says, blindman's buff, imitate a motion and pass it on. When you sense the children's readiness to do something more serious, tell them a story. Again, be sure that it is a simple story that they know and like. For very young children, "The Three Billy Goats Gruff" or "The Three Little Pigs" is good for creative playing. Have them act it, using music or drumbeat as they cross the bridge.

If the activity holds their interest, suggest that they might want to make paper-bag masks of the various characters. For "The Three Little Pigs," get large cardboard cartons from the custodian for the pigs' houses. The boxes can be painted to look like straw, wood, and brick, or they can be used just as they are.

Varied activities are better than is a complicated story for children whose attention span is short. Above all, remember that these children need structure. Unless there are serious problems, in time they will develop the self-discipline needed for creative work. Then you can push back the boundary lines and expect more of the group. For the present, however, start where the children are. Your objective right now is to help them achieve a focus and work cooperatively on a project to its completion.

11

GOING TO A PLAY

Playgoing is popular with children of all ages, but it has a special significance for those in the lower grades. It may be regarded as an occasional treat, enjoyed solely for its entertainment value; or it may be a richer experience, depending on its presentation and extension. Many 6- and 7-year-olds have never seen living theatre. They have been exposed to television since infancy, but live actors, performing a play on a stage in front of an audience, may constitute a brand-new experience. For that reason alone, we want the experience to be a good one. To ensure this, there are several important considerations to keep in mind.

First, there is the script. Is it of superior quality and appropriate for the age level of the audience? Second, is the play being performed by a good company of actors, either professional or amateur? It makes no difference whether the cast is a professional touring company or a group of students from the local high school or college, as long as the actors treat the material with care and the young audience with respect. Third, does the mounting—scenery and costumes—enhance the play? It need not be elaborate, but it should add to the overall impression. Finally, is the performance to take place in a room or an auditorium where every child can see and hear well? Inability to see the stage or hear the dialogue causes restlessness and discipline problems. What is worse, the magic of the theatre is lost for the young spectator, who is frustrated in his or her efforts to follow the story.

To appreciate theatre, it is necessary to understand the similarities and differences between it and film and to recognize the values of each. The accompanying chart shows the major components of the performing arts and the ways in which each of the three media handles them.

In schools where a video camera is available, drama sessions can be taped, affording advantages to both teachers and students. Video gives children the fun of seeing their own work; and it enables teachers to review sessions and thus evaluate progress throughout a semester. Comparing early and later sessions is often an eye opener that is possible only when performances are recorded.

The video presentation is also an excellent way to demonstrate the differences between live theatre and a performance shown on a screen. At no time, however, should it become so important that young "stars" are created. A relaxed, easy use of the equipment is far better than an emphasis on making a film.

	Theatre	*Film*	*Television*
Content	Dramatized stories, theatre-in-education programs Musicals and plays with music	Dramatized stories Documentaries Educational films	Dramatized stories Documentaries Serials Cartoons and animations
Actors	Live performers Small casts, performing on a stage or in a special area	Filmed performers Large casts, often crowds	Filmed performers, taped or live for the camera Casts smaller than for film but larger than for stage play
Structure	Play is divided into acts and scenes; length is from 30 or 40 minutes to 2 hours with an intermission	Play flows without intermission; length is from 60 to 90 minutes (occasionally longer)	Program is interrupted by commercials; length is from 30 minutes to 1 hour (occasionally longer)
Production	Stage with scenery, costumes, properties, lights, sound effects Performance in a theatre, school, or community center	Large screen with indoor and outdoor settings; can be elaborate because camera is not limited to a small area; play often filmed "on location" in the actual setting of the story	Small screen designed for home use or school room; plays filmed in studio or "on location" depending on story
Values	Direct communication with audience Performance often altered depending on audience and circumstances	Large variety possible, e.g., documentaries and educational films; can be shown repeatedly	Same values as film but programs are seldom repeated ("re-run") and are not usually available for rental or sale

TYPES OF PRODUCTIONS

The two types of productions most often designed for very young children are participatory plays and dramatizations of traditional stories performed on a proscenium stage. There are other kinds of entertainment that are popular with young audiences, however, and a number of types are most likely to be used for kindergarten to third-grade audiences.

Participatory Play

The participatory play is performed in the round in an all-purpose room or gymnasium with the audience seated on four sides so that it can become actively involved in the performance. The actors ask the children to help from time to time, either by responding to their questions or by coming into the playing space as fellow actors. Plays of this sort are frequently educational in purpose and are more successful with younger children than with older.

Dramatization of Traditional Stories

The dramatization of traditional stories includes adaptations of popular folk and fairy tales and children's classics. The stories are familiar and well loved, although their stage presentation may be new to the audience. Most companies who offer these traditional plays prefer to act *for* an audience rather than *with* it, regarding the theatre as an art form rather than a means of teaching.

Story Theatre

In story theatre, the actors are usually costumed and either speak or perform in pantomime while a narrator tells the story. There may be musical accompaniment throughout, and the pantomime may approach dance, depending on the interpretation and style of the troupe. Story theatre is a relatively new technique, so no hard-and-fast rules apply.

Puppet Show

Most children have seen puppet shows either on television or on a stage. Therefore, they know what to expect and usually respond enthusiastically to the announcement of a puppet show for assembly or a school field trip.

Children on the Salt River Indian Reservation enjoy a performance. (Courtesy of Lin Wright, Arizona State University; photograph by John Barnard)

Mixed Media

In the context of this chapter, mixed media refers to live actors and puppets performing together. The advantage of combining them is the variation in size that can be achieved. As puppets can range in height from a few inches to several feet, they may represent birds, elves, and giants, with the live actors taking the roles of human beings. These imaginative combinations appeal to audiences of all ages, but they are particularly popular with the very young, whose acceptance of mixed media is unqualified.

Storytelling

Storytelling would seem to need no definition. The reason one is given here, however, is that some modern storytellers perform stories rather than simply sharing a text with listeners. The traditional storyteller avoids any semblance of acting in an effort to stimulate the listeners to imagine the characters and the action. There is a growing trend, however, for the storyteller to dress up, even to change costumes between tales. In keeping with this concept, the modern storyteller often moves about freely, miming the action as he or she describes it and enacting the various roles. The result is a dramatic performance that—carefully planned, memorized, and rehearsed—can be very effective.

Some storytellers add music, taped or played by an accompanist on a piano, a guitar, or drums. One storyteller I know, who is herself an accomplished musician, has a piano on stage, which she plays as she performs. Her material consists of stories from or about classical music; hence her programs are both entertaining and educational. For example, she will tell the story of the "Golliwogg's Cake-walk" from Debussy's *Children's Corner* and then play it; next, perhaps a Mozart minuet, describing the courtly dance and the dancers in their costumes of the period. A piece like Debussy's *La Mer*, with its evocations of the gathering storm and the calm that comes afterward, suggests an imaginative treatment of the music for which she sometimes uses audience participation. The stage is colorfully decorated with toys and dolls, and she wears a floor-length gown.

Other storytellers may dress in the spirit of the material or theme. Peasant costumes, frontier clothes, and holiday outfits appear as frequently as do the quiet, understated garments of the librarian or teacher, who prefers to place the emphasis on the literature rather than on a performance of it. While storytelling in our country is generally thought of as more appropriate for young children, it can easily be adapted to all age levels by a judicious choice of the material.

Mime

Mime, or pantomime, is the art of conveying ideas or telling stories without the use of words. It has become a popular form of entertainment for both adults and children since the appearance of Marcel Marceau on the professional stage, but children find mime particularly engaging. Perhaps this is because expression in movement is so close to their own play that they have no difficulty following it; indeed, they often see at once what adults are slow to grasp.

CONSTITUENTS OF A GOOD PLAY FOR YOUNG CHILDREN

There are four elements to be considered in evaluating a play for a child audience: *plot, dialogue, production*, and *performance*. Let us begin with the script, for the finest production can go only so far unless the foundation is strong.

To begin with, a good play for children from 5 to 8 years of age differs in several respects from a play designed for older children. The scripts

The Little Match Girl: Sara's Dream Lullabye, *written by Xan Johnson, based on a Hans Christian Andersen story. (University of Utah Young People's Theatre; photograph by Robert Clayton. Courtesy of Xan Johnson)*

are generally shorter and simpler in structure than are those written for students in the middle and upper grades. Many of the same stories can be dramatized and produced to appeal to children up to 11 or 12, when there are elaborate costumes and scenic effects. The Rodgers and Hammerstein version of "Cinderella" is an example of a simple, well-known plot given Broadway musical treatment. Most educators lean toward age-level programming, however, despite the claim of some producers that their material will span audiences from the age of 3 to 15. In my experience, only the circus does that successfully.

There are a number of criteria for evaluating plays for the child audience.[1]

1. Is the story suitable for children in grades 1 to 3?
2. Is the story worth telling? Does it have content and meaning?

[1] Adapted from "CTAA Guidelines for Writing Children's Plays." By permission of the Children's Theatre Association of America.

3. Is it entertaining?
4. Does the play develop along clear, dramatic lines: that is, does it have a beginning, a properly built climax, and a satisfying conclusion?
5. Is the story told without interruption or without the introduction of extraneous action or characters?
6. Is it clearly established to which character the story belongs?
7. Is there an opportunity for identification? Usually a play is stronger if the audience can identify with the character to whom the story belongs.
8. Do characters react to one another naturally?
9. Are character and story developed through interaction?
10. If it is an adaptation, are the essential elements of the source material retained so that the audience will not be offended by the change?

Good Plot

Plots for younger children tend to have few complications, a clear story line, and a happy ending. Children of all ages need a leading character with whom to identify. This is especially important for the younger child because of the reality the characters have for him or her. Also, any fear that the story may have aroused must be relieved by the time the play is over. I remember one performance of the Southern folk tale "The Little Rabbit Who Wanted Red Wings," when there were a number of preschool children in the audience. In the scene where the Mother Rabbit did not know her own Little Rabbit with his red wings, some children were visibly upset. A few even cried and were not comforted until the Little Rabbit was finally rid of his wings and taken into his mother's embrace. These children were too young to attend such a play because they were unable to distinguish between real life and fantasy, and it made the identification with Little Rabbit too painful to handle. The story itself was appropriate for the age, but it would have been better told had the storyteller gauged the feelings of the 3- and 4-year-olds and deemphasized the upsetting parts. Although this was an extreme case, it was a clear illustration of the reaction of an immature audience. Some 6- and 7-year-olds are not emotionally ready to deal with material that frightens or upsets them, particularly if they have never seen live actors.

An adaptation of a familiar story must, under any circumstances, retain the basic elements. When children know a story well, they are offended by changes in plot or characterization. They can easily imagine scenes of magic that are technically impossible to create on stage, but they are unwilling to accept the omission of details that they consider important.

Convincing Dialogue

Dialogue should belong, as far as possible, to the period in which the play is set. Current slang and references to modern inventions and events are as out of place as inaccuracies in costumes and sets. Indeed, dialogue not only reflects the style and manners of a particular place, but also enriches the vocabulary of the audience with new words, appropriately used by the actors.

Effective Production

Children love color and spectacle. They are able to imagine costumes and sets if none are used in the production, but this does not mean that a production cannot be enhanced by them. Mounting a full production has many compensations, but it should be prepared as thoughtfully and carefully for children as for adults. Costumes should always be clean and fresh; settings, sturdy and in good condition. "Props," or properties, like costumes and sets, should belong to the period and locale of the story. Plastic baskets, modern toys, American daily newspapers, and the like do not belong in folk and fairy tales, although I have seen all of them used on occasion. Besides being anachronistic, they confuse children whose information is limited; moreover, they actually interfere with the learning that a well-researched play provides.

Some theatre groups prefer the uniform costume: jumpsuits or leotards in front of a plain black or beige curtain. This is effective and acceptable, but when it is the only type of costume children see, they are being deprived of the visual excitement that the theatre can provide.

Lively and Tasteful Performance

The performers bring life to the play and thus have the greatest appeal for a young audience. Their ability to create credible characters and to act with belief and vitality are the two most essential ingredients. Moreover, the actor in a children's play often finds that the physical demands of the performance offer a greater challenge than those found in adult drama. In addition to speech that is clear and audible, the actor must have the ability to sing, dance, fence, juggle, or perform any other skill that the script calls for.

Finally, there is the matter of respect for the child audience. "Playing down" has been all too common in the past, and the worst criticism that can be made of actors in a children's play is that they are condescending. Another thing that bothers children, although they do not understand why, is the "in joke" or deliberate attempt on the part of the actors to amuse the adults in the audience. The children are aware that something is humorous from the laughter around them, but they do not know what it is. This kind of pandering to the adult is inexcusable, for it is bad manners as well as bad taste. Conscientious, intelligent producers will not resort to such appeals to the sponsor for a laugh. While it is true that good children's theatre can appeal to adults, it is not true that all adult theatre will appeal to children. Some does, but not the double entendre.

While teachers ordinarily do not have an opportunity to preview productions that children will see in assembly, their opinion is often sought afterward. This is particularly true when attention has been poor or the audience has appeared to lack interest. The following guidelines were prepared by a committee of the Children's Theatre Association of America as an instrument to use in selecting plays for a showcase of children's entertainment. It is offered here for teachers and administrators, who may find it useful in determining what made for success or failure, and why.

Adapted From

EVALUATION FORM FOR CHILDREN'S THEATRE PREVIEWERS

Designed by Region 2, CTAA

Production title ______________________________

Date Previewed __________ Estimated Number in Audience ____

Name of Auditorium ______________ Seating Capacity ____

Producer ______________________________

(Name) (Address) (Tel. No.)

Note to Previewers: The prime criteria we use in children's theatre are the respect of the production for the audience and of the audience for the production. Does the production present an idea worthy of a child's consideration? Does it do so in a manner that honors his or her intelligence and integrity? Does it evoke his or her honest responses to quality in the theatre?

Report on this form by applying this rating code:

Excellent	Good	Adequate	Fair	Poor	TOTAL:
5	4	3	2	1	

Using the question as a guide, rate each category by the NUMBERS SHOWN ABOVE. Feel free to comment in answer to any specific question and enlarge on it.

1. DOES THE PRESENTATION RESPECT THE AUDIENCE IN THE PLAYSCRIPT?

   ☐ *Content:*
   Is it worth doing?
   Did you feel the children were involved enough to care about the people in the story and what happened to them?

   ☐ *Dramatic Development:*
   Is the story line clear and forward moving?
   Is the piece well paced, or does it drag? (Or is it too hectic?)
   Are suspense and fear relieved and finally resolved?
   Does the play allow for quiet moments?

   ☐ *Dialogue:*
   Does the vocabulary, which is essential to the comprehension of the plot, come within the range of the audience?
   Beyond that, does it offer enrichment?
   Is the dialogue suitable to the style and mood of the piece?

   COMMENT:

2. DOES THE PRESENTATION RESPECT THE AUDIENCE IN THE PRODUCTION?

   ☐ *Direction:*
   Is stage business pertinent to the situation and style? (Or is it inserted for its own sake?)
   Does the director have a point of view through which he or she unifies the elements of the play?
   Is the physical movement in keeping with character and style?
   Does the director achieve an ensemble performance?

   ☐ *Mounting:* (Costumes—Scenery—Lighting—Music)
   Are settings and costumes expressive of the style, the characters, the locale, and the period?
   If there is available equipment, is the lighting also consistent?
   Are settings and costumes fresh looking and attractively executed?

☐ *Acting:*
Do you believe the actor in his or her character? in relation to the style of the piece? (Or does he or she ever step out of character?)
Is there a sense of joy in the performance? (Or is it flat?)
Is dialogue well spoken (Voice? Diction? Interpretation?)
Are songs and dances well performed?
COMMENT:

Question: *DID YOU ENJOY IT?* ____________________

VALUES OF SEEING A PLAY

Many of the values of playgoing already have been suggested, but for the sake of clarity, they may be listed as follows:

1. *The pleasure of seeing favorite stories enacted on the stage.* For younger children, this is probably the greatest value, at least as far as they are concerned.
2. *The opportunity to learn new words and their meanings from hearing them in the context of the dialogue.* Children love words and often can be heard leaving the auditorium repeating words and phrases that the actors have used.
3. *Identification with admirable protagonists, both men and women.* The dramatist must be clear about which character the story belongs to, for children identify strongly with the one who interests them most. It is therefore important that the protagonist possess the qualities of character that are valued in our society. Children are impressionable, and through theatre, values can be stressed or taught.
4. *The opportunity to enjoy performance skills.* Performance skills include speech that is clear and audible; music, well played or sung; dances, choreographed and performed by well-trained dancers; and such other skills as juggling, fencing, and acrobatics that the script may call for.
5. *The pleasure of seeing beautiful visual effects.* Although not every play requires elaborate mounting and costumes, many do, and children respond to them with delight. No matter how simplified the production, it can and should be designed so as to give aesthetic satisfaction through the tasteful use of color, design, composition, lighting, and imaginative staging.

6. *The experience of being in an audience.* Going to the theatre is a social experience. It involves being part of a group, sharing a common adventure. For many young children, this may be the first time they have seen a play in the company of many other persons. Playgoing differs in this respect from television watching; children may have to be told about play structure (scenes and acts with no commercials) and what constitutes courtesy toward both the actors and the others in the audience.

7. *Involvement with the players.* This relates to being part of the audience. Another way in which the living theatre differs from television and film is the way the response of the audience affects the performance. Theatre is a form of direct communication; hence the rapport between actor and audience is an essential element. Incidentally, most actors love to perform for young children because of their willingness to suspend all disbelief and accept the characters and story as real.

8. *The opportunity to learn about other groups and cultures.* In plays, we see persons who are different from ourselves. Characters in other lands or living at other times come alive, often making an indelible impression. This is another reason for accurate, respectful portrayals. Far too many stereotypes have been imposed on children before they have even started attending school for us to assume their innocence. The time to correct such images is in the early grades, while strong impressions are still being formed. A stereotype, in which all members of a particular ethnic, racial, or religious group are presented as identical (often, unfortunately, in a denigrating way), is both untrue and difficult to erase later on. Elderly and handicapped persons often have been presented as irascible, even evil, in many children's stories, creating fear and dislike in those who may not know real old or disabled persons who contradict the stereotype.

9. *Strong emotional response.* Because young children believe in the characters, their emotional responses are immediate and strong. The play offers an opportunity for the expression of honest emotions—amusement, anger, fear, anxiety, excitement, joy, pity, and satisfaction. Expressed for the right reasons, these emotions are what Aristotle called the "catharsis" in theatre. As long as fear is relieved and poetic justice is done, the play offers a wonderful opportunity for children to express every human emotion under controlled and wholesome conditions.

10. *A foundation for theatre appreciation.* Good theatre experiences in childhood can lead to lifelong pleasure. The values can scarcely be overestimated. By carefully selecting what children see and orienting them to the experience, we are able to increase these values immeasurably.

PREPARING CHILDREN FOR THE OCCASION

The chances are that the play that children in the first three grades see will be given in a school assembly. The chances also are that it will be a play with audience participation. More and more producers these days are finding this an effective technique for reaching boys and girls in the lower grades. Many companies prepare teachers' packets, which they send to the schools in advance of the performance date. Packets contain information about the program or play, with suggestions about how classes may be oriented to it. If it is unfamiliar material, an introduction to the time, place, circumstance, and plot helps to prepare the prospective audience. If it is a well-known story, a brief review is all that is needed. Today, however, with so many children from different ethnic and racial backgrounds in a class, the teacher cannot take it for granted that every child is familiar with the same folk tales and legends. Some producers are beginning to choose stories from the Spanish culture, with which American children, brought up on the traditional folk and fairy tales of England and Germany, are unfamiliar. Because young children respond most readily to the stories they know, telling them the plot in advance increases their enjoyment.

Theatre Participation

If the play is to be done with full audience participation, additional preparation is necessary. Most companies handle this aspect themselves by offering to come into the classrooms in advance to talk to the children and explain the parts they will be asked to take in the performance. The actors may even rehearse the children in those scenes. The children may participate by singing, making appropriate sounds and motions when asked, or actually coming into the playing space to engage in certain actions with the cast.

The best audience participation is achieved in a large room, where the children can be seated on the floor on three or four sides of the players. Entrances are marked off on the floor with masking tape or chalk, and the audience is warned to keep these avenues open. When the children are needed, they are called or brought in by the actors. Occasionally, a child will not want to take part and should not be coerced. In time, he or she will feel ready to join in. The primary aim of participatory theatre is involvement, but the shy youngster will not become involved under protest.

Whether participating vocally, physically, or verbally, most children enjoy being spectators and participants in the same production. The play makes a deeper impression on them because they have "learned by doing," a sound educational principle. While the classroom teacher handles the first part of the orientation, the actors usually take over before and during the performance; many will come into the classrooms following the performance, if they are asked to do so.

When the play is given on a stage, the situation is quite different. Help from the audience sometimes is invited, but it can, of necessity, only be token, for it is too difficult to get children out of their seats and up on the platform for many to take part. The ideal participation includes the entire audience; the less singling out of individual children, the better. This is why many producers who use participation request an audience of no more than 200 persons.

Theatre Manners

One aspect of theatregoing that must be mentioned is manners. Accustomed to television, with its frequent breaks for commercials, children must be told that the theatre makes certain demands on the audience so that all can see and hear well. A good audience member:

1. *Does not talk aloud or annoy others.* Once seated, the members of the audience should refrain from whispering, standing up, or walking out without permission. When children can see and hear well, this rarely happens.

2. *Does not bring food into the auditorium.* Many schools bar eating in the auditorium or gym, a rule that makes the situation easier for the classroom teacher to control. Candy, gum, potato chips, and other

A member of the audience meets an actor following a performance. (Courtesy of Sunna Rasch, Periwinkle Productions, Inc., Monticello, New York)

foods interfere with attention in addition to causing clutter on the floor. The practice of eating while watching television has cultivated a habit that should be discouraged in the theatre. Eating should take place before or after the performance, but never in the auditorium or during a performance.

3. *Does not run around the auditorium during the intermission.* An intermission need not be a trying period for teachers and ushers, if its purpose is explained. It is a time to move and stretch, to go out for a drink, or to use the rest rooms while scenery is being changed. Some producers are afraid of intermissions, but I have never seen one misused when the play held the interest of the audience.

4. *Does not destroy printed programs.* Some companies provide printed programs. This is a theatre convention that children should understand. Programs are not to be made into airplanes or balls and thrown around the auditorium. If children are too young to read them, they should be kept for the suggestions they often include as to activities to try at home or in class after seeing the play.

5. *Waits for applause and curtain calls.* These are theatre conventions. Applause is our way of thanking the actors for the good time they have given us, and curtain calls let us see the actors as people instead of as characters in the play.

6. *Leaves the auditorium in an orderly manner.* Putting on coats, getting up before the curtain comes down, slamming seats, and running noisily up the aisles are bad manners. If children understand this, the majority of them will wait till the lights in the auditorium have been turned on, and it is time for the audience to go home.

Some casts make a practice of meeting the children in the lobby on the way out, and most youngsters enjoy this. I have mixed feelings about the practice, for it removes the mystique that the cast has taken pains to establish. But young children like seeing the characters at close range, and any lingering fears they may have are dispelled when they see that the witch is really a nice person after all. She may even be young and pretty!

Although carrying on conversations during a play has been mentioned as inconsiderate, this does not mean that an audience should observe total silence. Indeed, it is a pity when children are made to think they cannot utter a sound throughout the entire performance. There is nothing wrong with laughter, cheers, even calling out spontaneously to the actors when the comments are appropriate; an experienced cast can handle such responses, and most actors enjoy having this relationship with the audience.

THE FOLLOW-UP

Although follow-up activities are not necessary, they do enhance the experience and stimulate further learning. Older children, interested in the problem or conflict posed in the play, usually want to begin with discussion. After that, they will move on to further study or some creative expression. Younger children are more likely to be stimulated to immediate action: reenacting a scene that has amused them, drawing or painting pictures, repeating new words they have heard, or trying the steps of a dance. I remember after a matinee of *Mummenschantz* (a revue by a Swiss dance and mime troupe of the same name) in New York, the youngest members of the audience could not wait to get out of the lobby before trying some of the movements. Parents and teachers were literally picking children up off the floor so that other persons, amused at the situation, could get by. When I saw the troupe again several months later, it had incorporated this response into the matinee and was working creatively with children in the aisles and lobby during the intermission.

As in all teaching, we are most successful when we begin where the children are, following their lead before making suggestions as to how else their interests might be expressed.

An old-fashioned but still worthwhile activity is writing letters to the cast. This should not be imposed on children as a laborious assignment, but when it represents an honest expression of appreciation, it is an outlet for feelings, a courteous act, and a valid exercise in writing. Actors, incidentally, love the letters children write and often keep them in their scrapbooks.

Painting or drawing pictures of the play is another favorite activity. Teachers and actors are often astonished at what the children recall having seen. After viewing a play where little or no scenery was used, some children imagine an elaborate setting and paint it in colorful detail. I have seen pictures of castles and forests, although the play had been performed on a bare stage before curtains, and elaborate costumes, although the actors had appeared only in leotards. This is a tribute to the performers, who succeeded in giving the play reality, and to the children, who created through their imagination what was not physically there.

Creative drama is usually the most popular reaction to a play, and it can occupy children for many happy class hours. When they eventually tire of repeating scenes from that play, they will be ready to enact others and perhaps even make a play of their own. This is an ideal way to guide a class in creative drama.

Creative writing is often stimulated by creative playing and is even taught through it by some teachers. Poems and original stories by second and third graders are not uncommon after the children have seen plays that have stirred their feelings.

One final cautionary note. Preparatory and follow-up activities should increase the enjoyment of theatre, not detract from the performance. They should never come across as hidden methods of teaching or testing for right and wrong answers. When children feel that a play has been used for means other than enjoyment, they may be turned off and the entire experience, devalued. Teachers who are unsure as to how far to go in extending the play are always safe if they remember that "less is more." In time, they will sense the direction of the children's interest and can do their part to help make these first theatre experiences of young children some of the richest and most memorable of their lives.

SUMMARY

Playgoing has values for children of all ages, but for the younger child its greatest value may be an opportunity to experience the actor–audience relationship for the first time. Many children in the elementary grades know only television. They have never experienced the living theatre, in which the audience is an element of the performance. Writers of participatory plays recognize this and write scripts that involve the spectator intellectually, emotionally, verbally, and physically.

The best theatre on any level offers both entertainment and substance. This is not meant to imply that a play written and produced purely for entertainment is inferior or that the script that delivers a message is necessarily dull. There is a place for each, so long as the performers are skilled, the production is directed and designed with care, and, in the case of the educational program, the issue or subject is worthy of attention. The major values, however, are those discussed in this chapter:

1. The pleasure of seeing favorite stories on the stage
2. The opportunity to learn new words in the context of stage dialogue
3. The opportunity to identify with admirable protagonists
4. The opportunity to enjoy performance skills
5. The pleasure of seeing beautiful visual effects
6. The experience of being a member of an audience
7. The excitement of becoming involved with the players

8. A chance to learn about other groups and cultures
9. The opportunity to experience strong emotional responses
10. The opportunity to build a foundation for theatre appreciation

In order to receive the greatest value from a theatrical experience, children should be prepared for the occasion. A good orientation stimulates interest and provides information about what the class is going to see. A follow-up period or workshop, provided it is not presented as a lesson or test, helps deepen and enrich the experience. These days most producers send study guides, if they are requested, in advance of a class trip, so the classroom teacher is aided in preparing for and extending the performance.

12
PUTTING IT ALL TOGETHER

Although activities were suggested in most chapters, no step-by-step lesson plans were included. This chapter shows some specific ways in which teachers might approach and guide creative-drama classes, although they soon will develop strategies of their own. Also suggested are extensions of lessons, should themes be relevant to children's interests and concerns. The dynamic quality of drama provides a natural way of exploring social issues and studying curricular material, although it is not necessary to pursue further ends, nor is it always desirable. Teachers will sense how far to carry a lesson, but children's expressed interests usually offer the best guidance.

LESSON PLAN FOR MOVEMENT AND RHYTHMS (CHAPTER 3)

1. One of the first class sessions of the semester may involve movement and rhythms, the primary goal of which is to help children move freely and easily in space. It is hoped that the room will be large enough to permit the entire class to move at one time; if not, divide the class in half and alternate the two groups frequently. In either case, have the children form a large circle so that they have enough room to move without bumping into one another.
   a. Do deep knee bends, touching the floor; then reach up as high as possible—"being tall."
   b. Swing arms forward and backward, first together and then one arm at a time.

   c. Walk, trot, run, gallop, hop, jump, skip—stop with the command "Freeze!"
   d. Lie down on the floor, allowing for plenty of space around each person; breathe deeply, relax, be as quiet as possible.
2. Have the children stand (all should be thoroughly relaxed after moving their bodies) and move for a particular reason.
   a. Move out of the circle and tiptoe to another part of the room so as not to disturb "a sleeping person."
   b. Slide smoothly across the floor as though "moving on ice."
   c. Jump across the room as though taking part in a race with both legs tied together.
   d. Gallop like a herd of ponies on a plain.
   e. Skip like a group of happy children in the playground.
3. Ask each child in turn to start a movement, which the group will follow. This can continue as long as the interest holds, and it combines movement and creativity with observation.

LESSON PLAN FOR THE ENACTMENT OF A STORY (Chapter 6)

1. Start the class with physical warm-ups. Have the children form a large circle. If the class is too large for the space, divide it in half and alternate the two groups so that all have a chance to move often.
   a. Stretch, bend, and sway, using large body movements.
   b. Shake the arms, the hands, the fingers; then drop the head forward and roll it to the right, the back, the left, and up again.
   c. Be trees, swaying as the wind blows, bending as a cyclone hits, drooping in the heat, and reaching up for water as the rains come.
2. Have the children sit on the floor for a discussion of trees.
   a. Describe trees they know—in their yards, on their streets, in the park, in places they have visited.
   b. Show pictures of different kinds of trees.
3. Tell them the German tale "The Fir Tree Who Wanted Leaves."
   a. Talk about how the story might be acted; how to be trees. There are many ways in which this story can be handled. If the group is small, it can be played by individuals. Better, however, is group playing, with some children being the leaves and others being the goats, the wind, and the robbers. In this way, the imagination is stretched as the players experiment with different ways to show how green, glass, and gold leaves might look and move.

b. Improvise the story, scene by scene, changing parts each time the fir tree has a new suggestion. In this way, all the children will have a chance to create dialogue if they wish, although dialogue is not necessary.
c. Play music to create the mood and suggest the changes. This will help the children play the story.

4. After playing the story several times, bring up the theme of discontent. Dissatisfaction with one's lot is a theme that runs through folklore, and it is understood by quite young children.
   a. This discussion may bring out personal attitudes, wishes, and experiences.
   b. Ask for some ideas that the children might like to dramatize on the theme of discontent. The number and quality of the improvisations will determine how much time can be spent profitably on enactment.

THE FIR TREE WHO WANTED LEAVES

There was once a little fir tree who grew tired of his needles and wanted leaves like the other trees in the forest. One day, while he was complaining, a voice answered him, asking what kind of leaves he would like. "Oh, green leaves like the other trees," said the little fir. "I want leaves that are green in summer and change to red in the fall."

No sooner had he asked for them than his needles changed into smooth, bright green leaves. The little fir tree thought he looked very fine indeed. All that morning, he moved his branches and admired his appearance. Then, about noon, along came some goats. Seeing the fresh green leaves, they lifted their heads and greedily began to eat them. The poor little tree could do nothing to stop them, and soon all his leaves were gone.

He felt very bad. Finally, he said, "I wish I had glass leaves. They would be pretty, and no one would want to eat them."

Again, no sooner had he said the words than he found himself covered with sparkling glass. He was greatly pleased. "These leaves are much better than the others."

He moved his branches and watched them sparkle in the sunshine. About noon, however, a storm came up. The wind blew, and the leaves hit against each other. They were so brittle that as the storm grew worse, all the glass was broken and fell to the ground.

The little fir was discouraged, but not for long. "I know," he said, "I'd like gold leaves. They will sparkle, but the goats will not eat them, and they cannot break."

Suddenly, he was covered with yellow gold that gleamed in the sunlight. Surely he was the most beautiful tree in the forest! All day long, he admired his leaves. Then, as night fell, he saw some robbers approaching. When they saw the little fir tree, they could hardly believe their eyes. "A gold tree!" they said. "There's enough gold here to last us for the rest of our lives!"

They began picking off the leaves and putting them in sacks on their backs. In no time at all, every leaf was gone. The little tree stood cold and miserable in the forest.

"I wish," he began, "I wish I had my needles back again. They were the best of all."

Quick as a flash, his branches were covered with long, dark-green needles. And he never wished for leaves again.

LESSON PLAN FOR THE POSSIBILITIES IN POETRY (Chapter 7)

1. You might begin by talking about poetry. What is poetry? What poems do the children know? Can they think of any games they play with chants or verses?
   a. Say the chants and other familiar rhymes and verses.
   b. Suggest making a group poem on spring, fall, winter, snow, kittens, puppies, Thanksgiving, or a similar topic. Each child supplies a line, a phrase, or even a word, which the teacher writes on the board.
   c. Read the poem aloud and then have the class read it together.
   d. Continue discussion on the *feel* of words: their sounds, their meanings, appreciation of the language.
2. If the class is stimulated by the group poem, it is a good time to try writing individual poems. Poems can be illustrated, bringing in another art form.
3. This plan will have occupied two or three class sessions. It is a natural move from here to choral speaking or to improvising with poetry as a springboard.

LESSON PLAN FOR THE DRAMATIZATION OF A STORY

Each story brings its own challenge. Whereas "The Fir Tree Who Wanted Leaves" is static, with the action in the underlying theme, "A Bell for Ursli" is filled with action and offers a wonderful opportunity for the study of another country and its customs.

1. Put pictures and posters of Switzerland on the board so the children can visualize the setting. Switzerland may be more familiar to American children than are many other countries because of television and the fact that it is a favorite ski area.
2. Tell the class the story "A Bell for Ursli."
   a. Discuss how the story might be made into a play, mentioning the main characters, scenes, additional persons, and animals that belong in it.
   b. Have the children try, as a group, "trudging through the snow," "walking up the mountain," "fording icy streams," and "coming down the mountain, carrying a big bell."
3. Review or reread the story and start playing it, one scene at a time. The geography, climate, and customs of Switzerland will become real as they are experienced by being Ursli and his family.
   a. If the class is held in a large room, you have a wonderful opportunity to suggest the distance between Ursli's village and the mountain home. The neighbors' cottages can be located along the sides of the room, and the paths up the mountain can twist and turn through the center.
   b. Some children may want to put on caps, scarves, boots, or down jackets after improvising the story a few times. These are not to be construed as "costumes," but are an indication of the understanding the children have of the cold climate and the needs of the mountain climber.
4. What are the values of enacting "A Bell for Ursli"? I would list them as follows:
   a. The children's acquaintance with a new and worthwhile story.
   b. The experience of projecting themselves into a country and a culture different from their own.
   c. The realization that, despite certain differences, human beings are basically the same everywhere.
   d. The solution of problems involved in playmaking—planning of scenes, climaxes, character development, dialogue.
   e. The improvement of a product through discussion and criticism after each playing.
   f. The fun and discipline of working together on a project.
   g. The ultimate satisfaction of sharing work that, by this time, is as good as they can make it.

A BELL FOR URSLI

It is the custom in some Swiss villages for the children to ring bells one morning in March to call an end to the long winter and herald the coming of spring. One morning, a little boy named Ursli heard that this was the day that Uncle John, an old and beloved neighbor, would be giving out the bells. So he went with the other children to get one. When he arrived, the bigger boys pushed in ahead of him, and all that was left for Ursli was a tiny bell with almost no sound.

Disappointed, Ursli started home. Suddenly, he remembered the great bell that hung in the dining room of his family's mountain home. How could he get it? The house had been closed for the winter. The snow was still lying in drifts, and the streams were frozen. Nevertheless, he started out, making his way up and up to the very top of the mountain. When he finally arrived, he was so tired that he ate some of the hard bread the Swiss keep through the winter, and then he fell fast asleep. During the night, the animals, some deer and a fox, peered through the windows to see who had come to the empty house.

Meanwhile, Ursli's parents were greatly worried and went from cottage to cottage in the village, asking if anyone had seen their son. No one had. By morning, however, Ursli appeared with the big bell he had managed to carry down the dangerous paths over the mountain. His parents warned him never to go there again in the winter weather, but they were so glad to have him safe at home that they did not punish him. As for Ursli, he was just in time to join the other children on the village square, where he proudly rang the bell that he had carried down the mountain all by himself.

LESSON PLAN FOR LEARNING THROUGH DRAMA (Chapter 9)

Although the focus of this book is on drama as an art form, there is also value in using drama as a way of learning in other subject areas. Here a good approach is a topic of study, moving into drama when involvement in the topic clarifies and brings reality to it.

1. An example of a topic that might be handled by young children is a drought. This condition occurs in most parts of the country, and even young children are aware of it. The seriousness, however, can be impressed on them through a study of water and the ways in which we can conserve it.
   a. Discuss water—where it comes from, our many uses of water, how it is purified, and so on.
   b. What happens when there is too little water?
   c. What can we do in times of shortage? in the city? in the country?

   d. Bring in pictures of water supplies: wells, rivers, lakes, reservoirs. Bring photographs of drought conditions if they exist at the time of the study.
2. Suggest situations to be improvised.
   a. Be a family deciding how each member can conserve water.
   b. Pantomime watering a garden, brushing teeth, washing hands, and the like.
3. Develop a class project on "Water—an Essential Resource." This might include a display of photographs, drawings, and improvisations. The children probably will not be enacting a story but will be participants in a real situation, in which they are learning through *being*. (Children in the primary grades obviously cannot be expected to carry the subject into areas of engineering or chemistry, but they can gain an understanding of the importance of water to life. Through drama, they learn ways they can handle the problems of shortage, and they get insights into the problem of drought in other parts of the world.)

ABOUT PERFORMING

The question of performing is bound to come up. Children in the primary grades should not be subjected to the pressures of memorizing dialogue and performing before an audience. The effort to please or impress an audience is inevitably accompanied by competition for parts, long periods of drill, and self-consciousness. I am aware, however, that there is often an expectation on the part of school administrators and parents to view children's work, particularly plays and projects. If the teacher is faced with this situation, I urge as simple a performance as possible.

For parents, a far more desirable way of viewing their youngsters' work is through demonstration, with the teacher offering an oral or written explanation beforehand. This clarifies the learning objectives and procedure. The demonstration is best handled in a familiar location—the classroom or all-purpose room. As for assembly programs, the same approach is recommended, though the performance may have to take place on a stage.

For a more mature group of children who are eager to show their work, performing occasionally is fun and has some positive values. Poise, cooperation with others, and communication can be strengthened when spectators treat the occasion seriously. A small, understanding audience can even enhance the experience, when the occasion is handled with sensitivity and a clear understanding of the goals and expectations appropriate to the age of the players.

Guidelines for the Teacher

Involvement of the entire class. All class members should have some part in the performance—on stage, backstage, or in the auditorium as ushers. In other words, the project should be a group effort rather than a production featuring only a few.

Seating of audience. The spectators should be seated as close to the players as possible so that young voices can be heard easily and the distance between actors and audience is diminished or eliminated altogether.

Dialogue. Dialogue should be improvised, except for such repeated and familiar phrases and words as "Somebody's been sitting in my chair!"

Costumes. "Costumes" should not be used; garments suggestive of the characters are preferable. Shawls, boots, hats, scarves, and aprons are enough to define characters for young children.

Scenery. Scenery should be confined to a few chairs, stools, a small table, a bench, and perhaps a background painted by the children on brown wrapping paper and fastened to the stage curtains.

Properties. Baskets, artificial flowers, and simple, easily obtained items used by the players help to explain action.

Curtain call. If there is a curtain call, all the children should be included: those on stage, those backstage, *and* the ushers.

Announcing the play. For parents, the children could write invitations. This gives the occasion a personal touch, adds an opportunity for written communication, and stresses "showing work" rather than "showing off." Likewise, posters made by the class offer children who enjoy art a chance to contribute to the occasion in another way.

13
PUPIL EVALUATION

AN EVALUATION CHART

While grading children in the arts is to be avoided, a simple check list may be helpful in evaluating growth and development. The evaluation chart on page 000 was designed to show the major areas of concern and should serve as: (1) a guide to the emphases in teaching creative drama; and (2) an aid to the identification of children's individual needs and progress. It is suggested that children be evaluated three or four times a semester in order to note change and improvement.

We do not look for performance skills in elementary-school children, nor expect the level of achievement possible among high-school students. Involvement, sincerity, imagination, freedom of movement, and cooperation with the group are the basic goals in teaching creative drama. Beyond that, vocal expression, vocabulary, and the ability to plan and organize material are important, but they come with experience. The criteria applied to adult actors are inappropriate for children and should not be used. These criteria are audience-centered and therefore do not belong to creative drama, in which the participant is central. Even when children's work is shared with others, the goals remain the same, with the audience prepared for the occasion rather than the players drilled for a performance.

It is suggested that instead of giving children letter grades, teachers use the following three numbers to indicate quality of response in the specific category:

1. Shows good response
2. Is adequate
3. Needs special attention and, perhaps, help

EVALUATION SHEET

Date: ____________________

Students' Names	Listening	Concentration	Response	Imagination	Movement	Verbal ability	Cooperation	Organization	Attitude	Comments
Doe, John	1	2	2	1	3	1	3	1		

Teacher's evaluation of class progress:

Evaluation Key
1. Shows good response
2. Is adequate
3. Needs special attention and, perhaps, help

THE AREAS OF CONCENTRATION

1. *Listening.* Listening is an important skill for hearing instructions, discussing topics in class, responding to questions, and helping to create a climate in which all children can express themselves freely.
2. *Concentration.* The ability to hold an idea long enough to respond thoughtfully or creatively is essential in any discipline. It is particularly important in drama, for a breakdown in concentration on the part of one participant invariably affects the concentration of all. Group work requires the concentrated attention of every member.
3. *Response.* Responses can be varied; the important thing to note is whether or not the child is able to respond physically, verbally, or emotionally to the challenge.
4. *Imagination.* Imagination is the element that distinguishes a response as original, creative, or interesting.
5. *Movement.* Young children tend to be free in the use of their bodies as a primary means of expression. As they grow older, children become more inhibited in their physical responses. Tight, constricted movement suggests self-consciousness or fear. Unlocking the muscles, therefore, helps the performer to express ideas and feelings.
6. *Verbal ability.* The older the student, the greater verbal ability is to be expected. Increased vocabulary and added experience in speaking should improve oral communication. Creative drama offers a unique opportunity to develop this skill.
7. *Cooperation.* Cooperation includes the ability to offer and accept the ideas of others easily and graciously. It is an important part of successful living in a democracy.
8. *Organization.* Planning, seeing relationships, making choices and arranging the components of a project require thought, maturity, and patience. As children work together, they develop the ability to organize materials in such a way as to communicate with others.
9. *Attitude.* Attitude is the feeling or disposition toward the work and the other members of the class. A positive attitude not only enhances the quality of the individual student's work, but also contributes to the combined efforts of the group. A negative attitude, on the contrary, detracts and may even be a destructive force. A *good* attitude, therefore, is the most important element for achieving growth and success.

Although there are other important goals in teaching creative drama, those listed above are the most important in assessing the progress of children in the elementary and intermediate grades or, indeed, of beginners on any level. The evaluation sheet provided here was designed for easy duplication. Teachers may also want to keep brief anecdotal records as well as a check list. The space at the right, marked "Comments," provides for such entries. Specific instances of change, "breakthroughs," or problems can be written here.

"Class progress" is the overall picture of the group at work. In the adult theatre, this often is referred to as ensemble. Ensemble means the quality of work done as a group rather than by individual actors. It is not developed in a day or a week; after a month or so, a tentative evaluation can be made. This is because individuals develop at different rates of speed, and some have problems that must be resolved before it is possible for them to become absorbed in a group project. An accurate statement of group progress, therefore, cannot often be made until near the end of a semester.

OTHER YARDSTICKS

The best method of evaluating student progress is, of course, personal observation made on a daily basis. These observations lead to the information needed for a check list later on. Because the teacher's attention is on the lesson and the group, however, and because he or she must move on to other lessons, daily rating is impractical and actually undesirable. If there are student teachers in the room, ask them to be responsible for watching responses and variations in behavior from day to day. Should there be more than one student teacher assigned to the class, each can be given a group of children to observe over a period of time. This has two advantages: (1) it is a help to the classroom teacher, freeing him or her for teaching the group; and (2) it sharpens the student teacher's ability to discern growth and development. Again, it must be stressed that teaching comes first and that at no time should evaluation become important to the children or take on the appearance of assigning letter grades. When children try to *please* adults, they lose the most important value of the experience.

Another yardstick, possible in some schools but not in most, is videotaping of the class. This is an ideal way to compare work done at different periods in the semester and to take a second look at a performance that one does not clearly remember. The obvious disadvantage of taping is that when children know they are being filmed, they tend to become self-conscious, thus negating two of our principal goals: sincerity and involvement. Therefore, where videotaping is possible, it is suggested that it not be done until halfway through the semester, by which time the class is comfortable and working easily together. This should make it seem a natural way of recording group work.

To evaluate children's work in any area it is necessary to know the *characteristics, abilities, needs,* and *interests* of the particular age level.

Not that these are present to the same degree in all children, but they serve as guidelines for expectations. Human beings grow at different rates of speed, so there can be no arbitrary rules governing growth and development. Experienced teachers of the primary grades know what these children are like; but for the inexperienced teacher or one working with drama for the first time, an explanation may be helpful.

DEVELOPMENTAL CHARACTERISTICS OF CHILDREN IN THE PRIMARY GRADES

Characteristics of the First-Grade Child

Physical. Energetic, alert, active; responds with the entire body; enjoys frequent change of activity and position; needs quiet time after active periods; follows rules of the game

Mental. Capable of reproductive images and concrete operations as well as movement for its own sake; has ability to think independently; short attention span; is curious and investigative; enjoys symbolic play

Social. Begins decentering in cognitive and social areas; likes to be with other children of the same age; has strong feelings and is expressive; must learn to take turns

Interests. Family, home, local activities, and occupations; toys, animals, machinery; holidays and field trips

Activities. 15 to 20 minutes recommended; rhythms, imitative movements, and simple pantomimes; likes to enact short verses and nursery rhymes; favorite stories often played many times; should work in large groups rather than individually; enjoys having the teacher participate with class

Characteristics of the Second-Grade Child

Physical. Enjoys using the entire body; active, eager to participate; improved coordination and better control of small muscle movements than the 6-year-old

Mental. Is moving from concrete thinking to more conceptual mode of thought; vocabulary is expanding; developing critical ability; enjoys short discussion periods; creates anticipatory images as well as reproductive images

Social. Greater enjoyment of other children; more socialized and more independent

Interests. The community; holidays, guessing games, and riddles; animals; stories, both familiar and new

Activities. 30-minute periods of drama recommended; enjoys dramatizing stories and poems; likes fairy tales and fantasy; "Show and Tell" is a favorite activity; easily stimulated and can work in groups of two, three, or four as well as in large groups; enjoys pantomime

CHARACTERISTICS OF THE THIRD-GRADE CHILD

Physical. Developing well-coordinated movements; likes to run, jump, skip, gallop, and dance; noticeably finer development of small movements

Mental. Capable of critical and evaluative observation; able to organize ideas more quickly and clearly; plans scenes and sequences with ease; enjoys humor

Social. Strong sense of justice and fair play; often cites the moral of a story or fable; follows directions and works well with peers.

Interests. Interests broadening to include other peoples and other lands; interested in fantasy, royalty, folk and fairy tales, but moving toward stories of the here and now

Activities. 30 to 45 minutes recommended; enjoys challenging work on literature, projects, and exercises; will bring in relevant materials such as pictures, games, stories, songs, and other items of interest; likes to work on integrated projects involving social studies, literature, and the arts

BOOKS ON CHILD DEVELOPMENT

Bruner, Jerome. *The Process of Education.* Cambridge: Harvard University Press, 1960.

Day, B. D. *Early Childhood Education: Creative Learning Activities.* New York: Macmillan, 1983.

Dittman, L. L., and M. E. Ramsey, eds. *Today Is for Children.* Washington, D.C.: ACEI, 1982.

Flavell, J. H. *The Developmental Psychology of Jean Piaget.* Princeton, N.J.: Van Nostrand, 1963.

Gesell, Arnold, and Frances Ilg. *The Child from Five to Ten.* New York: Harper & Row, 1946.

Hendrick, J. *Total Learning for the Whole Child.* St. Louis: Mosby, 1980.

Maxim, G. *The Very Young Child: Guiding Children from Infancy through the Early Years,* 2d ed. Belmont, Calif.: Wadsworth, 1985.

Maynard, Olga. *Children and Dance and Music.* New York: Scribner, 1968.

Piaget, Jean, and Barbel Inhelder. *The Psychology of the Child.* New York: Basic Books, 1969.

——— and ———. *The Child's Conception of Movement and Speed.* New York: Basic Books, 1969.

Spodek, B., ed. *Handbook of Research in Early Childhood Education.* New York: Free Press, 1982.

GLOSSARY OF COMMON DRAMATIC TERMS

A number of the words listed in the glossary are discussed at greater length in the body of the text. They are repeated here, however, because of their frequent usage in discussions of drama and theatre. Many of the terms will obviously not be part of an elementary-school child's vocabulary, but in the event that they come up in class discussion the teacher will have brief definitions to share at his or her discretion.

Act. To perform or play a role. A division of a drama.

Actor. A person who performs in a play, who assumes the role of a character.

Adaptation. A play based on a story or novel rather than being an original plot.

Aesthetic growth. Development of sensitivity to art and beauty.

Amateur. A person who engages in an art or a sport for love of it, rather than for a livelihood.

Backstage. The area behind the stage, not visible to the audience.

Body awareness. The sense of the body as a means of enjoyment as well as an instrument of communication.

Border lights. Overhead lighting at the front of the stage.

Box office. The office where tickets are sold, located either in or in front of the lobby.

Choreographer. A person who designs and directs a dance.

Choreography. The design for a dance; the written representation of the steps of dancing.

Climax. The highest point of interest, usually near the end of the play.

Comedy. A play that ends satisfactorily for the hero or heroine; it is entertaining and usually lively, as opposed to a tragedy.

Community theatre. Theatre organized and run by persons living in the community; actors generally perform for the enjoyment of the experience rather than as a profession.

Cue. The signal for an actor to speak or perform an action, usually a line spoken by another actor.

Curtain call. The return of the entire cast to the stage after the end of a performance, when they acknowledge applause.

Denouement. The final unraveling of the plot of a play; the solution or outcome.

Dialogue. The lines of the play spoken by the actors.

Director. The person in charge; the one who gives directions to the actors and assumes ultimate responsibility for the production.

Double cast. To prepare two casts for a play, both of which will play the same number of performances.

Downstage. The front of the stage; the area nearest the audience.

Dramatist. Another name for a playwright.

Dramatization. The creation of a play from a story or poem.

Dress rehearsal. The final rehearsal or rehearsals of a play, when costumes are worn and all stage effects are completed.

Entr'acte. A song, dance, or short performance that takes place between the acts, most often in plays of an earlier period, although occasionally in children's theatre; it is designed to entertain the audience while scenery is being changed.

Epilogue. A short scene or speech at the end of the play; it is not often found in modern plays.

Expressive use of the body. Freedom to move so that the body reflects the player's true feelings.

Expressive use of the voice. The ability to speak audibly, clearly, and with color so as to reflect the speaker's thoughts and feelings.

Floodlights. Stage lights that throw a broad beam, as opposed to spotlights.

Footlights. The row of lights across the front of the stage, on a level with the actors' feet.

Hero. The central male character in a play; a man distinguished for valor.

Heroine. The central female character in a play; a woman distinguished for valor.

The house. The auditorium or seating area of a theatre.

Houselights. The auditorium lights, turned off or dimmed when the performance starts.

Imitative movement. Mime or movement that imitates the actions of human beings, animals, or mechanical objects.

Improvisation. A scene created by actors using spontaneous dialogue; the opposite of a memorized script.

Intermission. A recess or temporary stopping of action, usually about halfway through a play.

Lines. The dialogue or words spoken by the actors.

Lobby. The foyer or hall at the front of a theatre.

Mounting. The scenery and costumes used to dress the production.

Musical. A theatrical production characterized by music, songs, dances, and often spectacular settings and costumes.

Pantomime. The expression of ideas through action without the use of words.

Performance. A representation before spectators; an entertainment.

Playwright. A person who writes plays.

Plot. The story.

Production. The total theatrical product, including the play, the acting, the direction, scenery, costumes, lighting, and special effects.

Professional theatre. Theatre in which actors and all other employees earn their living.

Prologue. An introduction to a play, usually spoken by one of the actors; it occasionally is employed in plays for children to orient the audience to the piece or engage its attention.

Prompter. The person who watches the script backstage during the performance of a play; he or she gives the line to the actors, if they should forget.

"Props." The properties or small objects used by the actors.

Proscenium stage. A raised platform at one end of an auditorium with the audience seated out front.

Protagonist. The heroine or hero of a play; the actor who plays the chief part.

Puppetry. An art form in which puppets are the performers. While most puppets are small and resemble dolls, they may be made in any size or shape, so long as they can be easily moved and manipulated.

Rehearsal. The practice or repetition of a play in preparation for public performance.

Resident company. A company of actors who play in a home theatre, as opposed to a touring company.

Rhythmic movement. Movement that follows a rhythmic pattern: marching, folk dancing, repeated movements.

Scenario. The outline or story of a play.

Scene. A location or setting. A division of an act of a play.

Scenery. The large pieces (flats, backdrops, furniture, and so on) that are placed on the stage to represent the location.

Script. The manuscript or form in which the play is written; it contains the dialogue, stage directions, time, and place of each act and scene.

Sensory awareness. A recognition and appreciation of our five senses.

Shadow play. Enactment of a story or role in silhouette behind a screen or sheet. The play may be performed by human actors or puppets.

Soliloquy. Lines in a play, spoken by one character alone on the stage, in which his or her thoughts are revealed.

Spatial perception. A sense of space as related to body movement; something happening or existing in space.

Sponsor. A person or an organization engaging a theatrical company.

Spotlight. A strong beam of light used to illuminate a particular person or area of the stage, as opposed to floodlights.

Stage manager. The person in charge backstage; he or she helps the director during rehearsals and then takes charge backstage when the play is given.

Straight play. A drama without music or dance.

Subplot. A plot subordinate to the principal plot.

Theme. A topic or subject developed in a play; the subject on which the plot is based.

Theme song. A melody used throughout a dramatic presentation; a strain of music that establishes a mood through repetition.

Thrust stage. A stage or platform that extends into the auditorium, with the audience seated on three sides.

Touring company. A company of actors who take their show on the road, as opposed to a resident company.

Tragedy. A play that ends with the defeat or death of the main character; it is based on a serious theme or conflict, as opposed to a comedy.

Understudy. The actor who learns the part of another actor playing a major role; he or she is ready to go onstage should the other actor be unable to perform.

Upstage. The rear of the stage; the area farthest from the audience.

Villain. A character who commits a crime; the opponent of the hero or heroine.

Wings. The side areas of the stage out of view of the audience; the area where the actors wait for their entrances.

BIBLIOGRAPHY

The bibliography is divided into four parts, each of which is divided into categories. Each category of Part One represents a highly selective list of books based on the premise that classroom teachers will want to follow up on some areas but have little time to pursue all of them. Therefore, only the most relevant, recent, and landmark texts are included.

Prose and poetry for creative dramatization are listed in Part Two. This is also a selective list. Stories and poems that I have found particularly successful are included, but there are dozens more that other leaders might choose and that, indeed, I might have included had I not wanted to keep the list to a useful minimum. I have, however, cited a number of collections and anthologies containing a wealth of fine children's literature. Most of them are readily available in both school and public libraries. The folk and fairy tales are found in so many collections that they are listed by title rather than by any suggested source.

Part Three notes films on a number of subjects of interest to creative-drama teachers and students.

A list of mood music is included in Part Four for teachers who have access to record players or who play the piano. The music is grouped according to mood.

PART ONE: BOOKS

Creative Drama

In 1977, the Children's Theatre Association of America accepted this definition of creative drama: "Creative drama is an improvisational, nonexhibitional, process-centered form of drama in which participants are guided by a leader to imagine, enact, and reflect upon human experiences. Although creative drama traditionally has been thought of in relation to children and young people, the process is appropriate to all ages."[1]

Chambers, Dewey W. *Storytelling and Creative Drama.* Dubuque, Ia.: Brown, 1970.

This is an invaluable little book for the teacher, librarian, or group leader who wants to learn something of the ancient art of storytelling. Clear and succinct, it guides selection of material and offers simple techniques for effective presentation.

Fitzgerald, Burdette, ed. *World Tales for Creative Dramatics and Storytelling.* Englewood Cliffs, N. J.: Prentice-Hall, 1962.

In this book, the editor introduces a wide variety of stories not usually found in collections of this sort. She has drawn from the folklore of countries rarely represented in anthologies of children's literature, thus making an interesting contribution to the field.

Heinig, Ruth. *Creative Drama for the Classroom Teacher.* 2d ed. Englewood Cliffs, N. J.: Prentice-Hall, 1981.

Written by an experienced teacher in the field, this text suggests pantomimes, improvisations, songs, and games. They are arranged in order to guide the classroom teacher through simple to more advanced techniques, and each chapter has suggestions and assignments for the college student.

Koste, Virginia Glasgow. *Dramatic Play in Childhood: Rehearsal for Life.* New Orleans: Anchorage Press, 1978.

This beautiful book by a sensitive teacher discusses the values of play for young children. Filled with her observations and anecdotes, the book gives the reader insights and appreciation of dramatic play rather than methodology.

Kraus, Joanna H. *Sound and Motion Stories.* Rowayton, Conn.: New Plays, 1971.

Although not a text, this book shows how sounds and actions can be used to capture the attention and stimulate the imagination of younger children. The reader can learn from the author's inclusions how to handle other material in this way. The techniques are most valuable in classes where space is limited and where children are being introduced to creative drama.

McCaslin, Nellie, ed. *Children and Drama.* 2d ed. Lanham, Md.: University Press of America, 1981.

This is a collection of essays on creative drama written by 20 experts in the field. A variety of viewpoints are represented, and different methodologies are suggested. It is of greater interest to the experienced teacher than to the beginner.

[1] "Terminology of Drama/Theatre with and for Children: A Redefinition." *Children's Theatre Review* 27, no 1 (1978): 10–11.

Nobleman, Roberta. *Using Creative Drama Outside the Classroom.* Rowayton, Conn.: New Plays, 1974.

In this book, the author tells how creative drama may be taught successfully in nontraditional spaces and places. It is as valuable for the teacher as for the leader of community and camp groups.

Schwartz, Dorothy, and Dorothy Aldrich, eds. *Give Them Roots and Wings.* New Orleans, La.: Anchorage Press, 1985.

This is a guide to drama in the elementary school, prepared by leaders in the field and edited by the co-chairwomen of this project for the Children's Theatre Association. Published in workbook form, it offers the classroom teacher goals and dramatic activities with check lists for rating children's development.

Slade, Peter. *An Introduction to Child Drama.* London and Toronto: Hodder and Stoughton, 1976.

All the fundamental principles of Slade's methods are here. Children, if unhampered by adult imposition, can find self-expression and reach toward full human development. It is simply written, short, and to the point and is highly recommended for the beginner.

Van Tassel, Katrina, and Millie Greimann. *Creative Dramatization.* New York: Macmillan, 1973.

Here is a book with special value for the teacher of very young children. Based on sound educational principles, it is a guidebook for the stimulation of creativity through music, mime, movement, and language arts. It is clearly written, presented in an attractive format, and illustrated. The book is highly recommended.

Wagner, Jeannine, and Kitty Baker. *A Place for Ideas: Our Theatre.* Rev. ed. New Orleans: Anchorage Press, 1978.

This unique book describes with appreciation and beauty the theatre in which the authors work. It is not a children's theatre in the usual sense, but a "place for ideas," where the arts can be explored and experienced. Illustrations show children experimenting with color, movement, music, and creative drama. This is less a textbook than an inspiration to others who work with children in the arts.

Ward, Winifred. *Playmaking with Children.* New York: Appleton-Century-Crofts, 1957.

This landmark text by an American pioneer in the field still presents good basic material 30 years after its publication.

Choral Speaking

Brooks, Courtaney. *8 Steps to Choral Reading.* Claremont, Calif.: Belnice Books, 1983.

This is a simple introduction to choral speaking, giving clear instructions as to how to proceed, values in its use, and a number of selections for very young children to do. It probably is the best book available for the first three grades.

Rasmussen, Carrie. *Choral Speaking for Speech Improvement.* Boston: The Expression Company, 1942.

———. *Let's Say Poetry Together and Have Fun.* Minneapolis: Burgess, 1962.

These two books are among the best sources for choral speech in the elementary grades. Written at a time when the interest in this art was high, they are still relevant and useful.

DRAMA AS A WAY OF LEARNING

Green, Harriet H., and Sue Martin. *Sprouts.* Carthage, Ill.: Good Apple, 1981.

This is an amply illustrated collection of ideas for use with younger children. It is highly recommended.

Hall, Mary Ann, and Pat Hale. *Capture Them with Magic.* Rowayton, Conn.: New Plays, 1982.

This wonderful and useful collection of ideas will help kindergarten and primary-school teachers enliven classes in language arts and science, encourage reading, and improve self-esteem. Described by the authors as "real life" lessons, they deal with the magic of everyday experiences and activities.

Moffett, James, and Betty Jane Wagner. *Student Centered Language Arts and Reading, K–13.* Boston: Houghton Mifflin, 1976.

Written by two well-known educators, this book is an argument for the use of drama in language learning and comprehension.

Piaget, Jean. *Play, Dreams and Imitation in Childhood.* New York: Norton, 1962.

This landmark work is a study of child development in terms of systematic and representative imitation, the structure and symbolism of games and dreams, and the movement from sensorimotor schemas to conceptual schemas.

Stewig, John Warren. *Informal Drama in the Elementary Language Arts Program.* New York: Teachers College Press, 1983.

This text focuses on the value of drama in the development of language skills. The author deals with the various ways in which the classroom teacher can use movement and improvisation and can evaluate sessions in terms of the language arts. Its greatest value is for the generalist or classroom teacher.

———. *Teaching Language Arts in Early Childhood.* New York: Holt, Rinehart and Winston, 1980.

Although this book is a text on language arts by a specialist in the field, drama is stressed as to its value in English teaching. The author shares his enthusiasm with readers.

Wagner, Betty Jane. *Dorothy Heathcote—Drama as a Learning Medium.* Washington, D.C.: NEA Press, 1976.

The author has followed Heathcote's work for several years, and this text presents a faithful description of the educational philosophy and methods of one of the most influential teachers in the field. It is not a book on creative drama, but rather a detailed analysis of the strategies Heathcote uses to reach her educational and social goals through drama. It is the most thorough description of her work available.

MOVEMENT, MUSIC, AND DANCE

Aronoff, Frances Webber. *Music and Young Children.* Rev. ed. New York: Turning Wheel Press, 1984.

A widely used text for music teaching, this book has much to offer both specialist and generalist in drama. Ways in which music can enrich the lives of children are suggested and explained. It is an excellent resource.

Carr, Rachel. *See and Be: Yoga and Creative Movement for Children.* Englewood Cliffs, N.J.: Prentice-Hall, 1980.

This beautifully illustrated book shows parents and teachers ways of helping preschool-age children develop self-awareness and confidence through Yoga and creative movement.

Dorian, Margery, ed. *Ethnic Stories for Children to Dance.* San Mateo, Calif.: BBB, 1978.

This book includes stories from around the world with suggestions for rhythmic accompaniment on drums and other instruments. Years of experience as a dancer and as a teacher of dance give the author knowledge and insight. The choice of material is a valuable addition to the resources available to teachers in lower grades.

——— and Frances Gulland, eds. *Telling Stories Through Movement.* Belmont, Calif.: Fearon, 1974.

This is an invaluable little book for creative-drama teachers working with young children. The authors bring a rich background in dance, education, and drama to the task, and the result is practical and clear. Creative movement and rhythms are used to tell stories from many lands.

La Salle, Dorothy, ed. *Rhythms and Dance for Elementary Schools.* Rev. ed. New York: Ronald Press, 1951.

This collection of rhythms and dances should be extremely useful to the teacher of dramatic play and creative drama or to the children's-theatre director. It contains movement fundamentals, singing games, and folk dances, ranging from simple to advanced.

Lowndes, Betty. *Movement and Creative Drama for Children.* Boston: Plays, 1971.

First published in England, this practical and stimulating book should find enthusiastic readers in the United States. The author, an experienced teacher, explains the value and use of improvised movement and follows with chapters on body awareness, locomotion, mime, sensory awareness, and creative movement.

Maynard, Olga. *Children and Dance and Music.* New York: Scribner, 1968.

This book includes material not usually found in texts on creative drama. It is a good supplement to any text.

Ravosa, Carmino, ed. *Songs Children Act Up For.* Rowayton, Conn.: New Plays, 1974.

Twenty-two action songs were collected by an experienced teacher and composer for use with children. This is a good but, unfortunately, seldom-used way of stimulating creative drama.

Rowan, Betty. *Learning Through Movement: Activities for the Preschool and Elementary Grades.* New York: Teachers College Press, 1982.

The author suggests ways to use the child's natural movement for the teaching of language, science, numbers, and social studies. Lists of literature and recordings add to its value as a reference book.

Slade, Peter. *Natural Dance.* London: Hodder and Stoughton, 1977.

This book is particularly recommended for the teacher of creative drama. In it, Slade discusses "natural dance," or dance that is improvised, as opposed to formal-dance techniques. It deals with all ages, levels of experience, and levels of ability; the therapeutic aspects of dance are also included.

Puppets and Masks

Brooks, Courtaney. *Plays and Puppets Etcetera.* Claremont, Calif.: Belnice Books, 1981.

This book is designed as a starting point for readers who have little or no knowledge of puppets. Written in a conversational style, the text encourages the inexperienced person yet does not talk down to the reader.

Champlin, John, and Connie Brooks. *Puppets and the Mentally Retarded Student.* Austin, Tex.: Nancy Renfro Studios, 1980.

This book discusses methods of developing literary comprehension with the mentally retarded child. The text shows how to adapt books for telling stories and offers special techniques for utilizing puppets in kindergarten through the sixth grade.

Engler, Larry, and Carol Fijan. *Making Puppets Come Alive.* New York: Taplinger, 1973.

This is a charming and practical text for the beginner of any age. To be used by the teacher, it offers help in making and handling puppets, including experiences to develop the skills needed to produce a show.

Freericks, Mary, and Joyce Segal. *Creative Puppetry in the Classroom.* Rowayton, Conn.: New Plays, 1979.

As the title states, this book gives instruction for using puppets in the curriculum. Its suggestions about inexpensive materials and simple techniques add to its value for the teacher.

Hanford, Robert Ten Eyck. *The Complete Book of Puppets and Puppeteering.* New York and London: Drake, 1976.

This 157-page paperback concentrates on an overview of puppetry—past, present, and future; the tools of the trade; the production; and techniques and tips from the pros. It is an excellent book, written in a clear, definitive style with simple, yet complete instructions on all aspects of puppets and puppet productions.

Hunt, Tamara, and Nancy Renfro. *Puppetry in Early Childhood Education.* Austin, Tex.: Nancy Renfro Studios, 1982.

This is one of the most comprehensive books on the subject. Teachers, librarians, and recreation leaders will find it enormously helpful. It is highly recommended.

Jagendorf, Moritz. *Puppets for Beginners.* Boston: Plays, 1952.

This simple, comprehensive book with attractive illustrations is recommended for school and community use.

Krinsky, Norman, and Bill Berry. *Paper Construction for Children.* New York: Reinhold, 1966.

Masks and puppets are among the many projects described in this book. It is a delightful text with drawings and photographs to illustrate the brief but adequate explanations.

Luskin, Joyce. *Easy to Make Puppets.* Boston: Plays, 1975.

Instructions, patterns, and photographs show how to create 24 puppets: hand, glove, and marionette. It has a simple, attractive format.

McCaslin, Nellie. *Puppet Fun: Performance, Production and Plays.* New York: McKay, 1977.

This text, directed to the child from ages 7 to 10, can be used equally well by the teacher or recreation leader who wants to include puppetry but who has never worked with it. Diagrams and illustrations show the rudiments of making and manipulating hand puppets.

Nobleman, Roberta. *Mime and Masks.* Rowayton, Conn.: New Plays, 1979.

A gifted teacher brings two areas together in this book: mime, which is an actor's tool; and the mask, which is used for dramatic projection. In this text, the performing and visual arts meet.

Peyton, Jeffrey, and Barbara Koenig. *Puppetry: A Tool for Teaching.* New Haven, Conn.: P.O. Box 270, 1973.

Simplicity and economy characterize this 100-page guide to puppetry for the curriculum. Prepared for the New Haven public schools, it is adaptable to other systems and a variety of subject areas.

Renfro, Nancy. *Puppetry and the Art of Story Creation.* Austin, Tex.: Nancy Renfro Studios, 1979.

This guide to story creating with simple puppet ideas has a special section on puppetry for the disabled.

Storytelling

Bauer, Caroline. *Handbook for Storytellers.* Chicago: American Library Association, 1977.

All facets of storytelling are covered: planning, promotion, story sources, multimedia storytelling, and programs. It is a must for all storytellers.

Champlin, Connie. *Puppetry and Creative Drama in Storytelling.* Illustrated by Nancy Renfro. Austin, Tex.: Nancy Renfro Studios, 1980.

This excellent resource for teachers is by one of our best-known puppeteers, who combines her art with education and practical help for the nonspecialist.

Cullinan, Bernice E., and Carolyn W. Carmichael, eds. *Literature and Young Children.* Urbana, Ill.: National Council of Teachers of English, 1977.

This book presents a wealth of ideas for sharing literature with young children, especially the preschool child. It includes an annotated list of "The 100 Best Books and Authors for Young Children" prepared by the Committee on Literary Experiences for Preschool Children of the National Council of Teachers of English.

Ross, Ramon R. *Storyteller.* Westerville, Ohio: Merrill, 1975.

This superb book is on the development of skills in storytelling. Imaginatively and simply presented, it includes ideas on utilizing songs, puppetry, flannelboard, and game exercises to enrich storytelling.

Schimmel, Nancy. *Just Enough to Make a Story.* Berkeley, Calif.: Sisters' Choice Press, 1978.

This small book is filled with good advice for storytellers and is written in a refreshing, personal style. Samples include a finger play, a cante fable (story with a song in it), and a story accompanied by paperfolding.

Theatre for Children

Broadman, Muriel. *Understanding Your Child's Entertainment.* New York: Harper & Row, 1977.

This is the only book that discusses entertainment designed for the child audience in critical terms. The author, a critic, takes each of the performing arts in turn, pointing out common faults and offering guidelines to sponsors and parents. It is an invaluable aid for the adult who is responsible for selecting quality entertainment for young spectators.

Corey, Orlin. *Theatre for Children—Kids' Stuff or Theatre?* New Orleans: Anchorage Press, 1974.

This small collection of articles was written by a publisher and producer of plays for children and young people. A man of taste and judgment, Corey makes his points in a warm and lively style.

Davis, Jed, and Mary Jane Evans. *Theatre, Children and Youth.* New Orleans: Anchorage Press, 1982.

This is a college textbook on the subject, but it is included here for the use of some teachers of older children. Although the focus is on literature and production techniques, the text offers a wealth of information on the art, goals, and values of children's theatre.

Healy, Daty. *Dress the Show.* Rowayton, Conn.: New Plays, 1976.

This superb book on costume is for the teacher, community costumer, or parent faced with having to make and/or make over costumes. Written in a simple, readable style, it shows as well as describes the basic steps involved in this aspect of production. It probably is the best book available for the inexperienced costumer.

PART TWO: PROSE AND POETRY

Anthologies of Children's Literature

Arbuthnot, May Hill, ed. *The Arbuthnot Anthology of Children's Literature.* Rev. ed. Glenview, Ill.: Scott, Foresman, 1961.

This anthology contains the three classic Arbuthnot texts for children's literature: *Time for Fairy Tales, Time for Poetry,* and *Time for True Tales and Almost True*. Not all the stories and poems lend themselves to dramatization, but many do and many of the poems can be used for choral speaking.

——— et al., eds. *Children's Books Too Good to Miss.* 7th ed. Cleveland: The Press of Case Western Reserve University, 1980.

Here is a treasury of materials for the elementary-school classroom. Poetry, stories, biography, as well as study guides and explanations of literary and other items make this a useful and authoritative source.

Butler, Francelia, ed. *Sharing Literature with Children.* New York: Longman, 1977.

This well-known anthology is divided in a unique way: "Toys and Games," "Fools," "Masks and Shadows," "Sex Roles," and "Circles." The editor has included material for all age levels and provided a rich resource for the teacher to tell, read aloud, and use in creative playing.

Ciardi, John. *I Met a Man.* Boston: Houghton Mifflin, 1961.

These amusing verses for children, written by a well-known American poet, are useful for both creative drama and choral speaking.

———. *The Man Who Sang the Sillies.* Philadelphia: Lippincott, 1961.

Here is another collection of amusing verse for both younger and older children.

Cole, William, ed. *Poem Stew.* New York: Harper & Row, 1981.

Fun for children, this collection has over 50 poems for reading and dramatic enactment.

cummings, e. e. *Poems for Children.* New York: Liveright, 1983.

These 20 poems offer an introduction to the poet's work and provide an avenue to other modern experimental forms.

de la Mare, Walter, ed. *Come Hither: A Collection of Rhymes and Poems for the Young of All Ages.* New York: Knopf, 1957.

This collection of over 500 traditional poems with notes is interesting to children of all ages.

Fargeon, Eleanor. *Eleanor Fargeon's Poems for Children.* Philadelphia: Lippincott, 1951.

Some of these favorite poems by a well-known poet are good for dramatization and many, for choral speaking.

Fisher, Aileen. *Out in the Dark and Daylight.* New York: Harper & Row, 1980.

Selections from Aileen Fisher's books are compiled in a collection that is varied and representative of her work.

Fitzgerald, Burdette, ed. *World Tales for Creative Dramatics and Storytelling.* Englewood Cliffs, N.J.: Prentice-Hall, 1962.

This is a splendid collection of folk tales from around the world, many of which are little known.

Georgiou, Constantine. *Children and Their Literature.* Englewood Cliffs, N.J.: Prentice-Hall, 1969.

An excellent resource for teachers of all grades, this book treats the history and criticism of children's literature; divisions, genres, and analyses of old and new books. It includes extensive lists of stories for primary, intermediate, and upper grades.

Gruenberg, Sidoni M., ed. *More Favorite Stories.* Garden City, N.Y.: Doubleday, 1948.

This old but still good collection for primary and intermediate grades usually is available in public libraries.

Hopkins, Lee Bennett, ed. *The Sky Is Full of Song.* New York: Harper & Row, 1983.

This anthology of short poems arranged according to the seasons is particularly appropriate for the primary grades.

Jennings, Coleman A., and Aurand Harris, eds. *Plays Children Love.* Garden City, N.Y.: Doubleday, 1981.

This is an excellent collection of plays edited by two of our best-qualified practitioners: a child-drama specialist and a leading children's playwright. In the first part are plays for children to enjoy as spectators; in the second part are plays for older children to perform. The latter are shorter, making them practical for children to memorize and produce.

Johnson, Edna, Carrie E. Scott, and Evelyn R. Sickles, eds. *Anthology of Children's Literature.* Boston: Houghton Mifflin, 1948.

This classic text, still available, is filled with selections arranged according to subject matter and age level. Sections include fables, folk tales, myths, nature stories, travel, biography, literary fairy tales, and poetry.

Kase, Robert, ed. *Stories for Creative Acting.* New York: French, 1961.

Although compiled in 1961, this selection is well worth having in the library, for it includes stories used and recommended by leading creative-drama teachers. Many of them would be included today, if another such book were being assembled. The editor was a leading figure in the field and still devotes much time to drama/theatre, but with senior adults.

Lear, Edward. *A Book of Nonsense.* New York: Viking Press, 1980.

This collection of the poet's amusing limericks is always fun and good for all ages.

McCord, David. *One at a Time.* Boston: Little, Brown, 1977.

A collection of the poet's most popular work, this book is most useful to teachers of intermediate grades.

Mayer, Mercer. *A Poison Tree and Other Poems.* New York: Scribner, 1977.

For intermediate grades, these verses express children's feelings: anger, sadness, wishes, as well as less serious themes.

Merriam, Eve. *Rainbow Writing.* New York: Atheneum, 1976.

Light, descriptive verses covering a wide range of subjects, most useful on the intermediate level.

Milne, A. A. *Pooh's Library: Now We Are Six, The House at Pooh Corner, When We Were Very Young, and Winnie the Pooh.* New York: Dutton, 1961.

Moore, Lillian. *See My Lovely Poison Ivy*. New York: Atheneum, 1975.

These short verses with appeal for children in grades 3 to 6 are light and amusing.

Morton, Miriam, ed. *A Harvest of Russian Children's Literature.* Berkeley: University of California Press, 1967.

In this comprehensive collection of prose and poetry, the editor has included material for ages 5 to 7, 8 to 11, 12 to 15, and young adults. She has translated some material from the Russian, told some of the folk tales in her own words, and written introductions to each section. A wealth of material is presented for the classroom teacher as well as for the specialist.

Opie, Iona, and Peter Opie, eds. *The Oxford Book of Children's Verse.* New York: Oxford University Press, 1973.

In this classic text, teachers will find a wealth of material, some of which is suitable for choral speaking and creative drama.

Prelutsky, Jack. *The New Kid on the Block.* New York: Greenwillow Books, 1984.

These modern, childlike verses with a sense of humor can be enjoyed by children in lower and middle grades. The book is good for both creative-drama classes and choral speaking.

———, ed. *The Random House Book of Poetry for Children.* New York: Random House, 1984.

A collection of over 500 poems with more than 400 illustrations, this is a valuable addition to the library of books for creative playing. Amusing verse, witty rhymes, and serious poetry are all included in a source book for teachers and creative-drama leaders of children of all ages.

Sawyer, Ruth, ed. *The Way of the Storyteller.* Rev. ed. New York: Penguin Books, 1977.

This well-known book contains ways of telling and choosing stories, stories to tell, and a reading list.

Shedlock, Marie, ed. *The Art of the Story Teller.* 3d rev. ed. New York: Dover, 1977.

This is well-known and still one of the best books on the art of storytelling. In addition to chapters dealing with how to tell stories, it includes 18 selections and a list of others.

Siks, Geraldine Brain, ed. *Children's Literature for Dramatization: An Anthology.* New York: Harper & Row, 1964.

An anthology of poems and stories suitable for dramatization, assembled by a leader in the field. The stories are arranged for younger and older children. The poetry is categorized as "inviting action," "suggesting characterization," or "motivating conflict."

Stevenson, Robert Louis. *A Child's Garden of Verses.* New York: Random House, 1978.

These familiar verses are still interesting to children and good to use for both creative drama and choral speaking.

Viorst, Judith. *If I Were in Charge of the World and Other Worries.* New York: Atheneum, 1981.

The poet gives a variety of children's most secret thoughts, worries, and wishes in this collection. It is perceptive and humorous.

Ward, Winifred, ed. *Stories to Dramatize.* New Orleans: Anchorage Press, 1952.

In this volume, the author includes a rich collection of stories and poems from her own years of experience as a creative-drama teacher. It is arranged for players of various ages and contains material both classical and contemporary.

Annotated Bibliography of Children's Literature

Kimmel, Margaret Mary, and Elizabeth Segel. *For Reading Out Loud!* New York: Dell (Delacorte Press), 1983.

This book shows adults how to enrich children's lives and stimulate their interest by reading aloud to them. The authors explain why it is important to start early and how to do it successfully. The most valuable part of the book is a bibliography in which almost 150 books are described in detail. A long list of titles aids the teacher (or parent) in finding material for all age levels and interests.

Trelease, Jim. *The Read-Aloud Handbook.* New York: Penguin Books, 1982.

The author tells how reading aloud awakens the listeners' imagination, improves language arts, and opens doors to a new world of entertainment. An important inclusion is an annotated list of more than 300 fairy tales, short stories, poems, and novels that the author describes in detail, with suggested age and grade levels.

Traditional and Well-known Stories for Younger Children

Aesop's Fables
"The Elves and the Shoemaker"
"The Gingerbread Boy"
"Goldilocks and the Three Bears"
"Granny's Blackie" (East Indian Tale)
"Hansel and Gretel"
"Jack and the Beanstalk"
"The Lad Who Went to the North Wind" (Norse tale)
"Little Burnt Face" (North American Indian tale)
"Little Freddy with His Fiddle" (Norse tale)
"The Little Rabbit Who Wanted Red Wings" (Southern folk tale)
"Midas and the Golden Touch"
"The Musicians of Bremen"
"The Princess and the Pea"
"The Princess Who Couldn't Cry"
"The Ugly Duckling"

Stories for Younger Children

Bemelmans, Ludwig. *Madeline's Christmas.* New York: Viking Press, 1985.
Bianco, Pamela. *Valentine Party*. Philadelphia: Lippincott, 1955.
Bond, Michael. *A Bear Called Paddington.* Boston: Houghton Mifflin, 1960.
Bulla, Clyde Robert. *The Valentine Cat.* New York: Crowell, 1959.
Charlip, Remy, et al. *Handtalk.* New York: Parents' Magazine Press, 1974.
Collodi, C. *Pinocchio.* New York: Macmillan, 1951.
Duvosin, Roger. *Petunia.* New York: Knopf, 1950.
Flack, Marjorie. *Ask Mr. Bear.* New York: Macmillan, 1932.
Gag, Wanda. *Millions of Cats.* New York: Coward, McCann & Geoghegan, 1938.
Guy, Rosa. *Paris, Pee Wee, and Big Dog.* New York: Dell (Delacorte Press), 1985.

Jaffrey, Madhur. *Seasons of Splendor: Tales, Myths and Legends of India.* New York: Atheneum, 1985.

Jarret, Helen. *Angelo: The Naughty One.* New York: Viking Press, 1944.

Kipling, Rudyard. *Just-So Stories.* New York: Walker, 1970.

Laird, Elizabeth. *The Miracle Child (A Story from Ethiopia).* New York: Holt, Rinehart and Winston, 1985.

Lattimore, Eleanor Frances. *Little Pear.* New York: Harcourt Brace Jovanovich, 1931.

Lawson, Robert. *Rabbit Hill.* New York: Viking Press, 1944.

Lionni, Leo. *Cornelius.* New York: Pantheon Books, 1983.

Lobel, Anita. *King Rooster, Queen Hen.* New York: Morrow, 1975.

Lobel, Arnold. *Mouse Tales.* New York: Harper & Row, 1970.

Lundbergh, Holgar. *Great Swedish Fairy Tales.* New York: Dell (Delacorte Press), 1973.

Lurie, Alison. *Clever Gretchen and Other Forgotten Folk Tales.* New York: Harper & Row, 1980.

———. *Fabulous Beasts: Tales.* New York: Farrar, Straus & Giroux, 1981.

McCord, David. *Take Sky.* Boston: Little, Brown, 1962.

McGinley, Phyllis. *The B Book.* New York: Crowell-Collier, 1962.

Mayer, Mercer. *There's a Nightmare in My Closet.* New York: Dial Press, 1968.

Milne, A. A. *Winnie the Pooh.* New York: Dutton, 1954.

Minard, Rosemary. *Womenfolk and Fairy Tales.* Boston: Houghton Mifflin, 1975.

Paterson, Diane. *If I Were a Toad.* New York: Dial Press, 1977.

Pearson, Susan. *Monday I Was an Alligator.* Philadelphia: Lippincott, 1979.

Rojankowsky, Feodor. *Animals in the Zoo.* New York: Knopf, 1962.

Sawyer, Ruth. *Journal Cake Ho!* New York: Viking Press, 1966.

Sendak, Maurice. *Outside Over There.* New York: Harper & Row, 1981.

———. *Where the Wild Things Are.* New York: Harper & Row, 1963.

Steiner, Charlotte. *A Friend Is "Amie."* New York: Knopf, 1956.

Thurber, James. *The Great Quillow.* New York: Harcourt Brace Jovanovich, 1944.

Travers, P. L. *Mary Poppins.* New York: Harcourt Brace Jovanovich, 1963.

Uchido, Yoshiko. *Sumi's Prize.* New York: Scribner, 1964.

Wilde, Oscar. *Fairy Tales.* New York: Hart, 1975.

Zemach, Margot. *The Little Tiny Woman.* Indianapolis: Bobbs-Merrill, 1965.

Zolotow, Charlotte. *Big Sister and Little Sister.* New York: Harper & Row, 1966.

PART THREE: FILMS

Films and Videotapes

British Broadcasting Corporation (producer). *Three Looms Waiting*, 1972. 52 min., color

Three Looms Waiting shows Dorothy Heathcote, one of the leading British teachers of drama, working with a group of children. An excellent demonstration of her method, this film shows drama as a tool for learning rather than as an end in itself.

Distributed by Time-Life Films, 43 W. 16 Street, New York, NY 10016

Creative Dramatics: The First Steps, 1960. 29 min., color, sound

Creative Dramatics: The First Steps is a vintage film that demonstrates the teaching of creative drama to a group of fourth-grade children. Guided by an experienced teacher, the group moves from the faltering first steps to the creation of a drama.

Distributed by Northwestern University Film Library, 614 Davis Street, Evanston, IL 60201

Everyman in the Streets, 1969. 30 min., color

This film shows creative work in drama by neighborhood children in Brooklyn, New York. It is nontraditional in its approach. The greatest value of the film lies in the encouragement it gives to leaders of after-school and Saturday activity groups working in churches, museums, community centers, and alternative spaces.

Distributed by WNET, 304 W. 58 Street, New York, NY 10019

Feil, Edward (producer). *Aurand Harris Demonstrating Playwriting with Children,* 1983. 24 min., color (¾″ U-MATIC; ½″ VHS; ½″ BETA)

The most-produced children's playwright in the United States demonstrates teaching playwriting to children in intermediate grades. The lesson is interspersed with Harris's discussion of what he is doing and how playwriting strengthens writing.

Distributed by Edward Feil Productions, 4614 Prospect Avenue, Cleveland, OH 44103

Ideas and Me, 1964. 17 min., color

In *Ideas and Me*, children participate in the various aspects of creative drama at a well-known community theatre.

Distributed by Dallas Theatre Center, 3636 Turtle Creek Blvd., Dallas, TX 75200

Irwin, Eleanor C. *Playing: Spontaneous Drama with Children,* 1973. 20 min., black and white

Playing: Spontaneous Drama with Children describes a number of forms of spontaneous drama with primary- and intermediate-grade children. Activities showing creative movement, puppetry, role playing, and improvisation are demonstrated. The nature of creativity, the developmental roots of drama, the importance of impulse control and of impulse expression, the individuality of children and their fantasies, and the value of dramatic play in both cognitive and affective learning are discussed.

Distributed by Eleanor Irwin, Park Plaza, 128 North Craig Street, Pittsburgh, Pa. 15213

One of a Kind, 1978. 58 min., color, sound

Intended for audiences of all ages, *One of a Kind* deals with the relationship between a child and her troubled mother. Through participation in a traveling puppet show, the child is enabled to express her anguish and needs. This powerful film can be used effectively with teachers of special education, creative drama, and language arts.
Distributed by Phoenix Films, 468 Park Avenue South, New York, NY 10017

Theatre for Children: Designing the Setting, 1975. 27 min., color

This is an attractive, informative, and interesting film that shows different kinds of scenery and the criteria used in designing backgrounds for children's plays.
Distributed by University of Southern California, Department of Cinema, Film Distribution Center, University Park, Los Angeles, Calif. 90007

Why Man Creates, 1970. 25 min., color

Why Man Creates is a popular film that seeks to learn about the human need to create. It bears showing more than once.
Distributed by Pyramid Films, P.O. Box 1048, Santa Monica, CA 90406

Puppet Films

Manipulation of the Puppets

Blue Like an Orange, 1966. 25 min., color

Blue Like an Orange is a survey of puppetry as practiced around the world. It is considered to be one of the best of its kind.
Distributed by UNESCO, 345 E. 46 Street, New York, NY 10017

Chinese Shadow Play, 1947. 10 min., black and white

Chinese Shadow Play shows a production of a Chinese shadow theatre in New York City.
Distributed by the Donnell Library, 20 W. 53 Street, New York, NY 10019

Stop-Action Films

Reiniger, Lotte. *Caliph Stork, Carmen, The Frog Prince, Gallant Little Tailor, The Grass-hopper and the Ant, Hansel and Gretel, Jack and the Beanstalk, Puss in Boots, Sleeping Beauty, Snow White and the Seven Dwarfs, The Three Wishes, Thumbeline.* 10 min. each, black and white (*Jack and the Beanstalk* in color)

These films of charming silhouette puppetry are the work of a pioneer Berlin filmmaker of the 1920s. They are outstanding.
Distributed by Contemporary Films/McGraw-Hill, McGraw-Hill Training System, P.O. Box 641, Delmar, Calif. 92014

Trnka, Jiri. *The Hand,* 1966. 19 min., color; *Archangel Gabriel and Mother Goose,* 1965, 28 min., color; *Passion,* 1970, 10 min., color

These films by a Czech filmmaker are outstanding and treat serious modern themes in a sophisticated and compelling manner.
Distributed by Contemporary Films/McGraw-Hill, McGraw-Hill Training System, P.O. Box 641, Delmar, Calif. 92014

PART FOUR: MOOD MUSIC

The following mood music is suggested for creative drama. It is listed in categories, implying different moods and conditions. Many leaders find music a great asset in freeing children and inducing creative movement. All the selections are well known and available. This is by no means an exhaustive list, and many teachers will have ideas of their own.

It is suggested that children first listen to the music, and then either move to it or talk about the feelings it suggests. It often is a good idea to play it a second or even a third time before attempting to do anything with it.

Music Suggesting Activity

Beethoven, Ludwig van.	Sonata op. 10, no. 2 [fourth movement]
Bizet, Georges.	March and Impromptu from *Jeux d'Enfants*
Chopin, Frédéric.	Mazurka in B-flat
Gershwin, George.	*An American in Paris*
Grainger, Percy.	"Country Garden"
Mendelssohn, Felix.	Tarantella from *Songs Without Words* op. 102, no. 3
Paganini, Niccolò.	"Perpetual Motion"
Prokofiev, Sergei.	Symphony no. 1 in D [fourth movement]
Rimsky-Korsakov, Nicolai.	"Flight of the Bumble Bee"
Strauss, Johann, Jr.	"Thunder and Lightning, Galop"
Wagner, Richard.	"Spinning Song" from *The Flying Dutchman*

Music Suggesting Animals, Birds, and Insects

Dvořák, Antonin.	"Legent No. 7"
Grieg, Edvard.	"Little Bird"
———.	"Papillon [Butterfly]"

Respighi, Ottorino. *The Birds*
Rimsky-Korsakov, Nicolai. "Flight of the Bumble Bee"
Saint-Saëns, Camille. *Carnival of the Animals*
Schumann, Robert. *Papillons*
Stravinsky, Igor. Suite from *The Firebird*

Ballads and Folk Songs

Many well-known ballads and folk songs are appropriate for creative drama.

Environmental Music

Britten, Benjamin. "4 Sea Interludes" from *Peter Grimes*
Debussy, Claude. *La Mer [The Sea]*
Delius, Frederick. "Summer Night on the River"
Mendelssohn, Felix. *Fingal's Cave* Overture
Respighi, Ottorino. *The Fountains of Rome*
Smetana, Bedřich. "The Moldau" from *My Fatherland*
Strauss, Johann, Jr. "Blue Danube" Waltz

Happy Music

Dvořák, Antonin. Slavonic Dances
Mozart, Wolfgang Amadeus. Serenade in G [*Eine Kleine Nachtmusik*]
———. Symphony no. 40 in G Minor [first movement]
Nicolai, Otto. Overture to *Merry Wives of Windsor*
Offenbach, Jacques. *Gaité Parisienne*
Rossini, Gioacchino. *La Boutique Fantastique*
Scarlatti, Domenico. Harpsichord sonatas
Schumann, Robert. *Carnaval*
Telemann, Georg Philipp. *Don Quixote*

Lullabies

Brahms, Johannes. "Lullaby"
Godard, Benjamin Louis Paul. "Berceuse" from *Jocelyn*
Grieg, Edvard. "Cradle Song" from *Peer Gynt*
Khatchaturian, Aram. "Lullaby" from *Gayne*

Military Music

Elgar, Edward.	*Pomp and Circumstance* marches
Sousa, John Philip.	Any marches
Suppé, Franz von.	*Light Cavalry* Overture
Tchaikovsky, Peter Ilyich.	*1812* Overture

Music Suggesting Mystery

Dukas, Paul.	*The Sorcerer's Apprentice*
Grieg, Edvard.	"Abduction of the Bride" from *Peer Gynt*
———.	"The Hall of the Mountain King" from *Peer Gynt*
———.	"March of the Dwarfs" from *Huldigungmarsch*
Mussorgsky, Modesto.	*Night on Bald Mountain*
———.	*Songs and Dances of Death*
Saint-Saëns, Camille.	"Danse Macabre"
Schubert, Franz.	"The Erlking"
Sibelius, Jean.	*The Swan of Tuonela*
Strauss, Richard.	*Death and Transfiguration*

Romantic Music

Beethoven, Ludwig van.	Sonata no. 23 for Piano (*Appassionata*)
Brahms, Johannes.	"Valse"
Liszt, Franz.	"Liebestraum [Love Dream]"
Mendelssohn, Felix.	*Songs Without Words* op. 38, no. 2
———.	*Songs Without Words* op. 102, no. 1
Paderewski, Ignace.	"Love Song"
Rubinstein, Anton.	"Melody"
Tchaikovsky, Peter Ilyich.	Overture to *Romeo and Juliet*
———.	Symphony no. 5 [selections]
Wagner, Richard.	Prelude to *Tristan and Isolde*

Music Suggesting the Seasons

Beethoven, Ludwig van.	Sonata op. 24, no. 5 for Violin and Piano (*Spring*)
———.	Sonata op. 27, no. 2 (*Moonlight*)
———.	Symphony no. 6 (*Pastoral*)

Debussy, Claude. "Clair de Lune"
Delius, Frederick. "Summer Night on the River"
Grieg, Edvard. "Morning Mood"
———. "To the Spring" from *Lyric Pieces*
Grofe, Ferde. *Grand Canyon* Suite
Mendelssohn, Felix. Melody in F ("Spring Song")
Prokofiev, Sergei. "In Autumn"
———. *Summer Day* Suite
Ravel, Maurice. *Daphnis and Chloe*
Rossini, Gioacchino. "The Storm" from the Overture to *William Tell*
Sibelius, Jean. "Night Ride and Sunrise"
Vivaldi, Antonio. "Spring" from *The Four Seasons*

SERENE MUSIC

Bach, Johann Sebastian. Cantata no. 147 ("Sheep May Safely Graze")
Barber, Samuel. "Adagio for Strings" from Quartet for Strings op. 11
Bizet, Georges. *L'Arlésienne* [third movement]
Debussy, Claude. *Afternoon of a Faun*
Mendelssohn, Felix. *A Midsummer Night's Dream*
———. *Songs Without Words* op. 102, no. 6
Schubert, Franz. Quintet in A Major for Piano and Strings (*Trout*)
Schumann, Robert. *Traumerei*

MUSIC SUGGESTING STRONG MOVEMENT

Beethoven, Ludwig van. Sonata op. 27, no. 2 (*Moonlight* [third movement])
Falla, Manuel de. "Ritual Fire Dance" from *El Amor Brujo*
Holst, Gustav. "Mars" from *The Planets*
Khatchaturian, Aram. "Saber Dance" from *Gayne*
Prokofiev, Sergei. *Scythian* Suite [selections]
Shostakovich, Dimitri. Symphony no. 5 [fourth movement]
Tchaikovsky, Peter Ilyich. "Marche Slav"
———. Symphony no. 4

Music Suggesting Toys and Puppets

Bratton, John. "Teddy Bears' Picnic"
Coates, Eric. *Cinderella*
———. *The Three Bears*
Debussy, Claude. *Children's Corner*
Delibes, Léo. *Coppelia*
Elgar, Edward. *Nursery* Suite
———. *The Wand of Youth* Suites nos. 1 and 2
Herbert, Victor. "March of the Toys" from *Babes in Toyland*
Humperdinck, Engelbert. *Hansel and Gretel*
Jessel, Leon. "Parade of the Tin Soldiers"
Kleinsinger, George. "Peewee the Piccolo"
———. "Tubby the Tuba"
Mozart, Leopold. "Toy Symphony" from Cassation for Orchestra and Toys in G
Pierne, Gabriel. "March of the Little Lead Soldiers"
Prokofiev, Sergei. *Cinderella*
———. *The Love for Three Oranges*
———. *Peter and the Wolf*
Ravel, Maurice. *Mother Goose*
Rossini, Gioacchino. *La Cenerentola*
Tchaikovsky, Peter Ilyich. *The Nutcracker*
———. *The Sleeping Beauty*
———. *Swan Lake*

Whimsical Music

Grieg, Edvard. *Humoresque*
Mozart, Leopold. "Toy Symphony" from Cassation for Orchestra and Toys in G
Ponchielli, Amilcare. "Dance of the Hours" from *La Gioconda*
Strauss, Richard. *Till Eulenspiegel*
Tchaikovsky, Peter Ilyich. *Humoresque*

APPENDIX
SAMPLE STUDY GUIDES

LESSON PLANS FOR *THE MAGIC WORD*

PERIWINKLE PRODUCTIONS, INC., OF MONTICELLO, NEW YORK

I. *The Magic Word* is designed to help primary children discover or "rediscover" the joy and the fun of poetry. It is a play about a father who cannot smile; his two daughters, who have searched for a poem for a very long time; and the Spirit of Poetry, who takes them on a trip to the Isle of Poetry Laughter.

II. *The Magic Word* specifically follows directives laid down by educators as to the kind of poetry that *primary* children should be exposed to. Experts in the field agree that the experience must be a "fun" (and not a thinking) one.

   A. The test for successful verse with this age group is this:
      1. Is it simple?
      2. Is it entertaining?
      3. Does it have rhythm and rhyme?

   B. Studies show that it is an error to offer them "deeper" poetry at this time. At this age, children reject poetry of introspection, sadness, and loneliness; long poems; and even descriptive nature poems.

III. "Children entering kindergarten would have better speech habits, and first-grade children would have a greater power with and feeling for words, if more were done with *Mother Goose* in the home.

Knowing the verse expands the imagination, increases the vocabulary and develops an ear for the music of words . . . enjoying *Mother Goose* predisposes children to other books." [1]

IV. The nursery rhymes featured in *The Magic Word* include "Old King Cole," "Little Miss Muffet," "Pease Porridge Hot," and others.

A. Since the actors act out these rhymes (in the context of the story), this in itself becomes a motivating factor for both teacher and pupil in the classroom.

B. Children are encouraged to repeat the nursery rhymes that they know; and as the class has fun with nursery rhymes, the children who have not had this exposure in the home will gain it.

C. Kindergartners and first graders should be encouraged to bring their own *Mother Goose* books to class. The teacher usually has extra copies in the classroom. Sharing this experience brings new discoveries. Each *Mother Goose* book has fresh and different illustrations. Poring over illustrations is an education in art appreciation.

D. Art lesson in imagination. Have children draw their own versions of a nursery rhyme. For instance, see how many different "Humpty Dumpty's" you get, or how about "There was a crooked man who walked a crooked mile" or "Peter Peter Pumpkin Eater." Interesting results will occur, especially if you let children illustrate their favorite nursery rhymes.

E. Creative dramas. Children like to dramatize rhymes. Let them plan their own presentations of *Mother Goose*.

F. For children for whom English is a second language, the nursery rhymes provide excellent speech exercise. They will learn English rapidly and even catch the speech rhythms. Many teachers have cited the effectiveness of using nursery rhymes to involve the slow reader.

G. It is impossible to overestimate the importance of nursery rhymes in the literary and speech development of the primary child. As May Hill Arbuthnot phrased it, "Our goal is to see that no child goes out of our home, our kindergarten, or our first grades without knowing by heart dozens of these artless, picturesque, lyrical rhymes that, after all, constitute the child's most entertaining introduction to English poetry."

V. Nonsense verse. Nonsense verse helps children develop their sense of humor. It has been said that a lost day is that in which you have not laughed once.

A. Edward Lear is the master of nonsense verse. Children (of all

[1] May Hill Arbuthnot, *Children and Books* (Glenview, Ill.: Scott, Foresman, 1957), p. 74.

ages) love it! In *The Magic Word*, the children will see an actor discover:

There was an old man with a beard
Who said, "It is just as I feared"—
Two Owls and a Hen
Four larks and a wren
Have all built their nests in my beard!

Although Lear drew his own illustrations, why not have your class illustrate a Lear limerick?

B. It is important to remember that *nonsense verse feeds a child's imagination*. Adults have the tendency to forget that rhymes for children are written to entertain, rather than to instruct. It is the child's foundation in sounds and in books. Rhythm captivates children, and each verse has its own music. It sparkles and sings whether it is "Humpty Dumpty" or a Lear limerick.

C. Nonsense is fun that is impossible. Children understand this—and it becomes a stepping stone to humorous verse.

VI. Humorous verse is verse that deals with conceivably real people and the amusing things that happen to them—or *could* happen—maybe!

A. In his "Adventures of Isabel," Ogden Nash combines humorous verse with story-verse. Children like humorous story-poems, provided they are not too long.

B. All children see themselves in "After the Party," the story of a boy who gorges himself on goodies and then has a stomach ache. A good chance for group discussion on a time when "my eyes were bigger than my stomach."

VII. Children respond to sense impressions (seeing, smelling, hearing, feeling, tasting) *if it is something they are familiar with*. However, a young child cannot respond to detailed description. The poem has to be right to the point. Children like to talk about a poem but not to analyze it. A survey of college students revealed that it was this act of analyzing poetry at an early age that destroyed their love of poetry or their reception of it.

VIII. Conclusion

A. Poetry for younger children should be selected for entertainment only.

B. Children enjoy marked rhythms and crisp rhymes.

C. Young children cannot respond to detailed descriptions.

D. Children who have not had exposure to nursery rhymes automatically learn them by hearing them repeated in class. Children effortlessly memorize poetry just through repetition.

E. Through hearing poetry read aloud at an early age, children become attuned to sounds as well as words. Poetry helps to develop imagination and makes it possible for them to reach out to poetry at other levels when they are older.

F. Here's our thought for the day: a poem a day . . . to share . . . and then to hear again. Chiidren love to have "favorites" repeated. Please send us your list of your children's favorite poems. In addition, please share with us any of your children's first attempts at writing poetry.

STUDY GUIDE FOR *THE ICE WOLF*[2]

In the cold, icy lands of Canada, Greenland, Alaska, and Siberia live the Eskimos, which means "eaters of raw flesh." Every Eskimo man hunts each day in order to find food for his family. Seal, walrus, caribou, and fish are favorite foods. Sometimes families must travel many miles in one day to find food. Hunting is the Eskimos' most important job!

Long, long ago, Eskimos believed in many spirits. They were frightened of the forest because they believed that evil spirits lived there. When a seal was caught, the hunter always gave food to the spirits so that the spirits would send him another seal the next time he went hunting.

After a "good catch," many families gathered in a snowhouse to eat, tell stories, and sing songs. They hoped that the good spirits would like their stories and songs. There were no books, so children learned by listening to the tales on these happy occasions. When the children grew older, they would tell their children the very same stories!

One such story was about a little girl born to an Eskimo family. She did not look like them because her hair was pale and her skin was fair. Her parents named her Anatou—the Fair One. The villagers called her "the different one." She was the ice wolf!

When you enter Taylor Theatre, you will be transported to a *kashim*, a large snow dwelling used by the Eskimos as a place to sing, dance, and tell stories. The storyteller tells about a night a long time ago—the coldest night anyone remembers—when a baby girl was born!

THE ICE WOLF[3]

JOANNA H. KRAUS

The white curtain rises to reveal an igloo. Inside, Karvik, the father, and Arnaqik, the mother, welcome their friends who have

[2] Prepared by Cindy Garren, a member of the theatre department of the University of North Carolina at Greensboro, which is under the direction of Tom Behm.

[3] Joanna H. Kraus, *The Ice Wolf* (Rowayton, Conn.: New Plays, Inc., 1961).

come to see the new baby. The villagers are shocked because they have never seen a child with pale hair. They are afraid of the baby because she is different, and they believe that it is a sign from the spirits. Kiviog, Inuka, and Manik (the villagers) think the hunting will be spoiled because of the baby, and so they ask the parents to put the baby in the snow to die.

Karvik and Arnaqik assure their friends that their daughter will grow up to look and act like all the other Eskimos. The parents promise to teach her how to be an Eskimo, but they, too, are unsure if Anatou—the Fair One—will ever look like the rest.

Twelve years later, we see a group of children playing: Motomiak, a boy; Shikikanaq, a girl; and Tarto, another boy. Anatou accidentally disrupts the game, and Motomiak and Shikikanaq tease Anatou and call her names because she still has pale hair and fair skin. Tarto, Anatou's friend, defends her. But then the children accuse Anatou of casting a spell of famine on the village. The villagers hear the children and try to stop the fighting. Then they tell Anatou that her parents have disappeared while they were hunting.

The villagers and children believe that Anatou put a spell on her parents! Tarto is the only person who believes that Anatou loves her parents and would never hurt them. But the villagers do not understand, and they drive Anatou away from the village.

Anatou runs to the forest—even though Eskimos have been told never to go there—to find the Wood God. In this dark place, she finds the Wood God and asks him to transform her into a wolf. Anatou believes that she will not cry or have a broken heart if she can become a wolf and forget all about the Eskimos. The Wood God agrees, but warns Anatou never to leave the forest.

The fox, beaver, and ermine appear and help the Wood God turn Anatou into a wolf!

The wolf lives quite happily in the forest and forgets about her Eskimo life. One spring day, she leaves the forest and is surprised to see a group of Eskimos who have been hunting. She recognizes Tarto, who has become a good hunter. She also recognizes another villager, who had often called her names. The wolf quietly tries to get some meat, and the villager shoots his arrow at Anatou. In defending herself, Anatou (the wolf) kills the villager.

When the wolf returns to the forest, the Wood God is furious and tells her to learn to live in peace. But Anatou (the wolf) continues to prey on the Eskimos in order to seek her revenge. The villagers are frightened, so they decide to go into the forest to hunt the wolf!

The forest is dark and frightening, and Anatou (the wolf) tries to run away from the hunters. One of the hunters gets trapped in some fallen trees, and Anatou is surprised to see that it is Tarto, her friend.

Thinking he might be hurt, Anatou stops to help him. Tarto screams for help, the villagers rush in, the wolf flees, but it is too late. An arrow pierces the wolf!

Tarto tells the others that the wolf saved him. Everyone is confused. Why would a wolf help an Eskimo? They find the body, but it is no longer a wolf: it has been transformed back into Anatou, the fair Eskimo.

It is then that the Eskimos understand. Their ignorance and hatred drove Anatou away from the village. And her hate was so strong that she, too, hurt the Eskimos. In the end, Anatou knew she was wrong to hate, so she tried to save her friend. Anatou's spirit is seen, and she tells the Wood God that she forgives the Eskimos. The Eskimos leave the forest to go back to their village, where Tarto will be the first to tell the story "The Ice Wolf."

Before The Play

1. Discuss the differences among the theatre, movies, and television. Theatre happens right before our eyes—live onstage—while a movie or television show is a moving photograph. Also, there is some violence in the play. Be sure that your students understand that the actors are playing a role and do not really hurt one another!

2. Below is a list of vocabulary words used in the play. You can familiarize your students with these words and their definitions.

Blizzard. A terrible, blinding snowstorm.

Caribou. A reindeer that Eskimos use for food and clothing.

Famine. Extreme hunger. People can die from famine.

Harpoon. A spear with a rope attached that is used to capture seals and walruses.

Hudson Bay. An area of Canada where many Eskimos live.

Igloo. An Eskimo word for "house." We often think of dome-shaped snow-houses, although Eskimos also live in fur tents.

Nuliayuk. The seal goddess.

Shaman. A medicine man who cures sicknesses.

3. The Eskimos made masks that they wore when dancing or telling stories. Many characters in the play wear masks. You can make masks in your classroom by using paper plates. Make a nose or ears of stiff paper and attach to plate with staples. Finally, cut holes for the eyes and add a string. Now it's ready to wear!

4. Eskimos enjoy playing games. Play one of these favorite games.

Angugaurak (tag game). Eskimo children play a tag game in which everyone is a "wolf." The hunter is "it" and tries to tag a wolf. The tagged wolf then becomes the hunter, and the hunter becomes a wolf!

Muk (silence). Everyone stands in a circle, and the person who is "it" stands in the center. "It" walks to anyone in the circle, who then has to say "muk" without laughing. "It" then tries to make that person laugh by making faces or funny noises. If the person in the circle laughs, he or she becomes "it." If not, "it" goes on to another person.

5. Read some books about Eskimo culture or Eskimo folklore. Here is a list of some good choices:

Bringle, Mary. *Eskimos*. New York: Watts, 1973. Accurate information, maps, photographs, and drawings. Ages 4–7.

Bruemmer, Fred. *Seasons of the Eskimos*. Greenwich, Conn.: New York Graphic Society, 1971. Past and modern Eskimo life. Ages 6 and up.

Ginsburg, Maria. *The Proud Maiden, Tungak, and the Sun*. New York: Macmillan, 1974. Legends about why the nights are long, why there is a moon, and more. Ages K–2.

McDermott, Beverly Brodsky. *Sedna: An Eskimo Myth*. New York: Viking Press, 1975. The story of Sedna, the mother of all sea animals. Ages 2 and up.

After The Play

1. *The Ice Wolf* has been hailed as "the first tragedy for children." Discuss the following characteristics of a tragedy.

Reversal. A result that is the opposite of what was intended. What reversals do you remember in *The Ice Wolf*?

Tragic mistake. An error that causes the hero's change of luck. What tragic mistake does Anatou make?

Although audiences may feel sad at the end of a tragedy, there is often a feeling that something good will happen. What good things will come from the end of the play? Do you think the Eskimo villagers will make the same mistake again?

2. The Eskimos called Anatou a "freak" and "different." Have you ever felt disliked because you were different? Perhaps you wear glasses, and your friends tease you. How do you feel when people tease you? How do you feel different?

3. Pantomime—acting without sound—is a fun pastime. Try pantomiming the following and then create some of your own:

a. Building an igloo
b. Harpooning a seal
c. Skating on ice
d. Walking in a blizzard
e. Shooting a bow and arrow
f. Making a campfire
g. Sewing boots
h. Stalking an animal

4. Draw a picture of your favorite scene from the play.

5. Discuss the production with your class. What did they like and/or dislike? Why? Who were their favorite characters? Here are more detailed questions:

a. Why didn't the villagers like Anatou?

b. Why didn't Anatou's parents put her in the snow to die?

c. At what activity was Anatou very skilled? Why do you think she enjoyed this pastime?

d. Why were the animals afraid of Anatou, the wolf?

e. Was Anatou good or bad? Why?

f. How did you feel at the end of the play? Were you happy or sad?

During January, the director and cast members will be available to visit classrooms. These 30-minute visits can help you prepare your students for this exciting production of *The Ice Wolf.* Discussion can include background information on Eskimo culture, folklore, games, and art or on drama activities.

INDEX

Coláiste Oideachais Mhuire Gan Smál
Luimneach